IRELAND

TOP SIGHTS, AUTHENTIC EXPERIENCES

Neil Wilson, Isabel Albiston, Fionn Davenport,
Belinda Dixon, Catherine Le Nevez

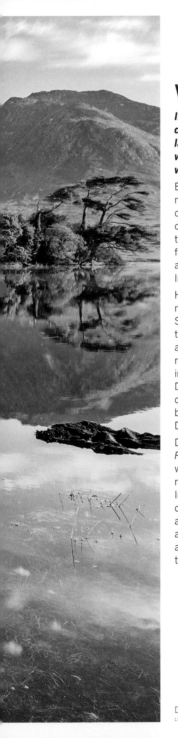

Welcome to Ireland

Ireland may be a small country but it deserves its big reputation for breathtaking landscapes and fascinating, friendly people, whose lyrical nature is expressed in the warmth of their welcome.

Everything you've heard is true: Ireland is a stunner. People will argue over the must-sees, but you can't go wrong if you put the brooding loneliness of Connemara, the dramatic wildness of Donegal, the majestic mountains of Mourne, the world-famous scenery of counties Kerry and Cork, and the celebrated Causeway Coast in Northern Ireland on your to-visit list.

History is everywhere, from the breathtaking monuments of prehistoric Ireland at Brú na Bóinne, Slea Head in Kerry and Carrowmore in Sligo, to the fabulous ruins of Ireland's rich monastic past at Glendalough, Clonmacnoise and Cashel. More recent history is visible in the Titanic Experience in Cobh and the forbidding Kilmainham Gaol in Dublin. And there's history so young that it's still considered the present, best experienced on a black-taxi tour of West Belfast or an examination of Derry's colourful political murals.

During your travels you might hear it said: *tá Fáilte romhat* (taw fall-cha row-at) – you're very welcome. Or, more famously, *céad míle fáilte* (kade meela fall-cha) – a hundred thousand welcomes. Irish friendliness is an oversimplification of a character that is infinitely complex, but the Irish are nonetheless genuinely warm and welcoming, and there are few more enjoyable ways of gaining a greater understanding of the island's inhabitants than a chat with a local.

Breathtaking landscapes and fascinating, friendly people

Derryclare Lough and the Connemara Mountains (p216)
LUKASZ PAJOR/SHUTTERSTOCK ©

ATLANTIC OCEAN

0 — 100 km
0 — 50 miles

Dungloe

Glencolumbcille

Donega

Donegal Bay

Pollatomish

Ballycastle

Sligo

Ballina

Boy

Newport

Castlebar

Knock

Westport

Lough Mask

Roscommon

Clifden

Cong

Lough Corrib

Cashel

Ballinasloe

Galway

Ballyvaughan

Gort

Loug Der

Doolin

Nenagh

Ennis

Kilkee

Limerick

Kilrush

Tipperary

Tralee

Mallow

Dingle

Killarney

Kenmare

Cork

Bantry

Skibbereen

In Focus

Survival Guide

Christ Church Cathedral (p59)
DAVID SOANES PHOTOGRAPHY/GETTYIMAGES ©

Plan Your Trip
Ireland's Top 12

Dublin

Capital city and the home of Guinness

Ireland's largest city by some stretch is the main gateway into the country, and it has enough distractions to keep visitors engaged for at least a few days. From world-class museums and entertainment, superb dining and top-grade hotels, Dublin (p35) has all the baubles of a major international metropolis. But the real clinchers are Dubliners themselves, who are friendlier, more easygoing and welcoming than the burghers of virtually any other European capital.

1

MEDIAPRODUCTION/GETTY IMAGES ©

STEFANO_VALERI/SHUTTERSTOCK ©

Ring of Kerry

Classic road trip through spectacular scenery

Driving around the Ring of Kerry (p158) is an unforgettable experience, but you don't need to limit yourself to the main route – there are countless opportunities for detours. Near Killorglin, it's a short hop up to the little-known Cromane Peninsula. Between Portmagee (pictured top) and Waterville, you can explore the Skellig Ring. The peninsula's interior offers mesmerising mountain views, so make the most of your camera! Bottom: Gap of Dunloe (p167)

2

AURÉLIEN POTTIER/GETTY IMAGES ©

Connemara

Gorgeous coast and wild mountains

Wandering Connemara's (p216) characterful roads brings you from one village to another, each with traditional pubs and restaurants serving seafood chowder cooked from recipes that are family secrets. Inland, the scenic drama is even greater. In fantastically desolate valleys, green hills, yellow wildflowers and wild streams reflecting the blue sky provide elemental beauty.

Roundstone harbour (p217)

3

4

Dingle

Picturesque peninsula strewn with ancient ruins

Dingle (p171) is the name of both the peninsula jutting into the Atlantic and its delightful main town, the peninsula's beating heart. Fishing boats unload fish and shellfish that couldn't be any fresher if you caught it yourself, many pubs are untouched since their earlier incarnations as old-fashioned shops, artists sell their creations (including beautiful jewellery with Irish designs) at intriguing boutiques, and toe-tapping trad sessions take place around roaring pub fires. Dick Mack's (p174)

5

Cork City

Gourmet delights in Ireland's foodie capital

The Republic's second city (p135) is second only in terms of size – in every other respect it will bear no competition. A tidy, compact city centre is home to an enticing collection of art galleries, museums and – most especially – places to eat. From cheap cafes to top-end gourmet restaurants, Cork city excels. At the heart of it is the simply wonderful English Market (p138; pictured), a covered produce market that is an attraction in itself.

ANDY GOSS/GETTY IMAGES ©

Glendalough

Ancient churches scattered amid scenic splendour

When St Kevin chose a remote cave on a lake nestled in a forested valley as his monastic retreat, he inadvertently founded a settlement that would later prove to be one of Ireland's most dynamic universities and, in our time, one of the country's most beautiful ruined sites (p86). The remains of the settlement (including an intact round tower, pictured), coupled with the stunning scenery, are unforgettable.

6

ROLF G #ACKENBERG/SHUTTERSTOCK ©

Kilkenny City

Arts, crafts and medieval monuments

From its regal castle to its soaring medieval cathedral, Kilkenny (p109) exudes a permanence and culture that makes it an unmissable stop. Its namesake county boasts scores of artisans and craftspeople and you can browse their wares at Kilkenny's boutiques. Chefs eschew Dublin to be close to the source of Kilkenny's wonderful produce and you can enjoy the local brewery's beer at scores of delightful pubs.

7

The Antrim Coast

Dramatic coastal scenery with geological wonders

County Antrim's Causeway Coast (p245) is a scenic backdrop for *Game of Thrones* filming locations. Put on your walking boots by the swaying Carrick-a-Rede rope bridge, then follow the rugged coastline for 16.5 spectacular kilometres, passing Ballintoy Harbour (aka the Iron Islands' Lordsports Harbour) and the famous Giant's Causeway's outsized basalt columns (pictured), as well as cliffs and islands, sandy beaches and ruined castles. Be sure to finish your day with a dram at the Old Bushmills Distillery.

NUMAN/SHUTTERSTOCK ©

Galway City

Ireland's liveliest city hums through the night

One word to describe Galway city (p212)? Craic! Discover music-filled pubs where you could hear three old guys playing spoons and fiddles, or maybe a hot young band. Join the locals as they bounce from place to place, never knowing what fun lies ahead but certain of the possibility. Add in local bounty such as the famous oysters and nearby adventure in the Connemara Peninsula and the Aran Islands – the fun never ends.

MILOSZ MASLANKA/SHUTTERSTOCK © ARCHITECT: ERIC KUHNE

JAMES KENNEDY NI/SHUTTERSTOCK ©

WILLY BARTON/SHUTTERSTOCK ©
SCULPTURE BY JOHN KINDNESS

Belfast

Victorian architecture, top museums and lively pubs

Northern Ireland's capital city (p221) is buzzing, having reinvented
itself as a major tourist hot spot. Historical attractions range from
Titanic Belfast (pictured), a multimedia celebration of the famous
ocean liner (built and launched here in 1911), to the fascinating
corridors of Crumlin Road Gaol, and tours of West Belfast's political
murals, a reminder of the strife that scarred the city. Bottom left: St
George's Market (p225); bottom right: *The Big Fish* sculpture

10

LM SPENCER / SHUTTERSTOCK ©

Brú na Bóinne

Mysterious prehistoric passage tombs

Ancient and yet eerily futuristic, Newgrange's immense, round, white stone walls topped by a grass dome is an extraordinary sight. Part of the vast Neolithic necropolis Brú na Bóinne (Boyne Palace; p100), it contains Ireland's finest Stone Age passage tomb, predating the Pyramids by some six centuries. Most extraordinary of all is the tomb's precise alignment with the sun at the time of the winter solstice.

11

SHUTTERUPEERE / SHUTTERSTOCK ©

Cliffs of Moher

Iconic sea cliffs of jaw-dropping beauty

Bathed in the golden glow of the late afternoon sun, the Cliffs of Moher (p180) are but one of the splendours of County Clare. From a boat bobbing below, the towering stone faces have a dramatic ruggedness that's enlivened by thousands of seabirds, including cute little puffins. Down south in Loop Head, pillars of rock towering above the sea are home to abandoned stone cottages whose very existence is inexplicable.

12

Plan Your Trip
Need to Know

When to Go

Belfast
GO May–Sep

Galway
GO May–Sep

Dublin
GO Any time;
lots of indoor
attractions

Kerry
GO May–Sep

Cork
GO May–Sep

High Season (Jun–mid-Sep)

o Weather at its best.

o Accommodation rates at their highest (especially in August).

o Tourist peak in Dublin, Kerry, southern and western coasts.

Shoulder (Easter–May, mid-Sep–Oct)

o Weather often good, sun and rain in May; 'Indian summers' and often warm in September.

o Summer crowds and accommodation rates drop off.

Low Season (Nov–Feb)

o Reduced opening hours from October to Easter; some destinations close.

o Cold and wet weather throughout the country; fog can reduce visibility.

Currency

Republic of Ireland: Euro (€)
Northern Ireland: Pound sterling (£)

Language

English, Irish

Visas

Not required by most citizens of Europe, Australia, New Zealand, USA and Canada.

Money

Visa and MasterCard credit and debit cards are widely accepted; American Express is only accepted by the major chains, and virtually no one will accept Diners or JCB.

Mobile Phones

All European and Australasian phones work in Ireland, as do North American phones not locked to a local network. Check with your provider. Prepaid SIM cards cost from €10/£10.

Time

Western European Time (UTC/GMT late October to late March; plus one hour late March to late October)

Daily Costs

Budget: Less than €80

○ Dorm bed: €14–25

○ Cheap meal in cafe or pub: €10–18

○ Intercity bus travel (200km): €14–25

○ Pint of beer: €5–6.50 (more expensive in cities)

Midrange: €80–180

○ Double room in hotel or B&B: €100–180 (more expensive in Dublin)

○ Main course in midrange restaurant: €17–30

○ Car rental (per day): from €32

○ Three-hour train journey: €60

Top end: More than €180

○ Four-star hotel stay: from €200

○ Three-course meal in good restaurant: around €70

○ Top round of golf (midweek): from €100

Useful Websites

Entertainment Ireland (www.entertainment.ie) Countrywide listings for every kind of entertainment.

Failte Ireland (www.discoverireland.ie) Official tourist-board website for the Republic – practical info and a huge accommodation database.

Lonely Planet (www.lonelyplanet.com/ireland, www.lonelyplanet.com/ireland/northern-ireland) Destination information, hotel bookings, traveller forum and more.

Northern Ireland Tourist Board (www.nitb.com) Official tourist-board site.

Opening Hours

Banks 10am–4pm Monday to Friday (to 5pm Thursday)

Pubs 10.30am–11.30pm Monday to Thursday, 10.30am–12.30am Friday and Saturday, noon–11pm Sunday (30 minutes 'drinking up' time allowed); closed Christmas Day and Good Friday

Restaurants noon–10.30pm; many close one day of the week

Shops 9.30am–6pm Monday to Saturday (to 8pm Thursday in cities), noon–6pm Sunday

Arriving in Ireland

Dublin Airport Private coaches run every 10 to 15 minutes to the city centre (€6). Taxis take 30 to 45 minutes and cost €20 to €25.

Dun Laoghaire Ferry Port Public bus takes around 45 minutes to the centre of Dublin; DART (suburban rail) takes about 25 minutes. Both cost €3.

Dublin Port Terminal Buses are timed to coincide with arrivals and departures; they cost €3.50 to the city centre.

Belfast International Airport Airport Express 300 bus runs hourly from Belfast International Airport (one way/return £8/11.50, 30 to 55 minutes). A taxi costs around £30.

George Best Belfast City Airport Airport Express 600 bus runs every 20 minutes from George Best Belfast City Airport (one way/return £2.60/4, 15 minutes). A taxi costs around £10.

Getting Around

Transport is efficient and reasonably priced to/from major urban centres; smaller towns and villages along those routes are well served.

Car The most convenient way to explore Ireland's every nook and cranny; can be hired in every major town and city. Drive on the left.

Bus An extensive network of public and private buses makes them the most cost-effective way to get around. There's service to/from most inhabited areas.

Bicycle Dublin operates a bike-share scheme with more than 100 stations throughout the city.

Train A limited (and expensive) network links Dublin to all major urban centres, including Belfast in Northern Ireland.

For more on **getting around**, see p305

Plan Your Trip
Hotspots For...

Irish Cuisine

Ireland's foodie revolution kicked off in County Cork in the 1970s and has now spread all over the country, with fine food and farmers markets everywhere.

LENSMEN/SHUTTERSTOCK ©

Cork City (p142)
The gourmet capital of Ireland, Cork is home to countless restaurants and the legendary English Market.

Best Dish
The Producers' Platter at Nash 19 (p145).

Dublin (p35)
Ireland's biggest city is a hotbed of modern Irish cuisine, with several Michelin star-rated restaurants.

Best Dish
Three-course set menu at Chapter One (p73).

Kinsale (p149)
This historic harbour town is famous for fine dining, and is the best place to sample fresh Irish seafood.

Best Dish
Irish oysters at Bastion (p151).

Coastal Scenery

Much of Ireland's most spectacular scenery is to be found around its wave-battered coastline, from beaches of golden sand to towering cliffs and sea stacks.

MICHAEL THALER/SHUTTERSTOCK ©

Dingle Peninsula (p171)
This remote finger of land is lined with beaches, mountains and cliffs, with views of the island-dotted Atlantic.

Slea Head Drive
The scenery on this coastal drive (pictured; p175).

Antrim Coast (p245)
Black basalt and white chalk cliffs plus stretches of golden sand make up the beautiful Antrim Coast.

Giant's Causeway
Hexagonal columns form the coast's (p248) centrepiece.

County Clare (p177)
Sculpted over aeons by Atlantic breakers, Clare's coast is a cornucopia of spectacular scenery.

Cliffs of Moher
Hauntingly beautiful 200m-high cliffs (p180).

Traditional Music

Western Europe's most vibrant folk music is Irish traditional music, best enjoyed in the convivial company of an old-fashioned pub.

PAOLO TROVO/SHUTTERSTOCK ©

Doolin (p189)
This west coast village is a major centre of Irish folk music, with daily sessions in its trio of pubs.

Gus O'Connor's
Atmospheric 19th-century hostelry (pictured; p189).

Galway City (p212)
Traditional pubs offer live music, while street performers belt out traditional classics.

Tig Cóilí
Authentic old pub with live *céilidh* every day (p209).

Derry (Londonderry; p262)
Friendly, atmospheric pubs, with live music happening somewhere every night of the week.

Peadar O'Donnell's
Rowdy traditional music sessions (p266) every night.

Monastic Sites

The 'land of saints and scholars' was a cradle of early Christianity, which has left a legacy of amazing ancient monastic sites.

STEFAN MISSING/SHUTTERSTOCK ©

Skellig Michael (p260)
Ireland's most spectacular monastic site, perched on top of a jagged rock pinnacle.

Beehive Cells
Sixth-century drystone monks' housing (pictured; p160).

Rock of Cashel (p126)
Medieval ruins atop a fortified, rock-girt hill dominate the landscape for miles around.

Cormac's Chapel
Houses Ireland's oldest mural paintings (p126).

Glendalough (p86)
Nestled between two lakes, haunting Glendalough is one of the most historic spots in the country.

St Kevin's Kitchen
An 11th-century church with a distinctive bell tower (p89).

Plan Your Trip
Essential Ireland

Activities

There's no better way of experiencing this wildly beautiful country than by exploring its varied landscapes – and the rewards can be spectacular. From majestic craggy mountains to lush lakeside woods, from broad sandy beaches to blankets of wild bog stretching as far as the eye can see, Ireland's great outdoors will never disappoint.

Shopping

Selling souvenirs to visitors is big business in Ireland, and many visitor attractions are accompanied by the inevitable gift shop. But look beyond the tourist kitsch of *shillelaghs* (Irish fighting sticks), cuddly leprechauns and shamrock key rings and you'll find plenty of good-value, high-quality items. Traditional Irish products such as crystal, knitwear and tweed remain popular choices, but a new wave of young Irish designers and craftspeople are turning out innovative ceramics, textiles and jewellery.

Entertainment

The big cities of Dublin, Belfast, Cork, Limerick and Galway offer a thriving entertainment scene. Big-name bands and singers play at venues like the **3 Arena** (☑01-819 8888; www.3arena.ie; East Link Bridge, North Wall Quay; tickets €30-100; ◷6.30-11pm; ☒The Point) in Dublin and the **SSE Arena** (www.ssearenabelfast.com; Odyssey Complex, 2 Queen's Quay; ☒G2) in Belfast, while any number of pubs and clubs host live performances by local and Irish bands.

More distinctively Irish are the traditional-music sessions that enliven many an evening in pubs the length and breadth of the country.

Eating

In the last couple of decades Ireland has 'rediscovered' its own native cuisine. A host of chefs and producers have led a foodie revolution that, at its heart, is about bringing to the table the kind of

BRIAN LOGAN PHOTOGRAPHY/SHUTTERSTOCK ©

meals that have long been taken for granted on well-run Irish farms. This 'local food' movement has gone from strength to strength, with farmers markets showcasing local produce, and restaurants all over the country championing the local sourcing of ingredients.

Drinking & Nightlife

Famed around the world for Guinness and whiskey, Ireland has a well-deserved reputation as a place to enjoy a drink or six. Every town and hamlet has at least one pub, usually several, and a visit to the pub is the best way to get a handle on what makes the country tick.

The traditional Irish pub is often the hub of a community, whether urban or rural, a meeting place and venue for quiz nights and live music. What makes the Irish pub scene unique is the survival of the 'spirit

★ Best Traditional Pubs

Long Hall (p74)

Monroe's Tavern (p209)

McGann's (p183)

Sin É (p146)

Crown Liquor Saloon (p230)

grocery', a combined pub and grocer's shop that emerged in the 19th century when a growing temperance movement forced many pub landlords to diversify their businesses in order to remain solvent.

In the last decade there has been a swing away from the big international brands in favour of beers made by small, local breweries – so-called 'craft beers'. Many of these have their own pubs, or even combine pub and brewery in one place.

From left: Long Hall; Crown Liquor Saloon

Plan Your Trip
Month by Month

February

Bad weather makes February the perfect month for indoor activities.

⚜ Audi Dublin International Film Festival

Most of Dublin's cinemas participate in the capital's film festival (www.diff.ie), a two-week showcase for new films by Irish and international directors, which features local flicks, arty international films and advance releases of mainstream movies.

☆ Six Nations Rugby

The Irish national rugby team (www.irishrugby.ie) plays its three home matches at the Aviva Stadium in the southern suburb of Ballsbridge. The season runs from February to April.

March

Spring is in the air, and the whole country is getting ready for arguably the world's most famous parade.

⚜ St Patrick's Day

Ireland erupts into one giant celebration on 17 March (www.stpatricksfestival.ie), but Dublin throws a five-day party around the parade (attended by 600,000), with gigs and festivities that leave the city with a giant hangover.

April

The weather is getting better, the flowers are beginning to bloom and the festival season begins anew.

☆ Circuit of Ireland International Rally

Northern Ireland's most prestigious rally race – known locally as the 'Circuit' (www.circuitofireland.net) – sees over 130 competitors throttle and turn through some 550km of Northern Ireland and parts of the Republic over two days at Easter.

Above: St Patrick's Day, Dublin

CLEARPIX / ALAMY STOCK PHOTO ©

☆ Irish Grand National

Ireland loves horse racing, and the race that's loved the most is the Grand National (www. fairyhouse.ie), the showcase of the national hunt season that takes place at Fairyhouse in County Meath on Easter Monday.

☆ World Irish Dancing Championships

There's far more to Irish dancing than *Riverdance*. Every April some 4500 competitors from all over the world gather to test their steps and skills against the very best. The location varies from year to year; see www.irishdancingorg.com.

May

The May Bank Holiday (on the first Monday) sees the first of the busy summer weekends as the Irish take to the roads to enjoy the budding good weather.

☆ North West 200

Ireland's most famous road race (www. northwest200.org) is also the country's

★ Best Festivals

St Patrick's Day, March

Galway International Arts Festival, July

Dublin Fringe Festival, September

All-Ireland Finals, September

Belfast International Arts Festival, October

biggest outdoor sporting event; 150,000-plus people line the triangular route to cheer on some of the biggest names in motorcycle racing. Held in mid-May.

🎵 Fleadh Nua

The third week of May sees the cream of the traditional music crop come to Ennis, County Clare, for one of the country's most important festivals (www.fleadhnua.com).

Above: Fleadh Cheoil na hÉireann (p24)

June

The bank holiday at the beginning of the month sees the country spoilt for choice as to what to do.

☆ Irish Derby

Wallets are packed and fancy hats donned for the best flat-race festival in the country (www.curragh.ie), run during the first week of the month.

✥ Bloomsday

Edwardian dress and breakfast of 'the inner organs of beast and fowl' are but two of the elements of the Dublin festival (www.jamesjoyce.ie) celebrating 16 June, the day on which Joyce's *Ulysses* takes place; the real highlight is retracing Leopold Bloom's steps.

July

There isn't a weekend in the month that a major festival doesn't take place, while visitors to Galway will find that the city is in full swing for the entire month.

✥ Galway International Arts Festival

Music, drama and a host of artistic endeavours are on the menu at the most important arts festival (p217) in the country, which sees Galway go merriment mad for the last two weeks of the month.

✥ Longitude

A mini-Glastonbury in Dublin's Marlay Park, Longitude (www.longitude.ie) packs them in over three days in mid-July for a feast of EDM, nu-folk, rock and pop. In 2019 Stormzy, Anne-Marie and Cardi B were the headliners.

August

Schools are closed, the sun is shining (or not!) and Ireland is in holiday mood.

☆ Galway Race Week

The biggest horse-racing festival (www. galwayraces.com) west of the Shannon is not just about the horses, it's also a celebration of Irish culture, sporting gambles and elaborate hats.

✥ Fleadh Cheoil na hÉireann

The mother of all Irish music festivals (www.fleadhcheoil.ie), held at the end of the month, attracts in excess of 400,000 music-lovers and revellers to whichever town is playing host.

✥ Rose of Tralee

The country's biggest beauty pageant (www.roseoftralee.ie) divides critics between those who see it as an embarrassing throwback to older days and those who see it as a throwback to older days. Wannabe Roses plucked from Irish communities throughout the world compete for the ultimate prize.

☆ All-Ireland Finals

The end of the summer sees the finals of the hurling and Gaelic football championships respectively, with 80,000-plus crowds thronging into Dublin's Croke Park for one of the biggest sporting days of the year.

September

Summer may be over, but September weather can be surprisingly good, so it's often the ideal time to enjoy the last vestiges of sunshine as the crowds dwindle.

✥ Dublin Fringe Festival

Upwards of 100 different performances take the stage, the street, the bar and the car in the fringe festival (www.fringefest.com) that is unquestionably more innovative than the main theatre festival that follows it.

October

The weather starts to turn cold, so it's time to move the fun indoors again. The calendar is still packed with activities and distractions.

✥ Belfast International Arts Festival

Northern Ireland's top arts festival (www. belfastinternationalartsfestival.com) attracts performers from all over the world for the second half of the month; on offer is everything from visual arts to dance.

Get Inspired

Read

The Glorious Heresies (Lisa McInerney; 2015) Fierce, funny novel set in Cork about a 15-year-old's descent into crime and his inept, debt-ridden father.

City of Bohane (Kevin Barry; 2011) The west of Ireland in 2053 is the setting for this award-winning novel where gangs run rampant and technology is rudimentary.

Normal People (Sally Rooney; 2018) Award-winning story of the fraught relationship between two friends in post-crash Dublin.

Brooklyn (Colm Tóibín; 2009) Beautifully recounted story of longing in New York and the pull of small-town Ireland; made into a film in 2015.

Watch

Bloody Sunday (2002) Unmissable account of events in Derry in 1972.

The Dead (1987) John Huston brings James Joyce's story to life in his last film, with powerful performances by Donal McCann and Anjelica Huston.

Sing Street (2016) John Carney's delightful coming-of-age musical set in 1980s Dublin is about a boy's efforts to start a band to impress a girl.

My Left Foot (1989) The true story of Dubliner Christy Brown and his struggle to create despite his cerebral palsy helped launch the career of Daniel Day Lewis.

Listen

Becoming a Jackal (Villagers; 2010) Stunning debut album by Conor O'Brien, one of Ireland's brightest talents.

Achtung Baby (U2; 1991) The band at its creative, rock 'n' roll best.

Music in Mouth (Bell X1; 2003) A beautiful album featuring the crafted songs of Paul Noonan.

The Lion and the Cobra (Sinéad O'Connor; 1987) O'Connor's debut album is as brilliant today as it was on its release.

Above: Exterior of the Irish Rock 'n' Roll Museum Experience, Dublin

Plan Your Trip
Five-Day Itineraries

Dublin to Meath

Short on time? Dublin has enough to entertain you for at least three days, leaving you with two to devote to day trips from the capital. Even on a quick trip here you'll see some of the country's top highlights.

County Meath (p97) On day five, head north into County Meath and visit Brú na Bóinne, Tara and the site of the Battle of the Boyne.

Dublin (p35) Spend two days in the capital, enjoying the top sights and restaurants, and perhaps a theatre performance.
🚗 1 hr to Powerscourt

County Wicklow (p81) Spend a day exploring the delights of Enniskerry and Powerscourt, and another touring the Wicklow Mountains and Glendalough.
🚗 1½ hrs to Brú na Bóinne

Northern Delights

Link Northern Ireland's two vibrant and historic cities with a scenic tour of the Antrim Coast and the iconic Giant's Causeway, taking in a string of locations made famous as settings for TV saga *Game of Thrones*.

Causeway Coast (p252)
Spend a day exploring the Glens of Antrim, Carrick-a-Rede Rope Bridge and the Giant's Causeway.
🚗 1 hr to Derry

₂

₃

rry (Londonderry) (p262)
e in the sights, walk
und the city walls, and view
Bogside murals.

Belfast (p221) Enjoy two days sightseeing, including a black-taxi tour. On the third take a *Game of Thrones* tour.
🚗 2 hrs to Giant's Causeway

₁

FROM LEFT: 1. FRANCESCO RICCIARDI EXP/GETTY IMAGES ©; 3. ROLF G WACKENBERG/SHUTTERSTOCK ©

Plan Your Trip
10-Day Itinerary

Dublin to Killarney

If you've only got 10 days and you must see the best of the country, you won't have time to linger too long anywhere. But if you manage it correctly, you'll leave with the top highlights in your memory – and on your memory card.

Dublin (p35) One day in the capital including visits to Trinity College and the *Book of Kells*, the National Museum of Ireland – Archaeology and the Guinness Storehouse. 🚗 3 hrs to Galway

Galway (p203) Three nights based here provides time to soak up the city's cultural delights, followed by a day's scenic drive along the Connemara coastline. 🚗 4hrs (via Cliffs of Moher) to Ennis

Ennis (p184) Drive south from Galway to visit the Cliffs of Moher, before an overnight in Ennis, where you can enjoy a trad music session in one of its pubs. 🚗 3 hrs to Dingle

Dingle (p171) Explore Dingle town the afternoon you arrive; the next day take a harbour cruise to see Fungie the dolphin, then motor around Slea Head Drive. 🚗 1 hr to Killarney

Killarney (p166) Stay for two nights and explore Killarney National Park, then drive (or take a coach tour) around the scenic splendours of the famous Ring of Kerry (180km).

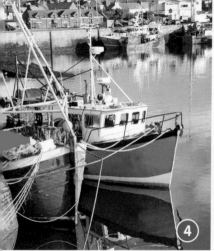

Plan Your Trip
Two-Week Itinerary

Belfast to Galway

This trail takes in many of Ireland's most famous attractions and passes through spectacular countryside. It's almost 1500km in length, so you could dash around it in less than a week, but what's the point of rushing? You won't be disappointed on this route.

Belfast (p221) **& County Antrim** (p245) Two nights in Belfast. Spend one day exploring the city's sights and one on a driving tour to the Giant's Causeway.
🚗 2 hrs or 🚌 2¼ hrs to Dublin

Dublin (p35) A one-day whistle-stop tour of the capital should include Trinity College, the National Museum of Ireland – Archaeology and the Guinness Storehouse.
🚗 1½ hrs or 🚌 1¾ hrs to Kilkenny

Galway (p203) Drive north to Galway via the Cliffs of Moher, and spend three nights there; follow the city sights with a Connemara coastal tour.

Killarney (p166) Two nights based in Killarney, exploring nearby Killarney National Park, and taking a tour around the Ring of Kerry (180km).
🚗 5 hrs via Cliffs of Moher or 🚌 4 hrs (direct) to Galway

Kilkenny (p109) Take a day to explore Kilkenny's medieval heritage – castle, cathedral, and city walls, plus arts-and-crafts shops and riverside walks
🚗 2½ hrs to Cork

Kinsale (p149) Indulge yourself with a day of shopping, eating and lounging around in the lovely yachting harbour of Kinsale.
🚗 1½ hrs to Killarney

Cork (p135) Take in Cashel and Blarney on the way to Cork, and spend the next day seeing the city's sights, including Spike Island.
🚗 40 mins or 🚌 50 mins to Kinsale

Plan Your Trip
Family Travel

Ireland loves kids. Everywhere you go you'll find locals to be enthusiastic and inquisitive about your beloved progeny. However, this admiration hasn't always translated into services such as widespread and accessible baby-changing facilities, or high chairs in restaurants – especially in smaller towns and rural areas.

For further general information see Lonely Planet's Travel with Children. Also check out www.eumom.ie for advice for pregnant women and parents with young children, as well as www.babygoes2.com, a travel site about family-friendly accommodation worldwide.

Restaurants & Pubs

There are no legal restrictions on kids in any restaurant or cafe, but in practice many places (especially in higher price brackets, but not exclusively so) would prefer if you left the kids at home, especially at busy times or in the evenings. Then, high chairs suddenly become unavailable: if you're booking ahead, be sure to specify if you need one.

Children between 15 and 17 are allowed into pubs unaccompanied; under 15s must be accompanied and can only be in a licensed premises between 10.30am (12.30pm on Sunday) and 9pm (10pm

between May and September), after which they must leave. In rural areas, however, some publicans will allow children to remain in the bar so long as they're under proper parental supervision.

Feeding & Changing

Although breastfeeding is not a common sight (Ireland has one of the lowest rates of it in the world), you can do so with impunity pretty much everywhere without getting so much as a stare. Nappy-changing facilities are generally only found in the newer, larger shopping centres – otherwise you'll have to make do with a public toilet.

Sightseeing

When it comes to activities for the whole family, Ireland is much better placed than it was even a decade ago, as many providers recognise the importance of catering to the whole family. Most activity centres offer kids programs for all ages; many museums have kid-friendly exhibits and some even offer guided tours to suit younger ages.

As far as parks, gardens and green spaces go, Ireland has an abundance of them but very few amenities such as designated playgrounds and other exclusively child-friendly spots. In Dublin, St Stephen's Green has a popular playground in the middle of it, but it is the exception rather than the rule.

Getting Around

Children under five years travel free on all public transport. Trains are ideal for families, as there's lots of room to move

★ Best Sights & Activities

Dublin Zoo (p67)
Muckross Traditional Farms (p164)
Titanic Belfast (p226)
Carrick-a-Rede Rope Bridge (p257)
Fungie the Dolphin (p173)

about and store all of your gear, including buggies and prams.

Child seats are mandatory in rental cars for children aged nine months to four years. All main car-hire companies can provide them (around €50/£35 per week), but you'll need to book them in advance or else risk being disappointed when you pick the car up. For insurance reasons most will insist that you fit the child seat yourself.

From left: Chimpanzees, Dublin Zoo (p67); Fungie the dolphin (p173)

Christ Church Cathedral (p59)

Trinity College (p38)

C.EDHEVESTE/SHUTTERSTOCK ©

Christ Church Cathedral (p59)

Arriving in Dublin

Dublin Airport Buses to the city every 10 to 15 minutes between 6am and midnight; taxis (around €25) take 30 to 45 minutes.

Dublin Port Terminal Buses (adult/ child €3.50/2, 20 minutes) coincide with arrivals.

Busáras All Bus Eireann services arrive at Busáras; private operators have stops in different parts of the city.

Train Stations Main-line trains from all over Ireland arrive at Heuston or Connolly Stations.

Where to Stay

A surge in tourist numbers and the relative lack of beds means hotel prices can skyrocket, especially at weekends. There are good midrange options north of the Liffey, but the biggest spread of accommodation is south of the river, from midrange Georgian townhouses to the city's top hotels. Budget travellers rely on the selection of decent hostels.

For more information on where to stay, see p79.

GIMAS/SHUTTERSTOCK ©

Trinity College

This calm retreat from the bustle of contemporary Dublin is Ireland's most prestigious university, a collection of elegant Georgian and Victorian buildings, cobbled squares and manicured lawns – a delightful place to wander.

The college was established by Elizabeth I in 1592 on land confiscated from an Augustinian priory in an effort to stop the brain drain of young Protestant Dubliners, who were skipping across to continental Europe for an education and becoming 'infected with popery'. Trinity went on to become one of Europe's most outstanding universities, producing a host of notable graduates – how about Jonathan Swift, Oscar Wilde and Samuel Beckett at the same alumni dinner?

It remained completely Protestant until 1793, but even when the university relented and began to admit Catholics, the Catholic Church held firm; until 1970, any Catholic who enrolled here could consider themselves excommunicated.

The campus is a masterpiece of architecture and landscaping beautifully preserved in Georgian aspic. Most of the

Great For...

☑ Don't Miss

The Long Room (pictured right), which starred as the Jedi Archive in the movie *Star Wars Episode II: Attack of the Clones.*

The Long Room

OLIVIER CIRENDINI/LONELY PLANET ©

ℹ Need to Know

Map p60; 📞01-896 1000; www.tcd.ie; College Green; 🕗8am-10pm; 🚌all city centre, 🚊Westmoreland or Trinity FREE

✕ Take a Break

Fade Street Social (p71) is an excellent lunch spot just a few blocks southwest.

★ Top Tip

Student-led **walking tours** (Authenticity Tours; www.tcd.ie/visitors/tours; tours €6, incl Book of Kells €15; 🕗9.30am-3.40pm Mon-Sat, to 3.15pm Sun May-Sep, fewer midweek tours Oct & Feb-Apr) depart from the Regent House entrance on College Green.

---

buildings and statues date from the 18th and 19th centuries, each elegantly laid out on a cobbled or grassy square. The newer bits include the 1978 Arts & Social Science Building, which backs on to Nassau St and forms the alternative entrance to the college. Like the college's Berkeley Library, it was designed by Paul Koralek; it houses the Douglas Hyde Gallery of Modern Art.

To the south of Library Sq is the **Old Library** (Library Sq; adult/student/family €11/11/28, fast-track €14/11/28; 🕗8.30am-5pm Mon-Sat, from 9.30am Sun May-Sep, 9.30am-5pm Mon-Sat, noon-4.30pm Sun Oct-Apr), built in a severe style by Thomas Burgh between 1712 and 1732. It is one of five copyright libraries across Ireland and the UK, which means it's entitled to a copy of every book published in these islands – around five million books, of which only a fraction are stored here.

Trinity's greatest treasures are kept in the Old Library's stunning 65m Long Room, which houses about 200,000 of the library's oldest volumes, including the **Book of Kells**, a breathtaking illuminated manuscript of the four Gospels of the New Testament, created around AD 800 by monks on the Scottish island of Iona. Other displays include a rare copy of the Proclamation of the Irish Republic, which was read out by Pádraig (Patrick) Pearse at the beginning of the Easter Rising in 1916.

Also here is the so-called harp of Brian Ború, which was definitely not in use when the army of this early Irish hero defeated the Danes at the Battle of Clontarf in 1014. It does, however, date from around 1400, making it one of the oldest harps in Ireland. You can visit the library as part of a tour of the Long Room. Your entry ticket also includes admission to temporary exhibitions on display in the East Pavilion.

Trinity College, Dublin

STEP INTO THE PAST

Ireland's most prestigious university, founded by Queen Elizabeth I in 1592, is an architectural masterpiece, mostly dating to the 18th and 19th centuries, and a cordial retreat from the bustle of modern life in the middle of the city. Step through its main entrance and you step back in time, the cobbled stones transporting you to another era, when the elite discussed philosophy and argued passionately in favour of empire.

Standing in Front Sq, the 30m-high ❶ Campanile is directly in front of you with the ❷ Dining Hall to your left. On the far side of the square is the Old Library building, the centrepiece of which is the magnificent ❸ Long Room, which was the inspiration for the computer-generated imagery of the Jedi Archive in *Star Wars Episode II: Attack of the Clones*. Here you'll find the university's greatest treasure, the ❹ Book of Kells. You'll probably have to queue to see this masterpiece, and then only for a brief visit, but it's very much worth it.

Just beyond the Old Library is the very modern ❺ Berkeley Library, which nevertheless fits perfectly into the campus's overall aesthetic. Directly in front of it is the distinctive ❻ Sphere Within a Sphere, the most elegant of the university's sculptures.

DON'T MISS

➡ Douglas Hyde Gallery, the campus's designated modern-art museum.

➡ A cricket match on the pitch, the most elegant of pastimes.

➡ A pint in the Pavilion Bar, preferably while watching the cricket.

➡ A visit to the Science Gallery, where science is made completely relevant.

Campanile
Trinity College's most iconic bit of masonry was designed in the mid-19th century by Sir Charles Lanyon; the attached sculptures were created by Thomas Kirk.

RPEDROSA/GETTY IMAGES ©

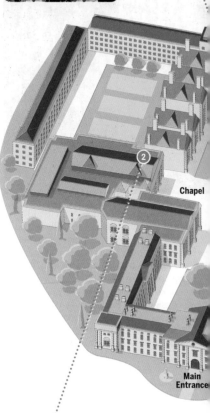

Chapel

Main Entrance

Dining Hall
Richard Cassels' original building was designed to mirror the Examination Hall directly opposite on Front Sq: the hall collapsed twice and was rebuilt from scratch in 1761.

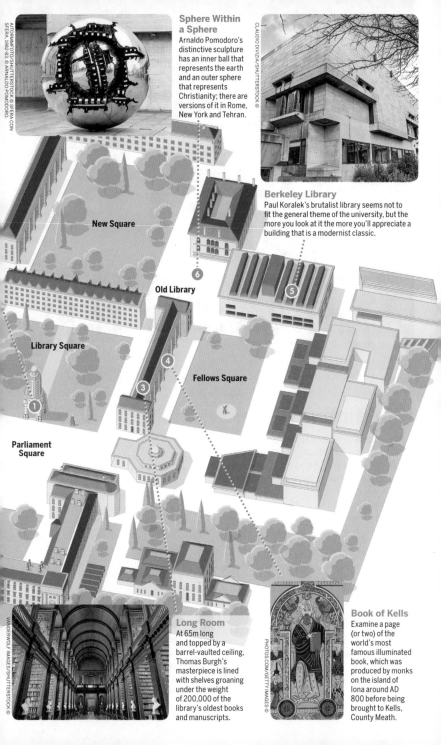

Sphere Within a Sphere

Arnaldo Pomodoro's distinctive sculpture has an inner ball that represents the earth and an outer sphere that represents Christianity; there are versions of it in Rome, New York and Tehran.

Berkeley Library

Paul Koralek's brutalist library seems not to fit the general theme of the university, but the more you look at it the more you'll appreciate a building that is a modernist classic.

New Square

Old Library

Library Square

Fellows Square

Parliament Square

Long Room

At 65m long and topped by a barrel-vaulted ceiling, Thomas Burgh's masterpiece is lined with shelves groaning under the weight of 200,000 of the library's oldest books and manuscripts.

Book of Kells

Examine a page (or two) of the world's most famous illuminated book, which was produced by monks on the island of Iona around AD 800 before being brought to Kells, County Meath.

SALVADOR MANIQUIZ/SHUTTERSTOCK ©

Kilmainham Gaol

If you have any desire to understand Irish history – especially the juicy bits about resistance to British rule – then a visit to this former prison is an absolute must.

Great For...

☑ Don't Miss

Kilmainham houses an outstanding museum dedicated to Irish nationalism and prison life.

This threatening grey building, built between 1792 and 1795, played a role in virtually every act of Ireland's painful path to independence and even today, despite closing in 1924, it still has the power to chill.

It took four years to build, and the prison opened – or rather closed – its doors in 1796. The Irish were locked up for all sorts of misdemeanours, some more serious than others. A six-year-old boy spent a month here in 1839 because his father couldn't pay his train fare, and during the Famine it was crammed with the destitute imprisoned for stealing food and begging. But it is most famous for incarcerating 120 years of Irish nationalists, from Robert Emmet in 1803 to Éamon de Valera in 1923. All of Ireland's botched uprisings ended with the leaders' confinement here, usually before their execution.

MATTHI/SHUTTERSTOCK ©

ℹ Need to Know

Map p64; 📞01-453 5984; www.kilmainham
gaolmuseum.ie; Inchicore Rd; adult/child
€9/5; 🕙9am-7pm Jun-Aug, 9.30am-5.30pm
Oct-Mar, 9am-6pm Apr, May & Sep; 🚌69, 79
from Aston Quay, 13, 40 from O'Connell St

✕ Take a Break

The 1845 Old Royal Oak pub (p75) is
just east of Kilmainham Gaol.

★ Top Tip

Book online as far in advance as possible to get your preferred visiting time.

It was the treatment of the leaders of
the 1916 Easter Rising that most deeply
etched the gaol into the Irish conscious-
ness. Fourteen of the rebel commanders
were executed in the stone breakers' yard,
including James Connolly who was so badly
injured at the time of his execution that he
was strapped to a chair at the opposite end
of the yard.

The gaol's final function was as a prison
for the newly formed Irish Free State, an
irony best summed up with the story of
Ernie O'Malley, who escaped from the gaol
when incarcerated by the British but was
locked up again by his erstwhile comrades
during the Civil War. This chapter is played
down on the tour, and even the passing
comment that Kilmainham's final prisoner
was the future president, Éamon de Valera,
doesn't reveal that he had been imprisoned
by his fellow Irish citizens. The gaol was
decommissioned in 1924.

An excellent audiovisual introduction to
the building is followed by a thought-
provoking tour of the eerie prison, the
largest unoccupied building of its kind in
Europe. Sitting incongruously outside in
the yard is the *Asgard*, the ship that successfully ran the British blockade to deliver
arms to Nationalist forces in 1914. The tour
finishes in the gloomy yard where the 1916
executions took place.

MADRUGADA VERDE/SHUTTERSTOCK ©

Dublin Castle

*This mostly 18th-century creation –
more hotchpotch palace than medieval
castle, though a 13th-century tower
survives – was the stronghold of British
power in Ireland for 700 years.*

The castle is now used by the Irish government for meetings and functions, and the best bits are only visible as part of a 70-minute guided tour (departing every 20 to 30 minutes, depending on numbers).

It was officially handed over to Michael Collins, representing the Irish Free State, in 1922, when the British viceroy is reported to have rebuked Collins on being seven minutes late. Collins replied, 'We've been waiting 700 years, you can wait seven minutes'.

As you walk into the grounds from the main Dame St entrance, there's a good example of the evolution of Irish architecture. On your left is the Victorian Chapel Royal (occasionally part of the Dublin Castle tours), decorated with more than 90 heads of various Irish personages and saints carved out of Tullamore limestone. Beside

Great For...

☑ **Don't Miss**

The view over Dublin from the top of the Bedford Tower.

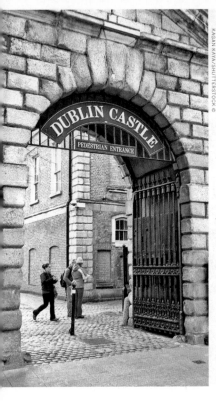

KAGAN KAYA/SHUTTERSTOCK ©

ℹ Need to Know

Map p60; ☏ 01-645 8813; www.dublincastle.
ie; Dame St; guided tours adult/child €12/6,
self-guided tours €8/4; ⏱ 9.45am-5.45pm, last
admission 5.15pm; 🚌 all city centre

✗ Take a Break

Head across the street to Queen of Tarts
(p70) for great cakes and coffee.

★ Top Tip

There's a self-guided tour option, but it
only includes the State Apartments.

this is the Norman Record Tower with its
5m-thick walls. It's currently closed to the
public pending a long-awaited revamp.
On your right is the Georgian Treasury
Building, the oldest office block in Dublin,
and behind you, yikes, is the uglier-than-sin
Revenue Commissioners Building of 1960.

Heading away from that eyesore, you
ascend to the Upper Yard. On your right
is a figure of Justice with her back turned
to the city – an appropriate symbol for
British justice, reckoned Dubliners. Next to
it is the 18th-century Bedford Tower, from
which the Irish Crown Jewels were stolen in
1907 and never recovered. Opposite is the
entrance for the tours.

The guided tours are pretty dry, but you
get to visit the State Apartments, many of

which are decorated in dubious taste. You
will also see St Patrick's Hall, where Irish
presidents are inaugurated and foreign
dignitaries toasted, and the room in which
the wounded James Connolly was tied to
a chair while convalescing after the 1916
Easter Rising, so that he could be executed
by firing squad.

Another highlight is a visit to the medieval undercroft of the old castle, discovered
by accident in 1986. It includes foundations
built by the Vikings (whose long-lasting
mortar was made of ox blood, egg shells
and horse hair), the hand-polished exterior
of the castle walls that prevented attackers
from climbing them, the steps leading
down to the moat and the trickle of the
historic River Poddle, which once filled the
moat on its way to join the Liffey.

Chester Beatty Library

The world-famous Chester Beatty Library, housed in the Clock Tower at the back of Dublin Castle, is not just Ireland's best small museum, but one of the best you'll find anywhere in Europe.

Great For...

☑ Don't Miss

Fragments of the Christian gospels written on papyrus, dating from around AD 200.

Sir Alfred Chester Beatty

An avid traveller and collector, Beatty was fascinated by different cultures and amassed more than 20,000 manuscripts, rare books, miniature paintings, clay tablets, costumes and any other objets d'art that caught his fancy and could tell him something about the world. Fortunately for Dublin, he also happened to take quite a shine to the city and made it his adopted home. In return, the Irish made him their first honorary citizen in 1957.

Artistic Traditions

The collection is spread over two levels. On the 1st floor you'll find Artistic Traditions, which begins with a collection of memorabilia from Beatty's life, before embarking on an exploration of the art of Mogul India, Persia, the Ottoman Empire, Japan and

ⓘ Need to Know

Map p60; ☎01-407 0750; www.cbl.ie; Dublin Castle; ⏰10am-5pm Mon-Fri, from 11am Sat & Sun Mar-Oct, 10am-5pm Tue-Fri, from 11am Sat & Sun Nov-Feb; 🚌all city centre FREE

✖ Take a Break

The library's own Silk Road Café (p70) is a great place for lunch.

★ Top Tip

The library regularly holds specialist workshops, exhibitions and talks on everything from origami to calligraphy.

China. Here you'll find intricately designed little medicine boxes and perhaps the finest collection of Chinese jade books in the world. The illuminated European texts are also worth examining.

Sacred Traditions

The 2nd floor is home to Sacred Traditions, which offers a fascinating insight into the rituals and rites of passage of the major world religions – Judaism, Christianity, Islam, Buddhism and Hinduism. There are audiovisual explorations of the lives of Christ and the Buddha, and of the Muslim pilgrimage to Mecca.

The collection of Qur'ans from the 9th to the 19th centuries is considered to be among the best examples of illuminated Islamic texts in the world. You'll also find ancient Egyptian papyrus texts (including Egyptian love poems from around 1100 BC), scrolls and exquisite artwork from Myanmar (Burma), Indonesia and Tibet – as well as the second-oldest biblical fragment ever found (after the Dead Sea Scrolls).

The Building

As if all of this wasn't enough for one visit, the library also hosts temporary exhibits that are usually too good to be missed. Not only are the contents of the museum outstanding, but the layout, design and location are also unparalleled, from the marvellous Silk Road Café and gift shop, to the Zen rooftop terrace and the beautiful landscaped garden out the front. These features alone would make this an absolute Dublin must-do.

Exterior of NMI – Archaeology

ANTON_IVANOV/SHUTTERSTOCK ©

National Museum of Ireland

The mother of all Irish museums and the country's most important cultural institution was established in 1877 as the primary repository of the nation's treasures.

The collection is so big that it is spread across three separate museums – the archaeology museum in Kildare St, the decorative arts museum at Collins Barracks and a country life museum in County Mayo, on Ireland's west coast. They're all fascinating, but the star attractions are to be found in the archaeology museum, mixed up in Europe's finest collection of Bronze and Iron Age gold artefacts, the most complete collection of medieval Celtic metalwork in the world, fascinating prehistoric and Viking artefacts, and a few interesting items relating to Ireland's fight for independence. If you don't mind groups, the themed guided tours will help you wade through the myriad exhibits.

Great For...

☑ **Don't Miss**

The extraordinary hoard of prehistoric gold objects in the archaeology museum.

Interior of NMI – Archaeology

ANTON_IVANOV/SHUTTERSTOCK ©

NMI Decorative Arts & History
O'Connell-GPO Abbey Street
Museum Jervis Smithfield Four Courts Westmoreland Dame St Trinity Pearse St
Thomas St High St Dawson
NMI Archaelology
St Stephen's Green

ⓘ Need to Know

NMI – Archaeology (Map p60; www.museum.ie; Kildare St; ⊙10am-5pm Tue-Sat, from 1pm Sun; 🚌all city centre) FREE
NMI – Decorative Arts & History (Map p64; www.museum.ie; Benburb St; ⊙10am-5pm Tue-Sat, from 2pm Sun; 🚌25, 66, 67, 90 from city centre, 🚇Museum) FREE

✗ Take a Break

There are several good places to eat on Merrion Row, just south of the archaeology museum.

★ Top Tip

You can travel between the two museum locations on a hop-on, hop-off tour bus.

National Museum of Ireland – Archaeology

Treasury

The Treasury is the most famous part of the collection, and its centrepieces are Ireland's best-known crafted artefacts, the Ardagh Chalice and the Tara Brooch. The 12th-century Ardagh Chalice is made of gold, silver, bronze, brass, copper and lead; it measures 17.8cm high and 24.2cm in diameter and, put simply, is the finest example of Celtic art ever found. The equally renowned Tara Brooch was crafted around AD 700, primarily in white bronze, but with traces of gold, silver, glass, copper, enamel and wire beading, and was used as a clasp for a cloak. It was discovered on a beach in Bettystown, County Meath, in 1850, but later came into the hands of an art dealer who named it after the hill of Tara, the historic seat of the ancient high kings. It doesn't have quite the same ring to it, but it was the Bettystown Brooch that sparked a revival of interest in Celtic jewellery that hasn't let up to this day. There are many other pieces that testify to Ireland's history as the land of saints and scholars.

Ór-Ireland's Gold

Elsewhere in the Treasury is the *Ór–Ireland's Gold* exhibition, featuring stunning jewellery and decorative objects created by Celtic artisans in the Bronze and Iron Ages. Among them are the Broighter Hoard, which includes a 1st-century-BC large gold collar, unsurpassed anywhere in Europe, and an extraordinarily delicate gold boat. There's also the wonderful Loughnasade bronze war trumpet, which also dates from the 1st century BC. It is 1.86m long and made of sheets of bronze, riveted together, with an intricately designed disc at the mouth. It produces a sound similar to the Australian didgeridoo, though you'll have to take our word for it. Running alongside the wall is a 15m log boat, which was dropped into the water to soften, abandoned and then pulled out 4000 years later, almost perfectly preserved in the peat bog.

Kingship & Sacrifice

One of the museum's biggest showstoppers is the collection of Iron Age 'bog bodies' in the *Kingship and Sacrifice* exhibit – four figures in varying states of preservation dug out of the midland bogs. The bodies' various eerily preserved details – a distinctive tangle of hair, sinewy legs and fingers with fingernails intact – are memorable, but it's the accompanying detail that will make you pause: scholars now believe that all of these bodies were victims of the most horrendous ritualistic torture and sacrifice – the cost of being notable figures in the Celtic world.

Other Exhibits

If you can cope with any more history, upstairs are Medieval Ireland 1150–1550, Viking Age Ireland – which features exhibits from the excavations at Wood Quay, the area between Christ Church Cathedral and the river – and our own favourite, the aptly named Clothes from Bogs in Ireland, a collection of 16th- and 17th-century woollen garments recovered from the bog. Enthralling stuff!

National Museum of Ireland – Decorative Arts & History

Once the world's largest military barracks, this splendid early neoclassical grey-stone building on the Liffey's northern banks was completed in 1704 according to the design of Thomas Burgh (he of Trinity College's Old Library). It is now home to the

NMI – Decorative Arts & History

Decorative Arts & History collection of the National Museum of Ireland, with a range of superb permanent exhibits ranging from a history of the Easter Rising to the work of iconic Irish designer Eileen Gray (1878–1976).

The Building

The building's central square held six entire regiments and is a truly awesome space, surrounded by arcaded colonnades and blocks linked by walking bridges. Following the handover to the new Irish government in 1922, the barracks was renamed to honour Michael Collins, a hero of the struggle for independence, who was killed that year in the Civil War; to this day most Dubliners refer to the museum as the Collins Barracks. Indeed, the army coat he wore on the day of his death (there's still mud on the sleeve) is part of the Soldiers and Chiefs exhibit, which covers the history of Irish soldiery at home and abroad from 1550 to the 21st century.

The Exhibits

The museum's exhibits include a treasure trove of artefacts ranging from silver, ceramics and glassware to weaponry, furniture and folk-life displays. The fascinating Way We Wore exhibit displays Irish clothing and jewellery from the past 250 years. An intriguing sociocultural study, it highlights the symbolism jewellery and clothing had in bestowing messages of mourning, love and identity.

The old Riding School is home to Proclaiming a Republic: The 1916 Rising, which opened in 2016 as an updated version of the long-standing exhibit dedicated to the rebellion. The exhibit explores the complicated socio-historical background to the Rising and also includes visceral memorabilia such as first-hand accounts of the violence of the Black and Tans and post-Rising hunger strikes, and the handwritten death certificates of the Republican prisoners and their postcards from Holloway prison.

Some of the best pieces are gathered in the Curator's Choice exhibition, which is a collection of 25 objects hand-picked by different curators and displayed alongside an account of why each object was chosen.

★ Top Tip

If you want to avoid crowds, the best time to visit is a weekday afternoon, when school groups have gone, and never during Irish school holidays.

TRABANTOS/SHUTTERSTOCK ©

★ Local Knowledge

A 10-minute walk east along the Liffey from the decorative arts museum is the atmospheric Legal Eagle (p72), a great spot for a pub lunch or dinner.

National Museum of Ireland

NATIONAL TREASURES

Ireland's most important cultural institution is the National Museum, and its most important branch is the original one, housed in this fine neoclassical (or Victorian Palladian) building designed by Sir Thomas Newenham Deane and finished in 1890. Squeezed in between the rear entrance of Leinster House – the Irish parliament – and a nondescript building from the 1960s, it's easy to pass by the museum. But within its fairly cramped confines you'll find the most extensive collection of Bronze and Iron Age gold artefacts in Europe and the extraordinary collection of the Treasury. This includes the stunning ❶ Ardagh Chalice and the delicately crafted ❷ Tara Brooch. Amid all the lustre, look out for the ❸ Broighter Gold Collar then pay a visit to the exquisite ❹ Cross of Cong, which was created after the other pieces but is just as beautiful. Finally, on the other side of the building is the unforgettable ❺ Kingship & Sacrifice exhibit, where you'll find 'bog bodies' - actual Celts preserved to an uncanny level of detail.

As you visit these treasures – all created after the arrival of Christianity in the 5th century – bear in mind that they were produced with the most rudimentary of instruments.

VIKING DUBLIN

Archaeological excavations in Dublin between 1961 and 1981 unearthed evidence of a Viking town and cemeteries along the banks of the River Liffey. The graves contained weapons such as swords and spears, together with jewellery and personal items. Craftsmen's tools, weights and scales, silver ingots and coins show that the Vikings, as well as marauding and raiding, were also engaged in commercial activities. The Viking artefacts are now part of the National Museum's collection.

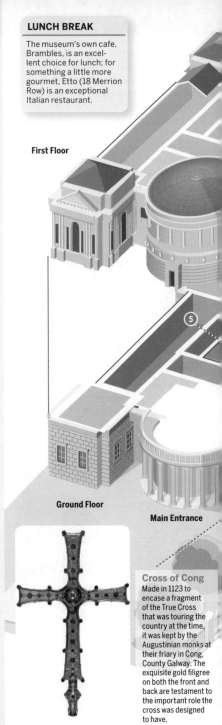

LUNCH BREAK

The museum's own cafe, Brambles, is an excellent choice for lunch; for something a little more gourmet, Etto (18 Merrion Row) is an exceptional Italian restaurant.

First Floor

Ground Floor

Main Entrance

Cross of Cong
Made in 1123 to encase a fragment of the True Cross that was touring the country at the time, it was kept by the Augustinian monks at their friary in Cong, County Galway. The exquisite gold filigree on both the front and back are testament to the important role the cross was designed to have.

Broighter Gold Collar
The most exquisite element of the larger Broighter Hoard, this beautiful gold neck ornament (called a torc) is decorated in the elaborate curved patterns of high Celtic art, called La Tène style.

Tara Brooch
Designed around AD 700 as a clasp for a cloak, this is the second superstar of the collection – its delicate craftsmanship has become a symbol of the excellence of Irish art.

Kingship & Sacrifice
One of the museum's biggest showstoppers is the collection of Iron Age 'bog bodies' in the Kingship and Sacrifice exhibit – four figures in varying states of preservation dug out of the midland bogs.

Ardagh Chalice
Made of gold, silver, bronze, brass, copper and lead, the 12th-century Ardagh Chalice is the finest example of Celtic art ever found.

VANDERWOLF IMAGES/SHUTTERSTOCK ©

Guinness Storehouse

More than any other beer produced anywhere in the world, Guinness has transcended its own brand. This beer-lover's Disneyland is a multimedia homage to Ireland's most famous export.

The mythology around Guinness is remarkably durable: it doesn't travel well; its distinctive flavour comes from Liffey water; it is good for you – not to mention the generally held belief that you will never understand the Irish until you develop a taste for the black stuff. All absolutely true, of course, so it should be no surprise that the Guinness Storehouse, in the heart of the St James's Gate Brewery, is the city's most-visited tourist attraction, an all-singing, all-dancing extravaganza that combines sophisticated exhibits, spectacular design and a thick, creamy head of marketing hype.

Great For...

☑ **Don't Miss**

Enjoying the view from the Gravity Bar with your free pint of Guinness (included with admission).

Guinness Storehouse Museum

The old Fermentation House, the only part of the massive, 26-hectare St James's Gate Brewery open to the public, is a suitable

THE TASTING ROOMS

COURTESY OF DIAGEO ©

Guinness Storehouse
Pim St
S Market St
Bellevue

❶ Need to Know

Map p64; www.guinness-storehouse.com; St James's Gate, S Market St; adult/child from €18.50/16, Connoisseur Experience €55; ⏰9.30am-7pm Sep-Jun, 9am-8pm Jul & Aug; 🚌13, 21A, 40, 51B, 78, 78A, 123 from Fleet St, 🚋James's

✕ Take a Break

Arthur's Pub (p75) on the 5th floor of the building serves up delicious bar lunches.

★ Top Tip

Avoid the queues (and save money) by buying your ticket in advance, online.

cathedral in which to worship the black gold. A stunning central atrium rises seven storeys in the shape of a pint of Guinness, with a dazzling array of audiovisual and interactive exhibits that cover most aspects of the brewery's story and explain the brewing process in overwhelming detail. The head is represented by the glass-walled Gravity Bar, which provides panoramic views of Dublin to savour with your complimentary half-pint.

The Perfect Pour

As you work your way to the top and your prize of arguably the nicest Guinness you could drink anywhere, you'll explore the various elements that made the beer the brand that it is and perhaps understand a little better the efforts made by the company to ensure its quasi-mythical status. From the (copy of) the original 9000-year lease (in a glass box embedded in the ground floor) to the near-scientific lesson in how to pour the perfect pint, everything about this place is designed to make you understand that Guinness isn't just any other beer.

Arthur Guinness

One fun fact you will learn is that genius can be inadvertent: at some point in the 18th century, a London brewer accidentally burnt his hops while brewing ale, and so created the dark beer we know today. Its name of 'porter' came because the dark beer was very popular with London porters. In the 1770s, Arthur Guinness, who had until then only brewed ale, started brewing the dark stuff to get a jump on all other Irish brewers. By 1799 he decided to concentrate all his efforts on this single brew. He died four years later, aged 83, but the foundations for world domination were already in place.

Dublin Crawl Walking Tour

If there's one constant, it's that Dubliners will always take a drink. Come hell or high water, the city's pubs will never be short of customers.

Start Lower Camden St
Distance 2.5km
Duration One hour to two days

Jervis

Ha'penny Bridge

Millennium Bridge

Wellington Quay

Temple Bar **FINISH**

TEMPLE BAR

Eustace St

Upper Fownes St

Crown Al

Cope St

7

Dame St

Lord Edward St

250 m
0.1 miles

Exchequer St

Castle Market

Dubhlinn Garden

S Great George's St

Fade St

4

6 **5**

Drury St

S William St

Lower Stephen St

6 Hogan's (35 S Great George's St; 1.30pm-11.30pm, Mon-Wed, to 1am Thu, to 2.30am Fri & Sat, 2-11pm Sun) has been one of the most popular watering holes in the city for longer than most of its clientele has been alive

5 Occupying the upstairs floor of an old townhouse, **No Name Bar** (3 Fade St; 12.30-11.30pm Sun-Wed, to 1am Thu, to 2.30am Fri & Sat; all city centre) is one of the city centre's most pleasant and handsome watering holes.

Coombe

Redmonds Hill

Lower Kevin St

Cuffe St

New St

New Bride St

Wexford St

Camden Row

Lower Camden St

Montague St

Harcourt St

Camden Pl

1 Start in the always excellent **Anseo** (4pm to 11.30pm Mon-Thu, to 12.30am Fri & Sat, 11am-11pm Sun; 14, 15, 65, 83) where hipsters rub shoulders with the hoi polloi.

Pleasants St

1 **START**

Grantham St

7 Finally, ring the doorbell to access the **Vintage Cocktail Club** (www.vintagecocktailclub.com; Crown Alley; ⊘5pm-1.30am Mon-Fri, 12.30pm-1.30am Sat & Sun; 🖵all city centre) If you've followed the tour correctly, you might not be able to find it. How many fingers?

Classic Photo: Grogan's Castle Lounge

4 Discuss the merits of that unwritten masterpiece with a clutch of frustrated writers in **Grogan's Castle Lounge** (p73).

2 Become a character in *Mad Men* at the whiskey bar at trendy **37 Dawson St** (☎01-902 2908; www.37dawsonstreet.ie ⊘10.30am-11.30pm Mon-Thu, to 12.30am Fri & Sat, noon-11pm Sun; 🖵all city centre).

3 Sink a glorious pint of plain (Guinness) in the atmospheric snug at **Kehoe's** (9 S Anne St; ⊘11am-11.30pm Mon-Thu, to 12.30am Fri & Sat, 12.30-11pm Sun; 🖵all city centre).

◎ SIGHTS

◎ Grafton St & Around

National Gallery
Museum

(Map p60; www.nationalgallery.ie; Merrion Sq W; ⓘ9.15am-5.30pm Tue-Wed, Fri & Sat, to 8.30pm Thu, 11am-5.30pm Sun-Mon; ☐4, 7, 8, 39A, 46A from city centre) **FREE** A magnificent Caravaggio and a breathtaking collection of works by Jack B Yeats – William Butler's younger brother – are the main reasons to visit the National Gallery, but not the only ones. Its excellent collection is strong in Irish art, and there are also high-quality collections of every major European school of painting.

Museum of Natural History
Museum

(National Museum of Ireland – Natural History; Map p60; www.museum.ie; Upper Merrion St; ⓘ10am-5pm Tue-Sat, from 1pm Sun; ☐7, 44 from city centre) **FREE** Affectionately known as the 'Dead Zoo', this dusty, weird and utterly compelling museum is a fine example of the scientific wonderment of the Victorian age. Its enormous collection of stuffed beasts and carefully annotated specimens has barely changed since Scottish explorer Dr David Livingstone opened it in 1857 – before disappearing into the African jungle for a meeting with Henry Stanley.

Little Museum of Dublin
Museum

(Map p60; ☎01-661 1000; www.littlemuseum. ie; 15 St Stephen's Green N; adult/student €10/8; ⓘ9.30am-5pm, to 8pm Thu, last admission 7pm; ☐all city centre, ☐St Stephen's Green) This award-winning museum tells the story of Dublin over the last century via memorabilia, photographs and artefacts donated by the general public. The impressive collection, spread over the rooms of a handsome Georgian house, includes a lectern used by JFK on his 1963 visit to Ireland and an original copy of the fateful letter given to the Irish envoys to the treaty negotiations of 1921, whose contradictory instructions were at the heart of the split that resulted in the Civil War.

There's a whole room on the 2nd floor devoted to the history of U2, as well as the personal archive of Alfred 'Alfie' Byrne (1882–1956), mayor of Dublin a record 10 times and known as the 'Shaking Hand of

Museum of Natural History

BOULENGER XAVIER/SHUTTERSTOCK ©

Dublin'. Visit is by guided tour, which goes on the hour every hour. The museum also runs the Green Mile walking tour (p67) of St Stephen's Green.

St Stephen's Green   Park

(Map p60; ⊙dawn-dusk; 🚇all city centre; 🚌St Stephen's Green) As you watch the assorted groups of friends, lovers and individuals splaying themselves across the nine elegantly landscaped hectares of Dublin's most popular green lung, St Stephen's Green, consider that those same hectares once formed a common for public whippings, burnings and hangings. These days, the harshest treatment you'll get is the warden chucking you out if you disturb the carefully tended flower beds.

◎ Temple Bar

You can visit all of Temple Bar's attractions in less than half a day, but that's not really the point: this cobbled neighbourhood, for so long the city's most infamous party zone, is really more about ambience than attractions. If you visit during the day, the district's bohemian bent is on display. You can browse for vintage clothes, get your nipples pierced, nibble on Mongolian barbecue, buy organic food, pick up the latest musical releases and buy books on every conceivable subject. You can check out the latest art installations or join in a pulsating drum circle. By night – or at the weekend – it's a different story altogether, as the area's bars are packed to the rafters with revellers looking to tap into their inner Bacchus: it's loud, raucous and usually a lot of fun.

Christ Church Cathedral   Church

(Church of the Holy Trinity; Map p60; www. christchurchcathedral.ie; Christ Church Pl; adult/student/child €7/5.50/2.50, with Dublinia €15/12.50/7.50; ⊙9.30am-5pm Mon-Sat, from 12.30pm Sun year-round, longer hours Mar-Oct; 🚌50, 50A, 56A from Aston Quay, 54, 54A from Burgh Quay) Its hilltop location and eye-catching flying buttresses make this the most photogenic of Dublin's cathe-

📖 Explore Literary Dublin

Newly opened in September 2019, the **Museum of Literature Ireland** (MoLI; Map p60; 📞01-477 9810; www.moli.ie; 85-86 St Stephen's Green S; adult/child under 3/ concession/family €8/free/6/17, guided tour €12; ⊙10am-6pm; 🚇all city centre, 🚌St Stephen's Green) is a digital, interactive exploration of Ireland's deep literary heritage, from the Middle Ages to the present day. Highlights include Joyce's *Ulysses* notebooks as well as the very first print of the novel. The museum is in two stunning Georgian townhouses collectively known as Newman House, which in 1865 saw the establishment of the Catholic University of Ireland, the alma mater of Joyce, Pádraig Pearse and Éamon de Valera.

Marsh's Library (Map p60; www. marshlibrary.ie; St Patrick's Close; adult/child €5/free; ⊙9.30am-5pm Mon & Wed-Fri, from 10am Sat; 🚌50, 50A, 56A from Aston Quay, 54, 54A from Burgh Quay) is a magnificently preserved scholars library, virtually unchanged in three centuries. It's one of Dublin's most beautiful open secrets and an absolute highlight of any visit. Atop its ancient stairs are beautiful dark-oak bookcases, each topped with elaborately carved and gilded gables, and crammed with 25,000 books, manuscripts and maps dating back to the 15th century.

Memorabilia aplenty and lots of literary ephemera line the walls and display cabinets of elegant **Dublin Writers Museum** (Map p68; www.writersmuseum.com; 18 N Parnell Sq; adult/child €7/6; ⊙9.45am-4.45pm Mon-Sat, 11am-4.30pm Sun; 🚌3, 7, 10, 11, 13, 16, 19, 46A, 123 from city centre), devoted to preserving the city's rich literary tradition up to 1970.

drals. It was founded in 1030 and rebuilt from 1172, mostly under the impetus of Richard de Clare, Earl of Pembroke (better

Temple Bar, Grafton St & St Stephen's Green

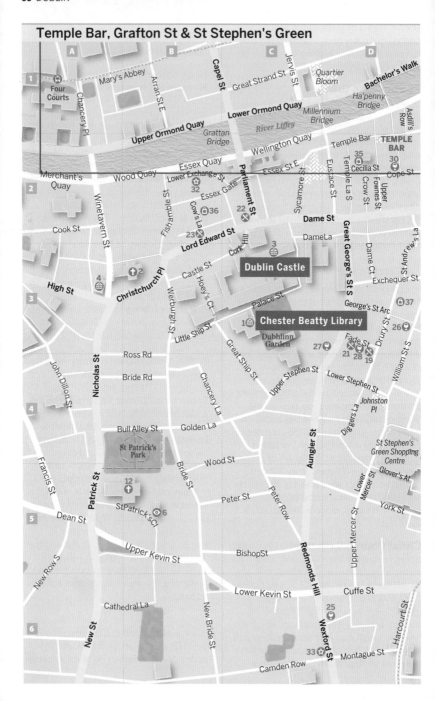

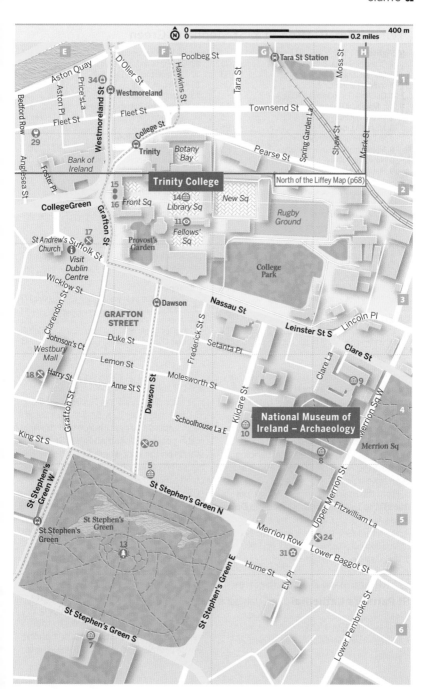

0 | 400 m
0 | 0.2 miles

E

Aston Quay
Price's La
Aston Pl
Bedford Row
Fleet St

F

Poolbeg St
D'Olier St
Hawkins St
Westmoreland St
34
Westmoreland
Fleet St
College St
Trinity
Bank of Ireland

G

Tara St Station
Moss St
Tara St
Townsend St
Spring Garden La
Pearse St
Shaw St
Mark St

H

1

Botany Bay

Trinity College

North of the Liffey Map (p68)

2

Foster Pl
Anglesea St

CollegeGreen
15
16 Front Sq
14 Library Sq
New Sq
Rugby Ground

Grafton St

St Andrew's Church
Suffolk St
17
Visit Dublin Centre
Wicklow St
Provost's Garden
Fellows' Sq
11

College Park

Clarendon St
Johnson's Ct
Westbury Mall
18 Harry St
King St S
Grafton St

Dawson
GRAFTON STREET
Duke St
Lemon St
Anne St S
Dawson St
Molesworth St
Schoolhouse La E

Nassau St
Frederick St S
Setanta Pl
Kildare St
10

Leinster St S
Lincoln Pl
Clare La
Clare St
9
Merrion Sq W

3

National Museum of Ireland – Archaeology

4

20
5
St Stephen's Green W
St Stephen's Green
St Stephen's Green
13
St Stephen's Green N
8
Merrion Sq
Upper Merrion St
Fitzwilliam La
Merrion Row
24
31
Lower Baggot St
Ely Pl
Hume St
St Stephen's Green E
St Stephen's Green S
7
Lower Pembroke St

5

6

Temple Bar, Grafton St & St Stephen's Green

known as Strongbow), the Anglo-Norman noble who invaded Ireland in 1170 and whose monument has pride of place inside.

Guided tours (Map p60; tour €11; ☉hourly 11am-noon & 2-4pm Mon-Fri, 2-4pm Sat) include the belfry, where a campanologist explains the art of bell-ringing and you can even have a go.

From the main entrance, a bridge, part of the 1871 to 1878 restoration, leads to **Dublinia** (Map p60; ☎01-679 4611; www.dublinia. ie; adult/student/child €10/9/6.50, with Christ Church Cathedral €15/12.50/7.50; ☉10am-5.30pm Mar-Sep, to 4.30pm Oct-Feb).

⊚ Kilmainham & The Liberties

St Patrick's Cathedral   Cathedral
(Map p60; ☎01-453 9472; www.stpatricks cathedral.ie; St Patrick's Close; adult/student €8/7; ☉9.30am-5pm Mon-Fri, 9am-6pm Sat,

9-10.30am, 12.30-2.30pm & 4.30-6pm Sun Mar-Oct, 9.30am-5pm Mon-Fri, from 9am Sat, 9-10.30am & 12.30-2.30pm Sun Nov-Feb; ☐50, 50A, 56A from Aston Quay, 54, 54A from Burgh Quay) Ireland's largest church and the final resting place of Jonathan Swift, St Patrick's stands on the spot where St Patrick himself reputedly baptised the local Celtic chieftains in the 5th century. Fiction or not, it's a sacred bit of turf upon which this cathedral was built between 1191 and 1270. The adjacent park was once an awful slum but is now a lovely garden to sit and catch some sunshine.

Like Christ Church Cathedral, the building has suffered a rather dramatic history of storm and fire damage and has been altered several times (most questionably in 1864 when the flying buttresses were added, thanks to the neo-Gothic craze that swept the nation). Oliver Cromwell, during his 1649 visit to

Ireland, converted St Patrick's to a stable for his army's horses, an indignity to which he also subjected numerous other Irish churches. Jonathan Swift, author of *Gulliver's Travels,* was the dean of the cathedral from 1713 to 1745, but after his tenure the cathedral was very neglected until its restoration in the 1860s. Also like Christ Church, St Patrick's is a Church of Ireland cathedral – which means that overwhelmingly Catholic Dublin has two Anglican cathedrals!

Entering the cathedral from the southwestern porch you come almost immediately, on your right, to the tombs of Swift and his long-time companion Esther Johnson, aka Stella. On the wall nearby are Swift's own (self-praising) Latin epitaphs to the two of them, and a bust of Swift.

The huge, dusty Boyle Monument to the left was erected in 1632 by Richard Boyle, Earl of Cork, and is decorated with numerous painted figures of members of his family. The figure in the centre on the bottom level is the earl's five-year-old son Robert Boyle (1627–91), who grew up to become a noted scientist. His contributions to physics include Boyle's Law, which relates to the pressure and volume of gases.

Irish Museum of Modern Art
Museum

(IMMA; Map p64; www.imma.ie; Military Rd; ⊙11.30am-5.30pm Tue-Fri, from 10am Sat, from noon Sun, tours 1.15pm Wed, 2.30pm Sat & Sun; 🚌51, 51D, 51X, 69, 78, 79 from Aston Quay, 🚆Heuston) FREE Ireland's most important collection of modern and contemporary Irish and international art is housed in the elegant, airy expanse of the Royal Hospital Kilmainham, designed by Sir William Robinson and built between 1684 and 1687 as a retirement home for soldiers. It fulfilled this role until 1928, after which it languished for nearly 50 years until a 1980s restoration saw it come back to life as this wonderful repository of art.

The building, which was inspired by Les Invalides in Paris, is a marvellous example of the Anglo-Dutch style that preceded the Georgian Age; at the time of its construction there were mutterings that it was altogether too fine a place for its residents.

St Patrick's Cathedral

Central Dublin

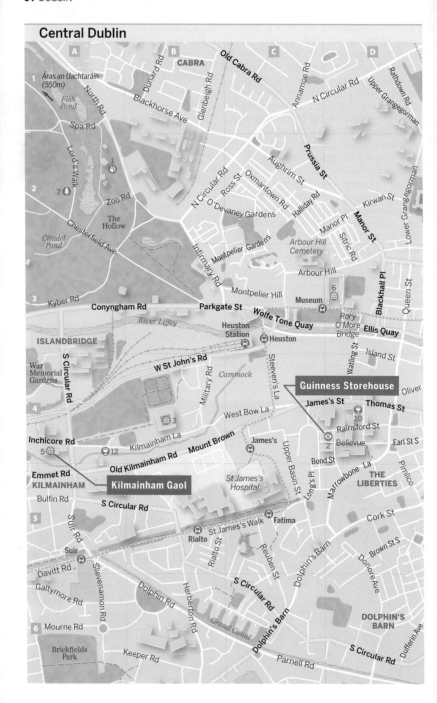

Áras an Uachtaráin (550m)

Fish Pond

CABRA

Old Cabra Rd

Dunard Rd

Glenbeigh Rd

North Rd

Blackhorse Ave

Annamoe Rd

N Circular Rd

Upper Grangegorman

Rathdown Rd

Spa Rd

Lord's Walk

Zoo Rd

The Hollow

Chesterfield Ave

Citadel Pond

Prussia St

Aughrim St

N Circular Rd

Ross St

Oxmantown Rd

Halliday Rd

O'Devaney Gardens

Kirwan St

Manor Pl

Manor St

Sitric Rd

Lower Grangegorman

Infirmary Rd

Montpelier Gardens

Arbour Hill Cemetery

Blackhall Pl

Queen St

Montpelier Hill

Arbour Hill

Kyber Rd

Conyngham Rd

Parkgate St

Museum

Wolfe Tone Quay

Rory O'More Bridge

Ellis Quay

River Liffey

Heuston Station

Heuston

ISLANDBRIDGE

Watling St

Island St

War Memorial Gardens

S Circular Rd

W St John's Rd

Military Rd

Cammock

Steeven's La

Guinness Storehouse

Oliver

James's St

Thomas St

West Bow La

Rainsford St

Earl St S

Inchicore Rd

Kilmainham La

Mount Brown

James's

Upper Basin St

Bellevue

Bond St

THE LIBERTIES

Pimlico

Emmet Rd

KILMAINHAM

Old Kilmainham Rd

Kilmainham Gaol

St James's Hospital

Marrowbone La

Bulfin Rd

S Circular Rd

Long's Pl

Cork St

Suir Rd

St James's Walk

Fatima

Brown St S

Rialto

Rialto St

Reuben St

Dolphin's Barn

Donore Ave

Suir

Davitt Rd

Slievenamon Rd

Dolphin Rd

Herberton Rd

S Circular Rd

S Circular Rd

Dufferin Ave

Galtymore Rd

DOLPHIN'S BARN

Mourne Rd

Brickfields Park

Keeper Rd

Grand Canal

Dolphin's Barn

Parnell Rd

S Circular Rd

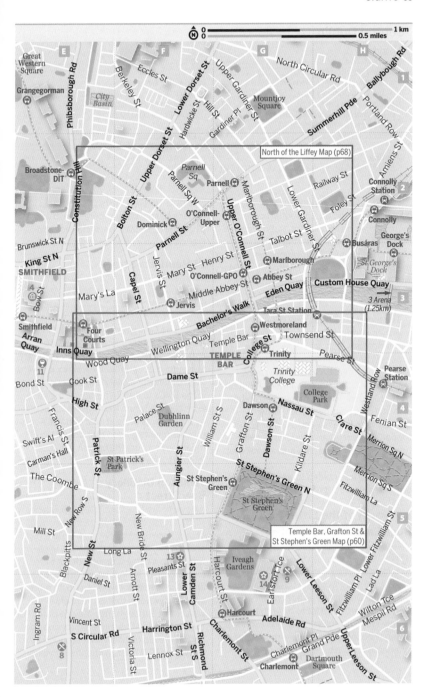

1 km
0.5 miles

Great Western Square

E

Grangegorman

Phibsborough Rd

Berkeley St

Eccles St

Lower Dorset St

Upper Gardiner St

F

Hill St

Hardwicke St

City Basin

Upper Dorset St

Gardiner Pl

G

North Circular Rd

Mountjoy Square

Summerhill Pde

Ballybough Rd

Portland Row

H

1

Constitution Hill

Broadstone-DIT

Parnell Sq

Parnell Sq W

Parnell

North of the Liffey Map (p68)

Railway St

Amiens St

Connolly Station

2

Brunswick St N

King St N

SMITHFIELD

Bolton St

Dominick

O'Connell-Upper

Parnell St

Upper O'Connell St

Marlborough St

Lower Gardiner St

Talbot St

Foley St

Connolly

Busáras

George's Dock

Jervis St

Mary St

Henry St

Capel St

Mary's La

Bow St

Smithfield

Arran Quay

4

Inns Quay

Four Courts

Jervis

Marlborough

O'Connell-GPO

Middle Abbey St

Abbey St

Eden Quay

St George's Dock

Custom House Quay

3 Arena (1.25km)

3

11

Wood Quay

Bachelor's Walk

Wellington Quay

Temple Bar

TEMPLE BAR

Westmoreland

College St

Townsend St

Trinity

Tara St Station

Pearse St

Westland Row

Pearse Station

Bond St

Cook St

High St

Dame St

Trinity College

College Park

4

Francis St

Swift's Al

Carman's Hall

The Coombe

Patrick St

Palace St

Dubhlinn Garden

St Patrick's Park

William St S

Grafton St

Aungier St

Dawson

Dawson St

Nassau St

Kildare St

Clare St

Fenian St

Merrion Sq N

Merrion Sq S

Fitzwilliam La

Mill St

New Row S

New St

New Bride St

St Stephen's Green

St Stephen's Green N

St Stephen's Green

Temple Bar, Grafton St & St Stephen's Green Map (p60)

Fitzwilliam Pl

Lower Fitzwilliam St

Upper Fitzwilliam St

Lad La

5

Blackpitts

Long La

Daniel St

13

Pleasants St

Lower Camden St

Harcourt St

Iveagh Gardens

Earlsfort Tce

9

14

Lower Leeson St

Wilton Tce

Mespil Rd

Ingram Rd

8

Vincent St

S Circular Rd

Harrington St

Arnott St

Victoria St

Lennox St

Richmond St S

Harcourt

Charlemont St

Adelaide Rd

Charlemont Pl

Charlemont

Grand Pde

Dartmouth Square

Upper Leeson St

6

Central Dublin

Following Irish independence it was briefly considered as a potential home for the new Irish Parliament, but it ended up as a storage facility for the National Museum of Ireland. Restorations began on the occasion of its 300th birthday in 1984 and it opened in 1991. A major restoration between 2012 and 2013 gave it an extra bit of sparkle.

The blend of old and new comes together wonderfully, and you'll find such contemporary Irish artists as Louis le Brocquy, Sean Scully, Barry Flanagan, Kathy Prendergast and Dorothy Cross featured here, as well as a film installation by Neil Jordan. The permanent exhibition also features paintings from heavy-hitters Pablo Picasso and Joan Miró, and is topped up by regular temporary exhibitions. There's a good cafe and a bookshop on the grounds.

There are free guided tours of the museum's exhibits throughout the year.

◎ North of the Liffey

Hugh Lane Gallery, Dublin   Gallery
(Map p68; ☑01-222 5550; www.hughlane.ie; 22 N Parnell Sq; ◷9.45am-6pm Tue-Thu, to 5pm Fri, 10am-5pm Sat, 11am-5pm Sun; ☑7, 11, 13, 16, 38, 40, 46A, 123 from city centre) FREE Whatever reputation Dublin has as a repository of world-class art has a lot to do with the simply stunning collection at this exquisite gallery, housed in the equally impressive Charlemont House, designed by William

Chambers in 1763. Within its walls you'll find the best of contemporary Irish art, a handful of impressionist classics and Francis Bacon's relocated studio.

14 Henrietta Street   Museum
(Map p68; ☑01-524 0383; www.14henriettastreet.ie; 14 Henrietta St; adult/child €9/6; ◷tours hourly 10am-4pm Wed-Sat, from noon Sun; ☑9, 13, 16, 40 from city centre) FREE Explore one of Dublin's Georgian townhouses, carefully restored to gently peel back layers of complex social history over 250 years. Part museum, part community archive, it covers the magnificent elegance of upper-class life in the 1740s to the destitution of the early 20th century, when the house was occupied by 100 tenants living in near squalor. Access is by 75-minute guided tour only, which means visitors get the benefit of lots of interesting detail.

Jameson Distillery Bow Street   Museum
(Map p64; www.jamesonwhiskey.com; Bow St; adult/student/child €19/18/11, masterclasses €60; ◷10am-5pm Mon-Sat, from 10.30am Sun; ☑25, 66, 67, 90 from city centre, ☐Smithfield) Smithfield's biggest draw is devoted to *uisce beatha* (ish-kuh ba-ha, 'the water of life'); that's Irish for whiskey. To its more serious devotees, that is precisely what whiskey is, although they may be put off by the slickness of this museum (occupying part of the old distillery that stopped production in 1971), which shepherds visitors

through a compulsory tour of the recreated factory (the tasting at the end is a lot of fun) and into the ubiquitous gift shop.

If you're really serious about whiskey, you can deepen your knowledge with the Whiskey Makers or the Whiskey Shakers, two 90-minute masterclasses that deconstruct the creation of Jameson whiskeys and teach you how to make a range of whiskey-based cocktails. If you're just buying whiskey, go for the stuff you can't buy at home, such as the excellent Red Breast or the super-exclusive Midleton, a very limited reserve that is appropriately expensive.

TOURS

Fab Food Trails
Walking

(www.fabfoodtrails.ie; tours €60; ⏰10am Sat) Highly recommended 2½- or three-hour tasting walks through the city centre's choicest independent producers. You'll visit up to eight bakeries, cheesemongers, markets and delis, learning about the food culture of each neighbourhood you explore. There is also a Food & Fashion walk. You meet in the city centre.

Green Mile
Walking

(Map p60; ☎01-661 1000; www.littlemuseum. ie; Little Museum of Dublin, 15 St Stephen's Green N; adult/student €15/13; ⏰11am Sat & Sun; ☒all city centre, ☒St Stephen's Green) Excellent one-hour tour of St Stephen's Green led by local historian Donal Fallon. Along the way you'll hear tales of James Joyce, the park's history and the drafting of the Irish Constitution. Book ahead as tours fill up pretty quickly. The tour also includes admission to and a guided tour of the Little Museum of Dublin (p58).

Historical Walking Tour
Walking

(Map p60; ☎01-878 0227; www.historical tours.ie; Trinity College Gate; adult/student/child €14/12/free; ⏰11am & 3pm May-Sep, 11am Apr & Oct, 11am Fri-Sun Nov-Mar; ☒all city centre) Trinity College history graduates lead this 'seminar on the street' that explores the

Dublin's Phoenix Park

Measuring 709 glorious hectares, **Phoenix Park** (Map p64; www.phoenix park.ie; ⏰24hr; ☒10 from O'Connell St, 25, 26 from Middle Abbey St) **FREE** is one of the world's largest city parks; you'll find joggers, grannies pushing buggies, ladies walking poodles, gardens, lakes, a sporting oval, a **zoo** (Map p64; www.dub linzoo.ie; adult/child/family €19.50/14/53; ⏰9.30am-6pm Mar-Sep, to dusk Oct-Feb; ♿) and 300 fallow deer. There are also cricket and polo grounds, a motor-racing track and some fine 18th-century residences, including those of the Irish president and the US ambassador.

The **Phoenix Park Visitor Centre** (☎01-677 0095; ⏰10am-6pm Apr-Dec, 9.30am-5.30pm Wed-Sun Jan-Mar) **FREE** has a self-guided exhibition on the history and wildlife of the park; you can also arrange and collect tickets for the Saturday tours of **Áras an Uachtaráin** (www.president.ie; ⏰guided tours hourly 10.30am-3.30pm Sat) **FREE**, the official residence of the Irish president.

Áras an Uachtaráin
SUETOT/SHUTTERSTOCK ©

Potato Famine, Easter Rising, Civil War and Partition. Sights include Trinity, City Hall, Dublin Castle and the Four Courts. In summer, themed tours on architecture, women in Irish history and the birth of the Irish state are also held. Tours depart from the College Green entrance.

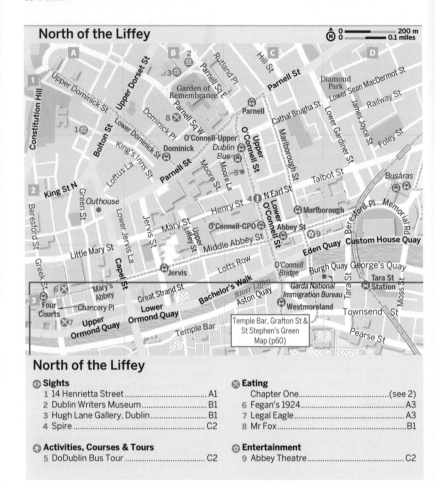

North of the Liffey

Dublin Musical Pub Crawl   Walking
(Map p60; ☏01-475 8345; www.musical
pubcrawl.com; Anglesea St; adult/student
€16/14; ☑7.30pm daily Apr-Oct, 7.30pm Thu-
Sat Nov-Mar; 🚍all city centre) The story of
Irish traditional music and its influence
on contemporary styles is explained and
demonstrated by two expert musicians
in a number of Temple Bar pubs over 2½
hours. Tours meet upstairs in the **Oliver
St John Gogarty** (Map p60; www.gogartys.
ie; 58-59 Fleet St; ☑10.30am-2.30am Mon-Sat,
noon-11.30pm Sun; 🚍all city centre) pub.

🛍 SHOPPING

If it's made in Ireland – or pretty much
anywhere else – you can find it in Dublin.
Grafton St is home to a range of largely
British-owned high-street chain stores;
you'll find the best local boutiques in the
surrounding streets. On the northside,
pedestrianised Henry St has international
chain stores, as well as Dublin's best de-
partment store, Arnott's.

Avoca Handweavers   Arts & Crafts

(Map p60; 01-677 4215; www.avoca.ie; 11-13 Suffolk St; 9.30am-6pm Mon-Wed & Sat, to 7pm Thu & Fri, 11am-6pm Sun; all city centre) Combining clothing, homewares, a basement food hall and an excellent top-floor **cafe** (mains €7-18; 9.30am-4.30pm Mon-Fri, to 5.30pm Sat, 10am-5pm Sun), Avoca promotes a stylish but homey brand of modern Irish life – and is one of the best places to find an original present. Many of the garments are woven, knitted and naturally dyed at its Wicklow factory. There's a terrific kids section.

Irish Design Shop   Arts & Crafts

(Map p60; 01-679 8871; www.irishdesign shop.com; 41 Drury St; 10am-6pm Mon-Sat, 1-5pm Sun; all city centre) Beautiful, imaginatively crafted items – from jewellery to kitchenware – carefully curated by owners Clare Grennan and Laura Caffrey. If you're looking for a stylish Irish-made memento or gift, you'll surely find it here.

Gutter Bookshop   Books

(Map p60; 01-679 9206; www.gutterbook shop.com; Cow's Lane; 10am-6.30pm Mon-Wed, Fri & Sat, to 7pm Thu, 11am-6pm Sun; all city centre) Taking its name from Oscar Wilde's famous line from *Lady Windermere's Fan* – 'We are all in the gutter, but some of us are looking at the stars' – this fabulous place is flying the flag for the downtrodden independent bookshop, stocking a mix of new novels, children's books, travel literature and other assorted titles.

Claddagh Records   Music

(Map p60; 01-677 0262; www.claddagh records.com; 2 Cecilia St; 10am-6pm Mon-Sat, from noon Sun; all city centre) An excellent collection of good-quality traditional and folk music is the mainstay at this centrally located record shop. The profoundly knowledgable staff should be able to locate even the most elusive recording for you. There's also a decent selection of world music. Another **branch** (Map p60; 01-888 3600; 5 Westmoreland St; 10am-6pm Mon-Sat, from noon Sun; all city centre) is on Westmoreland St; you can also shop online.

Irish Design Shop

ANNEMARIE MCCARTHY/LONELY PLANET ©

EATING

⊗ Grafton St & Around

Silk Road Café   Middle Eastern €

(Map p60; www.silkroadkitchen.ie; Chester Beatty Library, Dublin Castle; mains €12; ⊙10am-4.45pm Mon-Fri, from 11am Sat, from 1pm Sun May-Oct, closed Mon Nov-Apr; 🚌50, 51B, 77, 78A, 123) This vaguely Middle Eastern–North African–Mediterranean gem on the ground floor of the Chester Beatty Library (p46) is no ordinary museum cafe. Complementing house specialities including Greek moussaka and spinach lasagne are daily specials such as *djaj mehshi* (chicken stuffed with spices, rice, dried fruit, almonds and pine nuts). All dishes are halal and kosher.

Queen of Tarts   Cafe €

(Map p60; 🖉01-670 7499; www.queenoftarts.ie; 4 Cork Hill; mains €5-13; ⊙8am-7pm Mon-Fri, from 9am Sat & Sun; 🚌all city centre) This cute little cake shop does a fine line in tarts, meringues, crumbles, cookies and brownies, not to mention a decent breakfast: the smoked bacon and leek potato cakes with eggs

and cherry tomatoes are excellent. There's another, bigger, branch around the corner on **Cow's Lane** (Map p60; 3-4 Cow's Lane; mains €5-13; ⊙8am-7pm Mon-Fri, 9am-7pm Sat & Sun).

Coburg Brasserie   French €€

(Map p64; 🖉01-602 8900; www.thecoburg dublin.com; Conrad Dublin, Earlsfort Tce; mains €17-26; ⊙6.30am-11pm; 🚌all city centre) The French-inspired, seafood-leaning cuisine at this revamped hotel brasserie puts the emphasis on shellfish: the all-day menu offers oysters, mussels and a range of 'casual' lobster dishes, from lobster rolls to lobster cocktail. The bouillabaisse is chock-full of sea flavours, and you can also get a crab and shrimp burger and an excellent yellowfin tuna Niçoise salad. Top-notch.

Balfes   Irish €€

(Map p60; 🖉01-646 3353; www.balfes.ie; 2 Balfe St; mains €19-25; ⊙8am-10pm Mon-Thu, to 10.30pm Fri, 9am-10.30pm Sat, 9am-10pm Sun; 🚌all city centre) This all-day brasserie has a chic New York vibe, with leather banquettes and a small heated terrace luring a perpetually stylish crowd. While

TYLER W. STIPP/SHUTTERSTOCK ©

the menu focuses on hearty bistro dishes like duck liver pâté and steaks cooked on the Josper grill, it caters well to the healthier diner – think protein pancakes and superfood salads.

Fade Street Social   Modern Irish €€

(Map p60; ☑01-604 0066; www.fadestreet social.com; 4-6 Fade St; mains €20-36, tapas €6-17; ⓧ5-10.30pm Mon-Wed, 12.30-3pm & 5-10.30pm Thu, to 11pm Fri & Sat, to 10.30pm Sun; ☎; ⬚all city centre) ✔ Two restaurants in one, courtesy of renowned chef Dylan McGrath. At the front, the buzzy tapas bar, which serves gourmet bites from a beautiful open kitchen; at the back, the more muted restaurant specialises in Irish cuts of meat – from veal to rabbit – served with home-grown organic vegetables. There's a bar upstairs too. Reservations recommended.

Greenhouse   Scandinavian €€€

(Map p60; ☑01-676 7015; www.thegreen houserestaurant.ie; Dawson St; 2-/3-course lunch menu €45/55, 4-/6-course dinner menu €110/129; ⓧnoon-2pm & 6-9.30pm Tue-Sat; ⬚all city centre, ⬚St Stephen's Green) Chef Mickael Viljanen might just be one of the most exciting chefs working in Ireland to-day thanks to his Scandi-influenced tasting menus, which have made this arguably Dublin's best restaurant. The lunchtime set menu is one of the best bargains in town – a Michelin-starred meal for under €50. Reservations necessary.

Restaurant Patrick Guilbaud   French €€€

(Map p60; ☑01-676 4192; www.restaurant patrickguilbaud.ie; 21 Upper Merrion St; 2-/3-course set lunch €52/62, dinner menus €135-203; ⓧ12.30-2.30pm & 7-10.30pm Tue-Fri, 1-2.30pm & 7-10.30pm Sat; ☎7, 46 from city centre) This Michelin two-star is understand-ably considered the best in the country by its devotees, who proclaim Guillaume Lebrun's French haute cuisine the most exalted expression of the culinary arts. If you like formal dining, this is as good as it gets: the lunch menu is an absolute steal,

 The Spire of Dublin

The city's most visible landmark, the **Spire** (Map p68; O'Connell St; ⬚all city centre, ⬚Abbey) soars over O'Connell St and is an impressive bit of architectural engineering that was erected in 2001: from a base only 3m in diameter, it soars more than 120m into the sky and tapers into a 15cm-wide beam of light... it's tall and shiny and it does the trick rather nicely.

The brainchild of London-based architect Ian Ritchie, it is apparently the highest sculpture in the world, but much like the Parisian reaction to the con-struction of the Eiffel Tower, Dubliners are divided as to its aesthetic value and have regularly made fun of it. Among other names, we like 'the erection in the intersection', the 'stiletto in the ghetto' and the altogether brilliant 'eyeful tower'.

O'Connell Street and the Spire

at least in this stratosphere. Innovative and beautifully presented.

The room itself is all contemporary elegance and the service expertly formal yet surprisingly friendly – the staff are meticulously trained and as skilled at an-swering queries and addressing individual requests as they are at making sure not one breadcrumb lingers too long on the immaculate tablecloths. Owner Patrick Guilbaud usually does the rounds of the tables himself in the evening to salute regular customers and charm first-timers into returning. Reservations are absolutely necessary.

🛇 Kilmainham & the Liberties

1837 Bar & Brasserie   Brasserie €

(Map p64; 📞01-471 4602; www.guinness-storehouse.com; Guinness Storehouse, St James's Gate; mains €14-18; ⊗noon-3pm; 🚇21A, 51B, 78, 78A, 123 from Fleet St, 🚆James's) This lunchtime brasserie serves tasty dishes, from really fresh oysters to an insanely good Guinness burger, with skin-on fries and red-onion chutney. The drinks menu features a range of Guinness variants such as West Indian porter and Golden Ale. Highly recommended for lunch if you're visiting the museum.

Clanbrassil House   Irish €€

(Map p64; 📞01-453 9786; www.clanbrassil house.com; 6 Upper Clanbrassil St; mains €19-28; ⊗5-10pm Tue-Fri, 11.30am-2.30pm & 5-10pm Sat; 🚇9, 16, 49, 54A from city centre) With an emphasis on family-style sharing plates, this intimate restaurant consistently turns out exquisite dishes, cooked on a charcoal grill. Think rib-eye with bone marrow and anchovy, or ray wing with capers and brown shrimp butter. The hash brown chips are a

thing of glory, too. Order the full feast menu (€50) for the chef's choice.

🛇 North of the Liffey

Fegan's 1924   Cafe €

(Map p68; 📞01-872 2788; www.fegans1924. com; 13 Chancery St; mains €6-9; ⊗7.30am-4pm Mon-Fri, from 11am Sat & Sun; 🖭; 🚇25, 66, 67, 90 from city centre, 🚆Four Courts) A slice of rural Ireland in the city centre: this wonderful cafe is all distressed furniture and rustic charm, but there's nothing old-fashioned about the food and coffee. Fluffy scrambled eggs, perfectly made French toast and excellent brews...this is a place designed for lingering. Weekends also feature 40-minute creative workshops for kids (€6 each). No cash; cards only.

Legal Eagle   Irish €€

(Map p68; 📞01-555 2971; www.thelegal eagle.ie; 1/2 Chancery Pl; mains €22-30; ⊗9.30am-4pm Mon & Tue, to 10pm Wed-Fri, noon-10pm Sat, noon-9pm Sun; 🚆Four Courts) With the aesthetic of an old Dublin pub, combined with a kitchen churning out

Grogan's Castle Lounge

Long Hall (p74)

top-notch comfort food, this is one of Dublin's best new restaurants. There's a wood oven for potato flatbreads topped with Toonsbridge mozzarella and oxtail, and the retro-influenced Sunday menu is a contender for the best roast in town.

Chapter One   Irish €€€
(Map p68; ☎01-873 2266; www.chapter onerestaurant.com; 18 N Parnell Sq; 2-course lunch €36.50, 4-course dinner €80; ⊘12.30-2pm Fri, 5-10.30pm Tue-Sat; 🚌3, 10, 11, 13, 16, 19, 22 from city centre) Flawless haute cuisine and a relaxed, welcoming atmosphere make this Michelin-starred restaurant in the basement of the Dublin Writers Museum our choice for the best dinner experience in town. The food is French-inspired contemporary Irish; the menus change regularly; and the service is top-notch. The three-course pre-theatre menu (€44) is great if you're going to the **Gate** (Map p68; ☎01-874 4045; www.gatetheatre.ie; 1 Cavendish Row; ⊘performances 7.30pm Tue-Fri, 2.30pm & 7.30pm Sat; 🚌all city centre) around the corner.

Mr Fox   Irish €€
(Map p68; ☎01-874 7778; www.mrfox.ie; 38 W Parnell Sq; mains €20-30; ⊘noon-2pm & 5-9.30pm Tue-Sat; 🚌Parnell) In a gorgeous Georgian townhouse on Parnell Sq, the fantastic Mr Fox is cooking some of the finest food in the city. The plates celebrate Irish ingredients with a cheeky twist – think venison with black pudding, chestnut and blackberries, or pheasant with lentils and Toulouse sausage. A Michelin star can't be too far away.

🍷 DRINKING & NIGHTLIFE
🍸 Grafton St & St Stephen's Green
Grogan's Castle Lounge   Pub
(Map p60; www.facebook.com/groganscastle lounge; 15 S William St; ⊘10.30am-11.30pm Mon-Thu, to 12.30am Fri & Sat, 12.30-11pm Sun; 🚌all city centre) Known simply as Grogan's (after the original owner), this is a city-centre institution. It has long been a favourite haunt of Dublin's writers and painters, as well as others from the

Brazen Head

alternative bohemian set, who enjoy a fine Guinness while they wait for that inevitable moment when they're discovered.

Long Hall
Pub

(Map p60; 51 S Great George's St; ⊘noon-11.30pm Mon-Thu, to 12.30am Fri & Sat, 12.30-11pm Sun; 🖵all city centre) A Victorian classic that is one of the city's most beautiful and best-loved pubs. Check out the ornate carvings in the woodwork behind the bar and the elegant chandeliers. The bartenders are experts at their craft, an increasingly rare attribute in Dublin these days.

Vintage Cocktail Club
Bar

(Map p60; ☑01-675 3547; www.vintagecocktail club.com; Crown Alley; ⊘5pm-1.30am Mon-Fri, from 12.30pm Sat & Sun; 🖵all city centre) The atmosphere behind this inconspicuous, unlit doorway initialled with the letters 'VCC' is that of a Vegas rat pack hang-out or a '60s-style London members' club. It's so popular you'll probably need to book for one of the 2½-hour evening sittings, which is plenty of time to sample some of the excellent cocktails and finger food.

No Name Bar
Bar

(Map p60; www.nonamebardublin.com; 3 Fade St; ⊘1.30-11.30pm Mon-Wed, to 1am Thu, 12.30pm-2.30am Fri & Sat, noon-11pm Sun; 🖵all city centre) A low-key entrance next to the trendy French restaurant **L'Gueuleton** (Map p60; ☑01-675 3708; www.lgueuleton. com; 1 Fade St; mains €20-31; ⊘12.30-4pm & 5.30-10pm Mon-Wed, to 10.30pm Thu-Sat, noon-4pm & 5.30-9pm Sun; 🖵all city centre) leads upstairs to one of the nicest bar spaces in town, consisting of three huge rooms in a restored Victorian townhouse plus a sizeable heated patio area for smokers. There's no sign or a name – folks just refer to it as the No Name Bar.

Against the Grain
Craft Beer

(Map p60; www.galwaybaybrewery.com/against thegrain; 11 Wexford St; ⊘noon-midnight Mon-Thu, to 2am Fri & Sat, 12.30pm-midnight Sun; 🖵all city centre) An excellent pub for the craft-beer fans, which is no surprise considering it's owned by the Galway Bay Brewery. There's an impressive selection of ales and beers on tap, and the barkeeps are generous when it comes to offering tasters to help in your decision-making. Order some chicken wings for soakage if you plan on staying a while...

Toner's
Pub

(Map p60; www.tonerspub.ie; 139 Lower Baggot St; ☺10.30am-11.30pm Mon-Thu, to 12.30am Fri & Sat, 11.30am-11.30pm Sun; ☐7, 46 from city centre) Toner's, with its stone floors and antique snugs, has changed little over the years and is the closest thing you'll get to a country pub in the heart of the city. Next door, Toner's Yard is a comfortable outside space. The shelves and drawers are reminders that it once doubled as a grocery shop.

🍺 Kilmainham & the Liberties

Old Royal Oak
Pub

(Map p64; 11 Kilmainham Lane; ☺5pm-midnight Mon-Thu, 3pm-1am Fri, 12.30pm-1am Sat, 12.30-11pm Sun; ☐68, 79 from city centre) Locals are fiercely protective of this gorgeous traditional pub, which opened in 1845 to serve the patrons and staff of the Royal Hospital (now the Irish Museum of Modern Art). The clientele has changed,

but everything else remains the same, making this one of the nicest pubs in the city in which to enjoy a few pints.

Arthur's
Pub

(Map p64; ☎01-402 0914; www.arthurspub. ie; 28 Thomas St; ☺11am-11.30pm Mon-Thu, to 12.30am Fri & Sat, to 11pm Sun; ☐21A, 51B, 78, 78A, 123 from Fleet St, ☐James's) Given its location, Arthur's could easily be a cheesy tourist trap, and plenty of Guinness Storehouse (p54) visitors do pass through the doors tempted by another taste of the black stuff. Instead it's a friendly, cosy bar with a menu full of good comfort food. Best visited in winter so you get the full benefit of the roaring fireplace and soft candlelight.

Brazen Head
Pub

(Map p64; ☎01-679 5186; www.brazenhead. com; 20 Lower Bridge St; ☺10.30am-midnight Mon-Thu, to 12.30am Fri & Sat, 12.30pm-midnight Sun; ☐51B, 78A, 123 from city centre) Reputedly Dublin's oldest pub, the Brazen Head has been serving thirsty patrons since 1198 when it set up as a Norman

Arthur's

ANNEMARIE MCCARTHY/LONELY PLANET ©

Smock Alley Theatre

tavern. It's a bit away from the city centre, and the clientele consists of foreign-language students, tourists and some grizzly auld locals.

Though the pub's history is uncertain, the sunken level of the courtyard indicates how much street levels have altered since its construction. Robert Emmet was believed to have been a regular visitor, while in *Ulysses,* James Joyce reckoned 'you get a decent enough do in the Brazen Head'.

⭐ ENTERTAINMENT

Believe it or not, there is life beyond the pub. There are comedy clubs and classical concerts, recitals and readings, marionettes and music – lots of music. The other great Dublin treat is the theatre, where you can enjoy a light-hearted musical alongside the more serious stuff by Beckett, Yeats and O'Casey – not to mention a host of new talents.

O'Donoghue's   Traditional Music
(Map p60; 📞01-660 7194; www.odonoghues.ie; 15 Merrion Row; ⊙from 7pm; 🚌all city centre)

There's traditional music nightly in the old bar of this famous boozer. Regular performers include local names such as Tom Foley, Joe McHugh, Joe Foley and Maria O'Connell.

Devitt's   Live Music
(Map p64; 📞01-475 3414; www.devittspub.ie; 78 Lower Camden St; ⊙from 9pm Mon & Tue, 9.30pm Wed & Thu, 7.45pm Fri & Sat, 6.30pm Sun; 🚌14, 15, 65, 83) Devitt's – aka the Cusack Stand – is one of the favourite places for the city's talented musicians to ply their trade, with sessions as good as any you'll hear in the city centre. Highly recommended.

Whelan's   Live Music
(Map p60; 📞01-478 0766; www.whelanslive. com; 25 Wexford St; 🚌16, 122 from city centre) Perhaps the city's most beloved live-music venue is this midsized room attached to a traditional bar. This is the singer-songwriter's spiritual home: when they're done pouring out the contents of their hearts on stage, you can find them filling up in the bar along with their fans.

Smock Alley Theatre — Theatre

(Map p60; ☎01-677 0014; www.smockalley.
com; 6-7 Exchange St; ☐all city centre) One of
the city's most diverse theatres is hidden
in this beautifully restored 17th-century
building. It puts on a broad program of
events (expect anything from opera to
murder mystery nights, puppet shows and
Shakespeare) and many events also come
with a dinner option.

Abbey Theatre — Theatre

(Map p68; ☎01-878 7222; www.abbeytheatre.
ie; Lower Abbey St; ☐all city centre ☐Abbey)
Ireland's national theatre was founded by
WB Yeats in 1904 and was a central player
in the development of a consciously native
cultural identity. Expect to see a mix of
homegrown theatre from Irish playwrights,
as well as touring performances from
around the world.

National Concert Hall — Live Music

(Map p64; ☎01-417 0000; www.nch.ie; Earlsfort
Tce; ☐all city centre) Ireland's premier
orchestral hall hosts a variety of concerts
year-round, with an increasingly diverse
roster of performances including author
interviews and spoken-word events.

ℹ️ INFORMATION

Visit Dublin Centre (Map p60; www.visit
dublin.com; 25 Suffolk St; ⊙9am-5.30pm Mon-
Sat, 10.30am-3pm Sun; ☐all city centre) General
visitor information on Dublin and Ireland, as well
as an accommodation and booking service.

ℹ️ GETTING THERE & AWAY

AIR

Dublin Airport (p304) is 13km north of the city
centre and has two terminals: most international
flights (including most US flights) use Terminal
2; Ryanair and select others use Terminal 1.
Both terminals have the usual selection of pubs,
restaurants, shops, ATMs and car-hire desks.

BOAT

The **Dublin Port Terminal** (☎01-855 2222; Alexandra Rd; ☐53 from Talbot St) is 3km northeast
of the city centre.

National Concert Hall

BUS

Dublin's central bus station, **Busáras** (Map p68; 01-836 6111; www.buseireann.ie; Store St; Connolly) is just north of the River Liffey, behind the Custom House. It has different-sized luggage lockers costing from €6 to €10 per day.

TRAIN

All trains in the Republic are run by Irish Rail (p308). Dublin has two main train stations: **Heuston Station** (01-836 6222; Heuston), on the western side of town near the Liffey; and **Connolly Station** (01-703 2359; Connolly, Connolly Station), a short walk northeast of Busáras, behind the Custom House.

 GETTING AROUND

BUS

The office of **Dublin Bus** (Map p68; 01-873 4222; www.dublinbus.ie; 59 Upper O'Connell St; 9am-5.30pm Tue-Fri, to 2pm Sat, 8.30am-5.30pm Mon; all city centre) has free single-route timetables for all its services. Buses run from around 6am (some start at 5.30am) to about 11.30pm.

TAXI

Numerous taxi companies, such as **National Radio Cabs** (01-677 2222; www.nrc.ie), dispatch taxis by radio. You can also try MyTaxi (www.mytaxi.com), a taxi app.

TRAIN

The **Dublin Area Rapid Transport** (DART; 01-836 6222; www.irishrail.ie) provides quick train access to the coast as far north as Howth (about 30 minutes) and as far south as Greystones in County Wicklow. Pearse Station is convenient for central Dublin south of the Liffey, and Connolly Station for north of the Liffey. There are services every 10 to 20 minutes, sometimes more frequently, from around 6.30am to midnight Monday to Saturday. Services are less frequent on Sunday.

TRAM

The Luas (www.luas.ie) light-rail system has two lines: the Green Line (running every five to 15 minutes) runs from Broombridge in the north of the city down through O'Connell St and St Stephen's Green to Sandyford in south Dublin (via Ranelagh and Dundrum); the Red Line (every 20 minutes) runs from the Point Village to Tallaght via the north quays and Heuston Station.

Where to Stay

Dublin is always bustling, so book your accommodation well in advance, especially for weekend visits.

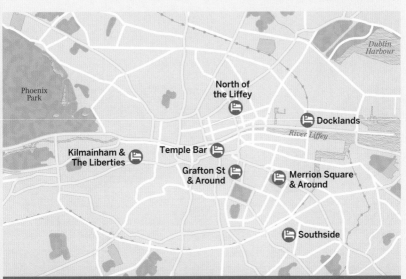

Neighbourhood	Atmosphere
Grafton St & Around	Close to sights, nightlife, etc; a good choice of midrange and top-end hotels. Not always good value for money and rooms tend to be smaller.
Merrion Square & Around	Lovely neighbourhood, elegant hotels and townhouse accommodation; some of the best restaurants in town. Not a lot of choice; virtually no budget accommodation.
Temple Bar	In the heart of the action; close to the party. Noisy and touristy; not especially good value for money.
Kilmainham & the Liberties	Close to the old city and the sights of west Dublin. No good accommodation; only a small selection of restaurants.
North of the Liffey	Good range of choices; within walking distance of sights and nightlife. Budget accommodation not always good quality.
Docklands	Excellent contemporary hotels with good service, including some top-end choices. Isolated in a quiet neighbourhood; reliant on taxis or public transport to get to city centre.
Southside	More bang for your buck; generally bigger rooms and properties with gardens. If not on the Luas line, bus transfers into town can take up valuable time.

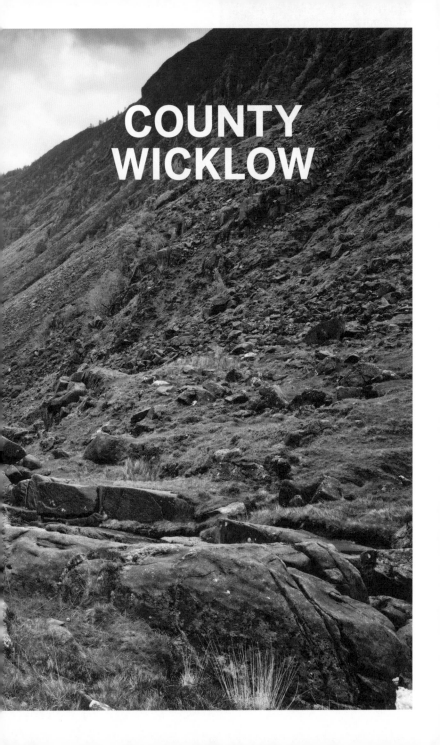

COUNTY
WICKLOW

County Wicklow

Just south of Dublin, County Wicklow (Cill Mhantáin) is the capital's favourite playground, a wild pleasure garden of coastline, woodland and daunting mountains through which runs the country's most popular walking trail, Wicklow Way. The wild topography is marvellously desolate and raw, with deep glacial valleys (notably Glenmacnass, Glenmalure and Glendalough) and corrie lakes gouged by the ice of long-gone glaciers. In the foothills you can explore monastic ruins, handsome gardens and magnificent 18th-century mansions. The coastal towns and rolling valleys of eastern Wicklow play second fiddle to the mountains in terms of dramatic scenery, but have a subtle charm.

One Day in County Wicklow

With only one day available, head straight to **Powerscourt Estate** (p85) and pass the morning walking around its glorious gardens. After lunch in the cafe at Powerscourt House, head south to **Glendalough** (p86) to explore its ancient monastic site before enjoying a late-afternoon walk along the shores of the scenic Upper Lake.

Two Days in County Wicklow

With two days you can be more relaxed. On day one, after visiting **Powerscourt Estate** (p85) and Enniskerry village, drive over to **Avoca Handweavers** (p91) at Kilmacanogue for lunch and shopping. On day two, visit **Glendalough** (p86) in the morning and devote the afternoon to one of Wicklow's famous gardens, such as **Mt Usher** (p91) or **Kilmacurragh Botanic Gardens** (p91).

Previous page: Wicklow Mountains

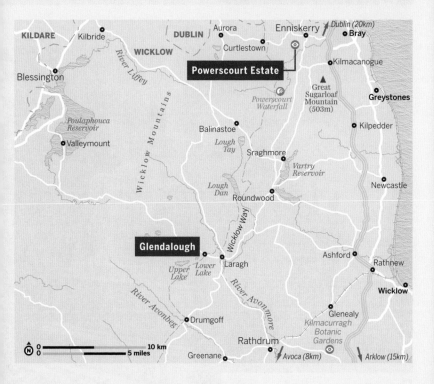

Arriving in County Wicklow

Enniskerry is 18km south of Dublin, just 3km west of the M11 along the R117. From here, getting to Powerscourt House on foot is not a problem (it's 500m from the town).

St Kevin's Bus (www.glendaloughbus. com) runs twice daily from Dublin and Bray to Roundwood and Glendalough. Dublin Bus 65 runs regularly as far as Blessington.

Where to Stay

As far as accommodation goes, County Wicklow has a bit of everything, from walkers hostels and camping grounds to farmhouse B&Bs and luxurious country-house hotels. As it's a popular weekend escape for Dubliners, it's wise to book a bed in advance.

Enniskerry is the best base from which to explore Powerscourt, while both Enniskerry and Blessington are good options for visiting Glendalough.

NIALL DUNNE/SHUTTERSTOCK ©

Powerscourt Estate

Wicklow's most visited attraction is this magnificent 64-sq-km estate. At the heart of it is a 68-room Palladian mansion, but the real draw is the formal gardens and the stunning views that accompany them.

Great For...

☑ Don't Miss

The animal cemetery in the estate gardens, final resting place of the Wingfield pets and horses.

History

The estate has existed more or less since 1300, when the LePoer (later anglicised to Power) family built themselves a castle here. The property changed Anglo-Norman hands a few times before coming into the possession of Richard Wingfield, newly appointed Marshall of Ireland, in 1603. His descendants were to live here for the next 350 years. In 1730 the Georgian wunderkind Richard Cassels (or Castle) was given the job of building a 68-room Palladian-style mansion around the core of the old castle.

The Wingfields left during the 1950s, after which the house had a massive restoration. Then, on the eve of its opening to the public in 1974, a fire gutted the whole building. The estate was eventually bought by the Slazenger sporting-goods family who have overseen a second restoration

RICHARD SEMIK/SHUTTERSTOCK ©

❶ Need to Know

☎01-204 6000; www.powerscourt.com; Bray Rd; house free, gardens adult/child Mar-Oct €10/5, Nov-Feb €7.50/3.50; ⊙9.30am-5.30pm Mar-Oct, to dusk Nov-Feb

✗ Take a Break

Enjoy lunch on the terrace at the cafe in Powerscourt House, with lovely views towards Great Sugarloaf mountain.

★ Top Tip

If you're driving, plan a picnic lunch at nearby Powerscourt Waterfall.

as well as the addition of all the amenities the estate now has to offer, including the two golf courses and the fabulous **hotel** (☎01-274 8888; www.powerscourthotel.com; d/ste from €244/333; 🅿 🛜 🏊), now part of Marriott's Autograph collection.

The Gardens

The star of the show is the 20-hectare landscaped gardens, originally laid out in the 1740s but redesigned in the 19th century by gardener Daniel Robinson. Robinson was one of the foremost horticulturalists of his day and his passion for growing things was matched only by his love of booze: the story goes that by a certain point in the day he was too drunk to stand and so insisted on being wheeled around the estate in a barrow.

Perhaps this influenced his largely informal style, which resulted in a magnificent blend of landscaped gardens, sweeping terraces, statuary, ornamental lakes, secret hollows, rambling walks and walled enclosures replete with more than 200 types of trees and shrubs, all beneath the stunning natural backdrop of the Great Sugarloaf mountain to the southeast. Tickets come with a map laying out 40-minute and hour-long walks around the gardens.

The Waterfall

The house itself is every bit as grand as the gardens, but with most areas closed to the public, there's not much to see beyond the bustle of the ground-floor cafe and gift shop. A 6km drive to a separate part of the estate takes you to the 121m-high Powerscourt Waterfall. It's the highest waterfall in Ireland, and at its most impressive after heavy rain. A nature trail has been laid out around the base of the waterfall, taking you past giant redwoods, ancient oaks, beech, birch and rowan trees.

REMIZOV/SHUTTERSTOCK ©

Glendalough

Glendalough is one of the most beautiful corners of the whole country and the epitome of the kind of rugged, romantic Ireland that probably drew you to the island in the first place.

Great For...

☑ **Don't Miss**

The 33m-tall, 1000-year-old Round Tower at the heart of the site.

History

In AD 498 a young monk named Kevin arrived in **Glendalough** (www.glendalough. ie) **FREE**, known as Gleann dá Loch, which means 'Valley of the Two Lakes', looking for somewhere to kick back, meditate and be at one with nature. He pitched up at what had been a Bronze Age tomb on the southern side of the Upper Lake and for the next seven years slept on stones, wore animal skins, maintained a near-starvation diet and – according to the legend – became bosom buddies with the birds and animals. Kevin's ecofriendly lifestyle soon attracted a bunch of disciples, all seemingly unaware of the irony that they were flocking to hang out with a hermit who wanted to live as far away from other people as possible. Over the next couple of centuries his one-man operation mushroomed into a proper settlement and

Entrance

ATTORMMFOTO/GETTY IMAGES ©

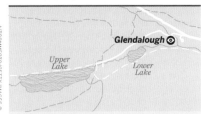

❶ Need to Know

📞0404-45352; www.heritageireland.ie; adult/child €5/3; ⏱9.30am-6pm mid-Mar–mid-Oct, to 5pm mid-Oct–mid-Mar

✖ Take a Break

Wicklow Heather (📞0404-45157; www.wicklowheather.ie; Glendalough Rd, Laragh; mains €13-29; ⏱8am-9.30pm Mon-Thu, to 10pm Fri & Sat, to 9pm Sun) is the best place for anything substantial.

★ Top Tip

Take a look around the visitor centre to get a feel for the history before touring the monastic site itself.

by the 9th century Glendalough rivalled Clonmacnoise as the island's premier monastic city. Thousands of students studied and lived in a thriving community that was spread over a considerable area.

Inevitably, Glendalough's success made it a key target for Viking raiders, who sacked the monastery at least four times between 775 and 1071. The final blow came in 1398, when English forces from Dublin almost destroyed it. Efforts were made to rebuild and some life lingered on here as late as the 17th century when, under renewed repression, the monastery finally died.

Upper Lake

The original site of St Kevin's settlement, Teampall na Skellig is at the base of the cliffs towering over the southern side of the Upper Lake and is accessible only by boat;

unfortunately, there's no boat service to the site and you'll have to settle for looking at it across the lake. The terraced shelf has the reconstructed ruins of a church and early graveyard. Rough wattle huts once stood on the raised ground nearby. Scattered around are some early grave slabs and simple stone crosses.

Just east of here and 10m above the lake waters is the 2m-deep artificial cave called St Kevin's Bed, said to be where Kevin lived. The earliest human habitation of the cave was long before St Kevin's era – there's evidence that people lived in the valley for thousands of years before the monks arrived. In the green area just south of the car park is a large circular wall thought to be the remains of an early Christian stone fort (caher).

Follow the lakeshore path southwest of the car park until you come to the considerable remains of Reefert Church above the tiny River Poulanass. It's a small, plain,

11th-century Romanesque nave-and-chancel church with some reassembled arches and walls. Traditionally, Reefert (literally 'Royal Burial Place') was the burial site of the chiefs of the local O'Toole family. The surrounding graveyard contains a number of rough stone crosses and slabs, most made of shiny mica schist.

Climb the steps at the back of the churchyard and follow the path to the west and you'll find, at the top of a rise overlooking the lake, the scant remains of **St Kevin's Cell**, a small beehive hut.

Lower Lake

While the Upper Lake has the best scenery, the most fascinating buildings lie in the lower part of the valley east of the Lower Lake, huddled together in the heart of the ancient monastic site.

Just round the bend from the Glendalough Hotel is the stone arch of the monastery gatehouse, the only surviving example of a monastic entranceway in the country. Just inside the entrance is a large slab with an incised cross.

Beyond that lies a graveyard, which is still in use. The 10th-century round tower is 33m tall and 16m in circumference at the base. The upper storeys and conical roof were reconstructed in 1876. Near the tower, to the southeast, is the Cathedral of St Peter and St Paul with a 10th-century nave. The chancel and sacristy date from the 12th century.

At the centre of the graveyard to the south of the round tower is the Priest's House. This odd building dates from 1170 but has been heavily reconstructed. It may have been the location of shrines of St

Kevin. Later, during penal times, it became a burial site for local priests – hence the name. The 10th-century St Mary's Church, 140m southwest of the round tower, probably originally stood outside the walls of the monastery and belonged to local nuns. It has a lovely western doorway. A little to the east are the scant remains of St Kieran's Church, the smallest at Glendalough.

Glendalough's trademark is St Kevin's Kitchen or Church at the southern edge of the enclosure. This church, with a miniature round tower-like belfry, protruding sacristy and steep stone roof, is a masterpiece. The oldest parts of the building date from the 11th century – the structure has been remodelled since but it's still a classic early Irish church.

At the junction with Green Rd as you cross the river just south of these two churches is the Deer Stone, in the middle of a group of rocks. Legend claims that when St Kevin needed milk for two orphaned babies, a doe stood here waiting to be milked. The stone is actually a *bullaun* (a stone used as a mortar for grinding medicines or food).

The road east leads to St Saviour's Church, with its detailed Romanesque carvings. To the west, a nice woodland trail leads up the valley past the Lower Lake to the Upper Lake.

Tours

Wild Wicklow Tours (☎01-280 1899; www.wildwicklow.ie; adult/child €33/28; ☺departs 8.50am) offers award-winning day trips from Dublin to Glendalough via Avoca Handweavers (p91) and the Sally Gap that never fail to generate rave reviews for atmosphere and all-round fun. Pick-ups are throughout Dublin, starting at the Shelbourne hotel, and returning at around 6pm.

Getting to Glendalough

St Kevins Bus (www.glendaloughbus.com) departs from the bus stop on St Stephen's Green North in Dublin (11.30am and 6pm daily, one way/return €13/20, 1½ hours); from March to October the evening bus leaves at 7pm on Saturday and Sunday. It also stops at the Town Hall in Bray. Departures from Glendalough are at 7am and 4.30pm weekdays, and 9.45am and 5.40pm on weekends. Buy your ticket on the bus. On weekdays in July and August there's an additional service from Glendalough to Dublin at 9.45am.

☑ Don't Miss

If you have time, don't miss the walk from the monastic site along the south side of the Lower Lake to the Upper Lake.

JIR/CASTKA/SHUTTERSTOCK ©

✗ Take A Break

If the weather's good, pack a picnic basket and head for the gravel beach at the east end of the Upper Lake for lunch with a view.

Enniskerry

◉ SIGHTS

Powerscourt Waterfall   Waterfall

(www.powerscourt.com/waterfall; Powerscourt Estate; adult/child €6/3.50; ⊘9.30am-7pm May-Aug, 10.30am-5.30pm Mar, Apr, Sep & Oct, 10.30am-4pm Nov-Feb) On the southern edge of the Powerscourt Estate (p85), 6km south of Powerscourt House, is this pictur-esque waterfall. At 121m it's the highest in Ireland (though it's a cascade, rather than a single drop) and is at its most impressive after heavy rain. The waterfall is signposted from the main estate entrance; walking in is not recommended, as the route lies on narrow roads with no footpath.

A nature trail around the base of the waterfall takes you past giant redwoods, ancient oaks, beech, birch and rowan trees. There are plenty of birds in the vicinity, including the chaffinch, cuckoo, chiffchaff, raven and willow warbler.

Great Sugarloaf   Hill

At 503m it's nowhere near Wicklow's highest summit, but the Great Sugarloaf is one of the most distinctive hills in Ireland, its conical peak visible for many kilometres around. The mountain towers over the small village of Kilmacanogue, on the N11 about 35km south of Dublin, and can be climbed from a car park on the L1031 minor road (off the R755 road, 7.5km south of Enniskerry). It's a steep but straightforward hike (one hour return).

✪ ACTIVITIES

Powerscourt Golf Club   Golf

(☑01-204 6033; www.powerscourtgolfclub.com; Powerscourt Estate; green fees Apr-Oct €75, Nov-Mar €55; ⊘8am-dusk) You have a choice between two stunning par-72 courses here: the West Course, with streams and ravines, was designed by David McLay Kidd (who also designed Bandon Dunes in Oregon, USA) and is a shade tougher than the East Course, designed by Peter McEvoy, which

Powerscourt Waterfall

BOYAN GEORGIEV GEORGIEV/SHUTTERSTOCK ©

is arguably the more scenic, with hedges, ancient oaks and beech trees.

☞ TOURS

DoDublin Bus Tour   Bus

(Map p68; www.dodublin.ie; 59 Upper O'Connell St; adult/child €27/12; ⊙10.30am daily May-Sep, 10.30am Mon, Fri & Sat Apr, Oct & Nov, 10.30am Fri & Sat Mar) Departing from the Dublin Bus office in Dublin, this tour takes in both Glendalough and Powerscourt in County Wicklow, returning to Dublin at 5pm.

🛍 SHOPPING

Avoca Handweavers   Arts & Crafts

(☏01-274 6900; www.avoca.com; Main St, Kilmacanogue; ⊙9am-6pm Mon-Fri, 9.30am-6pm Sat & Sun) Avoca has 13 branches across Ireland and a widespread reputation for creating stylish traditional rural handicrafts. Its operational HQ is set in a 19th-century arboretum 5km southeast of Enniskerry. The bustling shop is crammed with knitwear, textiles, ceramics, toys, homewares, gourmet foodstuffs and cookbooks; also here is an excellent cafe (dishes €6 to €15) utilising Avoca's own-grown produce.

🍴 EATING

Poppies Country Cooking   Cafe €

(☏01-282 8869; www.facebook.com/poppies ireland; The Square; mains €6.50-12; ⊙8am-5pm Mon-Fri, to 6pm Sat & Sun) Hearty Irish breakfasts are served until noon at this red cafe with a butter-yellow interior, while wholesome salads, filling sandwiches and daily specials such as shepherd's pie and veggie quiches make it a great option for lunch. You can also drop by for cakes, pastries and scones served with Kilmurry-made jam.

Johnnie Fox's   Seafood €€

(☏01-295 5647; www.johnniefoxs.com; Glencullen; mains €15-26, seafood platters €28-130, 3-course Hooley menu €59.50; ⊙kitchen 12.30-9.30pm, bar 11am-11.30pm Mon-Thu, to 12.30am

🔭 County Wicklow Gardens

Wicklow's nickname, 'the Garden of Ireland', is justified by green idylls such as the 8-hectare **Mt Usher Gardens** (☏0404-49672; www.mountushergardens. ie; Ashford; adult/child €8/4; ⊙10am-5pm), just outside the unremarkable town of Ashford, about 10km south of Greystones on the N11. Trees, shrubs and herbaceous plants from around the world are laid out in Robinsonian style – ie according to the naturalist principles of famous Irish gardener William Robinson (1838–1935) – rather than in the formalist manner of preceding gardens.

There's also an Avoca cafe on the premises, as well as a 'shopping courtyard' where you can buy freshly baked goods, ice cream, plants, furniture, clothing and art, including photography.

Surrounding the ruins of an 18th-century mansion are the ornamental gardens of **Kilmacurragh Botanic Gardens** (☏0404-48844; www. botanicgardens.ie; Kilbride; ⊙9am-5pm daily Mar-Sep, 9am-4.30pm Mon-Fri, 10am-4.30pm Sat & Sun Oct-Feb), originally laid out in 1712 and replanted in the 19th century to reflect the wilder, antiformal style of William Robinson (1838–1935). Particularly notable are the South American conifers, the colourful rhododendrons and the avenue of yews. The gardens are 7km east of Rathdrum.

Kilmacurragh Botanic Gardens

Johnnie Fox's (p91)

Fri & Sat, noon-11pm Sun; 🛜📷♿) Just over the County Dublin border, 5.5km northwest of Enniskerry, traditional 19th-century pub Johnnie Fox's fills with busloads of tourists for its knees-up Hooley Show of Irish music and dancing. But it's even more worthwhile entering its warren of rooms, nooks and crannies for standout seafood spanning Roaring Bay oysters, Dublin Bay prawns, Annagassan crab, Kilmore Quay lobster and more.

Vegetarian, kids and babies menus are available.

🛈 GETTING THERE & AWAY

Car Enniskerry is 18km south of Dublin, just 3km west of the M11 along the R117.

Bus Dublin Bus (www.dublinbus.ie) services link Dublin (Dublin City University) with Enniskerry (€3.30, 1½ hours, hourly).

Bray

Right on the County Dublin border and less than 25km from the centre of the capital, County Wicklow's biggest town stretches along a 1.6km sand and shingle beach fronted by a broad promenade.

Bray (Bré in Irish) evolved into a seaside resort after the arrival of the railway in 1854. Although tourism later declined when cheap flights made it easier for Dubliners to head to sunnier climes, grand buildings from its 19th-century heyday still line the waterfront and it remains a popular day-trip destination. Visitor numbers peak during late July, when Bray hosts the country's largest air show, the Bray Air Display.

◎ SIGHTS

Killruddery House & Gardens House
(📷01-286 3405; www.killruddery.com; Southern Cross Rd; house & gardens adult/child €15.50/5.50, garden only €8.50/3; ⊙house 9.30am-6pm Sat-Thu May-Sep, Sat & Sun only Apr & Oct, gardens 9.30am-6pm daily May-Sep, Sat & Sun only Apr & Oct) A stunning mansion in the Elizabethan Revival style, Killruddery has been home to the Brabazon family

(the earls of Meath) since 1618 and has one of the oldest gardens in Ireland, with a magnificent orangery built in 1852; it's chock-full of statuary and plant life. Compulsory 45-minute guided tours lead you through the impressive house, designed by architects Richard Morrisson and his son William in 1820. It's 2km south of Bray just off the R768.

The house was reduced to its present-day still-huge proportions by the 14th earl in 1953; he was obviously looking for something a little more bijou.

An excellent farmers market sets up from 10am to 3pm on Saturday year-round.

Brave Maeve Story Trail   Public Art

(www.bray.ie; The Promenade; ⊘24hr; 🚻) Along Bray's seafront promenade, this kids walking trail links up five brightly coloured murals created by children's author and illustrator Chris Judge and 50 local children. Together, the murals tell the story of Maeve, a young giant who is searching for a home for her family, encountering monsters and mythical figures along the way. The trail is 1.5km long; download a free map from the website (there's also a free app).

✖ EATING & DRINKING

Dockyard No 8   Cafe €€

(📞01-276 1795; www.dockyardno8.ie; 8 Dock Tce; breakfast & lunch dishes €7-19, dinner mains €16-24; ⊘9am-4.30pm Sun-Wed, 9am-4.30pm & 5.30-9.30pm Thu-Sat; 🛜) By day this harbourside cafe opposite the shipyard is a fantastic spot for breakfast (ham hock eggs Benedict; Belgian waffles with smoked bacon) and lunch (chowder with chorizo; seafood baskets with calamari, tiger prawns and daily-caught fish), especially when the retractable roof opens up. At dinner, refined mains might include Parma-ham-wrapped cod on white-bean cassoulet.

Harbour Bar   Pub

(www.theharbourbar.ie; 1-4 Dock Tce; ⊘1-11.30pm Mon-Thu, to 12.30am Fri, noon-12.30am Sat, noon-11pm Sun; 🛜) Four former fisherman's terraces make up this maze of rooms with vintage maritime bric-a-brac

Killruddery House & Gardens

(and a resident cat). Craft-beer options by local brewers include County Wicklow's Wicklow Wolf (made in Bray), Larkin's Brewing (from nearby Kilcoole), and County Kildare's Whiplash (from Cellbridge). The beer garden gets rammed on sunny days; live music plays from Wednesday to Sunday.

It's been a pub since 1872; James Joyce, Katharine Hepburn, Peter O'Toole, Laurence Olivier, Roddy Doyle and U2's Bono are among its past patrons.

Vale of Avoca

One of the most scenic spots in County Wicklow is the Vale of Avoca, a darkly wooded valley that begins where the Rivers Avonbeg and Avonmore come together to form the River Avoca. The aptly named Meeting of the Waters was made famous by Thomas Moore's 1808 poem of the same name.

The tiny village of Avoca (Abhóca in Irish) is best known as the birthplace of the superstar of all Irish cottage industries, Avoca Handweavers.

🔒 SHOPPING

Avoca Handweavers   Arts & Crafts

(📞0402-35105; www.avoca.com; Main St; ⊙shop 9.30am-5pm, cafe 9.30am-4pm Mon-Fri, to 5pm Sat & Sun, mill 9.30am-4.30pm) Ireland's oldest working mill is the birthplace of Avoca Handweavers, a company that is now famous across Ireland and the world. The mill has been turning out woollen and other fabrics since 1723, and many of Avoca's clothing and homewares (blankets, cushion covers and more) are produced here and sold in the neighbouring shop.

You're free to wander around the weaving sheds and to chat with the weavers. The cafe serves warming soups, salads, sandwiches and pastries. Arrive early or late to avoid coach tour groups.

❎ EATING

Mickey Finns Pub   Pub Food €€

(📞0404-41661; www.wicklowbrewery.ie; Main St, Redcross; mains €13-25; ⊙kitchen 12.30-9.30pm, bar to midnight; 🛜🚼) Many dishes at this cosy, low-ceilinged pub incorporate

Avoca Village

TRISH PUNCH/GETTY IMAGES ©

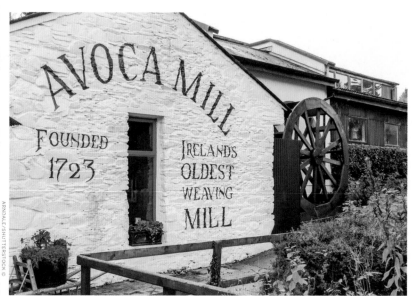

Avoca Handweavers

beers brewed at the adjacent **Wicklow Brewery** (📞0404-41661; www.wicklowbrewery.ie; Main St, Redcross; tour €15; ⊙brewery beer hall 2-11pm Sat & Sun, tours by reservation) 🌿 and come with pairing suggestions, such as Wicklow Black Stout beef pie matched with a Black 16, or the artisan 8oz burger with maple-smoked bacon and Helles Lager chutney accompanied by a Hopknut Pale Ale. There's trad music on Wednesday year-round.

ℹ INFORMATION

Tourist Office (📞0402-35022; www.visit wicklow.ie; Old Courthouse, Main St; ⊙9am-4pm Mon-Fri) Pick up information about local walks here in Avoca village.

ℹ GETTING THERE & AWAY

Bus Éireann (www.buseireann.ie) links Dublin (Georges Quay) with the Meeting of the Waters (€14, 1¾ hours, two per day) and Avoca village (€14, two hours).

COUNTIES MEATH & LOUTH

Counties Meath & Louth

Meath's rich soil, laid down during the last ice age, drew settlers as early as 8000 BC. They worked their way up the banks of the River Boyne, transforming the landscape from forest to farmland. One of the five provinces of ancient Ireland, Meath was at the centre of Irish politics for centuries. Across the Boyne, Louth – Ireland's smallest county – was at the centre of ecclesiastical Ireland during the 5th and 6th centuries, with wealthy religious communities at the monastery at Monasterboice and the Cistercian abbey at Mellifont. There are numerous must-see attractions here, including many tangible reminders of Ireland's absorbing history.

One Day in Counties Meath & Louth

From Dublin, head to Brú na Bóinne and plan to spend most of the day there learning about the remarkable prehistoric passage tombs of **Newgrange** (p101), **Knowth** (p102) and **Dowth** (p102). Midafternoon visit the **Battle of the Boyne site** (p106) on the way to Drogheda, where you'll spend the night.

Two Days in Counties Meath & Louth

On day two, after a wander around the town, explore the fascinating ecclesiastical ruins of **Monasterboice** (p106) and **Old Mellifont Abbey** (p106); in the afternoon, on your way back towards Dublin, visit the ancient capital of the High Kings of Ireland at the atmospheric **Hill of Tara** (p106).

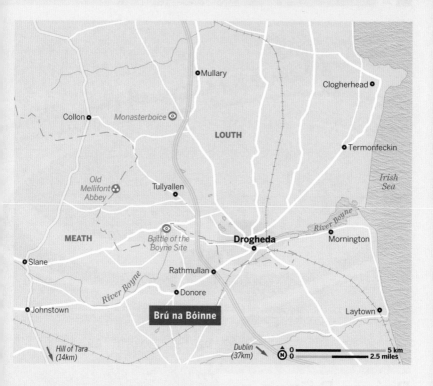

Arriving in Counties Meath & Louth

County Meath has numerous Bus Éireann (www.buseireann.ie) services, but to get off the beaten track your own wheels are best. Tour companies ply the main sights; most depart from Dublin.

Trains on the Dublin–Belfast line stop in Drogheda and Dundalk; the towns are also served by bus. Buses link Carlingford with Dundalk.

Where to Stay

Most villages and towns throughout County Meath have good sleeping options. Beautiful manor houses dot the countryside.

While there are some B&Bs, hotels and hostels near Brú na Bóinne and Tara, Drogheda and Trim have a more comprehensive range of sleeping options and offer good transport links. Counties Louth and Meath can also be explored as a day trip from Dublin.

Newgrange

MNSTUDIO/SHUTTERSTOCK ©

Brú na Bóinne

The vast Neolithic necropolis of Brú na Bóinne is one of the most extraordinary sites in Europe. A thousand years older than Stonehenge, it's an evocative testament to the achievements of prehistory.

Great For...

☑ **Don't Miss**

The beautifully carved stone decoration in the passage entrance to Newgrange tomb.

The complex of Brú na Bóinne (the Boyne Palace) was built to house the remains of those who were at the top of the social heap – its tombs were the largest artificial structures in Ireland until the construction of the Anglo-Norman castles 4000 years later. The area consists of many different sites; the three principal ones are New-grange, Knowth and Dowth.

Over the centuries the tombs decayed, were covered by grass and trees, and were plundered by everybody from Vikings to Victorian treasure hunters, whose carved initials can be seen on the great stones of Newgrange. The countryside around the tombs is home to countless other ancient tumuli (burial mounds) and standing stones.

Entrance to Newgrange

POWEROFFOREVER/GETTY IMAGES ©

Drogheda

Brú na Bóinne

ℹ Need to Know

📞041-988 0300; www.worldheritageireland.
ie; Donore; adult/child visitor centre €4/3,
visitor centre & Newgrange €7/4, visitor centre
& Knowth €6/4, all 3 sites €13/8; ⊘9am-7pm
Jun–mid-Sep, 9am-6.30pm May & mid-Sep–
early Oct, 9.30am-5.30pm Feb-Apr & early
Oct-early Nov, 9am-5pm early Nov-Jan

✕ Take a Break

The visitor centre cafe has excellent
food, and extensive vegetarian options.

★ Top Tip

Tours are mostly outdoors so wear
comfortable hiking shoes or boots and
bring rain gear.

Newgrange

A startling 80m in diameter and 13m high,
the white, round stone walls of **Newgrange**
(www.worldheritageireland.ie; visitor centre &
Newgrange €7/4; ⊘9am-7pm Jun–mid-Sep,
9am-6.30pm May & mid-Sep–early Oct, 9.30am-
5.30pm Feb-Apr & early Oct-early Nov, 9am-5pm
early Nov-Jan), topped by a grass dome, look
eerily futuristic. Underneath lies the finest
Stone Age passage tomb in Ireland – one
of the most remarkable prehistoric sites
in Europe. Dating from around 3200 BC,
it predates Egypt's pyramids by some six
centuries.

The tomb's precise alignment with
the sun at the time of the winter solstice
suggests it was also designed to act as a
calendar.

Newgrange Winter Solstice

At 8.20am on the winter solstice (between
18 and 23 December), the rising sun's rays
shine through the roof-box above the entrance, creep slowly down the long passage
and illuminate the tomb chamber for 17
minutes. There is little doubt that this is
one of the country's most memorable, even
mystical, experiences.

There's a simulated winter sunrise for
every group taken into the mound. To be in
with a chance of witnessing the real thing
on one of six mornings around the solstice, enter the free lottery that's drawn in
late September; 50 names are drawn and
each winner is allowed to take one guest
(be aware, however, that over 30,000 people apply each year). Fill out the form at
the Brú na Bóinne Visitor Centre or email
brunaboinne@opw.ie.

Knowth

Northwest of Newgrange, the burial mound of **Knowth** (www.worldheritage ireland.ie; visitor centre & Knowth €6/4; ⏱9am-7pm Jun–mid-Sep, 9am-6.30pm May & mid-Sep–early Oct, 9.30am-5.30pm Feb-Apr & early Oct-early Nov, 9am-5pm early Nov-Jan) was built around the same time. It has the greatest collection of passage-grave art ever uncovered in Western Europe. Early excavations cleared a passage leading to the central chamber, which at 34m is much longer than the one at Newgrange. In 1968 a 40m passage was unearthed on the opposite side of the mound.

Also in the mound are the remains of six early-Christian souterrains (underground chambers) built into the side. Some 300 carved slabs and 17 satellite graves surround the main mound.

Dowth

The circular mound at **Dowth** (L1607) FREE is similar in size to Newgrange – about 63m in diameter – but is slightly taller at 14m high. Due to safety issues, Dowth's tombs are closed to visitors, though you can visit the mound (and its resident grazing sheep) from the L1607 road between Newgrange and Drogheda.

North of the tumulus are the ruins of **Dowth Castle** and **Dowth House**.

Newgrange Farm

One for the kids, this hands-on, family-run 135-hectare working **farm** (☎041-982 4119; www.newgrangefarm.com; Newgrange; per person €9, tractor ride €3; ⏱10am-6pm mid-Mar–Aug) allows visitors to feed the ducks, lambs and goats, milk a cow, pet a rabbit and take

Knowth

a tractor ride. Children's play areas include a straw maze and toy tractors; there are indoor and outdoor picnic areas and a cafe. Follow the signs on the N51.

Visiting Brú na Bóinne

Advance planning will help you get the most out of your visit.

○ All visits to Brú na Bóinne start at the Brú na Bóinne Visitor Centre (p106), from where there's a shuttle bus to the tombs. If you turn up at either Newgrange or Knowth first, you'll be sent to the visitor centre, 4km from either site. Walking is discouraged, as the lanes are narrow and dangerous due to passing tour buses.

○ Allow plenty of time: an hour for the visitor centre alone, two hours to include a trip to Newgrange or Knowth, and half a day to see all three.

○ Dowth's tombs are closed to the public but you can freely visit the surrounding site.

○ In summer, particularly at weekends, Brú na Bóinne gets very crowded; on peak days more than 2000 people can show up. As there are only 750 tour slots, you may not be guaranteed a visit to either of the passage tombs. Tickets are sold on a first-come, first-served basis (no advance booking). Arrive early in the morning or visit midweek and be prepared to wait. Alternatively, visiting as part of an organised tour, such as Mary Gibbons Tours, guarantees a spot.

○ Tours are primarily outdoors with no shelter so bring rain gear, just in case.

Tours

Brú na Bóinne is one of the most popular tourist attractions in Ireland, and there are plenty of organised tours. Most depart from Dublin.

Mary Gibbons Tours   Tours
(☑086 355 1355; www.newgrangetours.com; tour incl entrance fees adult/child €40/35) These excellent tours depart from numerous Dublin hotels, beginning at 9.30am Monday to Friday, and 7.30am Saturday and Sunday, and take in the whole of the Boyne Valley including Newgrange and the Hill of Tara. Expert guides offer a fascinating insight into Celtic and pre-Celtic life in Ireland. No credit cards; pay cash on the bus.

> **Where to Stay**
>
> While there are some B&Bs, hotels and hostels near Brú na Bóinne and Tara, Drogheda and Trim have a more comprehensive range of sleeping options.

DESIGN PICS / STUART WESTMORLAND/GETTY IMAGES ©

> ★ **Did You Know?**
>
> In August 1843 a crowd of 750,000 gathered at Tara to hear Daniel O'Connell, leader of the opposition to union with Great Britain, speak.

Brú na Bóinne

All visits start at the ① **visitor centre**, which has a terrific exhibit that includes a short context-setting film. From here, you board a shuttle bus that takes you to ② **Newgrange**, where you'll go past the ③ **kerbstone** into the ④ **main passage** and the ⑤ **burial chamber**. If you're not a lucky lottery winner for the solstice, fear not – there's an artificial illumination ceremony that replicates it. If you're continuing on to tour ⑥ **Knowth**, you'll need to go back to the visitor centre and get on another bus; otherwise, you can drive directly to ⑦ **Dowth** and visit, but only from outside (the information panels will tell you what you're looking at).

Newgrange Interior Passage
The passage is lined with 43 orthostats, or standing stones, averaging 1.5m in height: 22 on the left (western) side, 21 on the right (eastern) side.

Knowth
Roughly one third of all megalithic art in Western Europe is contained within the Knowth complex, including more than 200 decorated stones. Alongside typical motifs like spirals, lozenges and concentric circles are rare crescent shapes.

TOP TIP
Best time to visit is early morning mid-week during summer, when there are fewer tourists and no school tours.

Newgrange Entrance Kerbstone
Newgrange is surrounded by 97 kerbstones (24 of which are still buried), numbered sequentially from K1, the beautifully decorated entrance stone.

Newgrange
Newgrange's passage grave is designed to allow for a solar alignment during the winter solstice.

FACT FILE

The winter solstice event is witnessed by a maximum of 50 people selected by lottery and their guests (one each). In 2018, 28,595 people applied.

Dowth
There is no public access to the two passage chambers at Dowth. The crater at the top was due to a clumsy attempt at excavation in 1847.

⑦

Newgrange Burial Chamber
The corbelled roof of the chamber has remained intact since its construction, and is considered one of the finest of its kind in Europe.

①

Brú na Bóinne Visitor Centre
The spiral design of this wonderful interpretative centre is designed to echo the construction and decoration of Newgrange. Inside are exhibits on prehistoric Ireland and passage tombs.

©NATIONAL MONUMENTS SERVICE DEPT OF ARTS, HERITAGE AND THE GAELTACHT

Around Brú na Bóinne

Hill of Tara

The Hill of Tara is Ireland's most sacred stretch of turf, occupying a place at the heart of Irish history, legend and folklore. It was the home of the mystical druids, the priest-rulers of ancient Ireland, who practised their particular form of Celtic paganism under the watchful gaze of the all-powerful goddess Maeve (Medbh). Later it was the ceremonial capital of the high kings, all 142 of them, who ruled until the arrival of Christianity in the 5th century. It is also one of the most important ancient sites in Europe, with a Stone Age passage tomb and prehistoric burial mounds that date back some 5000 years.

Although little remains other than humps and mounds on the hill (named from ancient texts), its historic and folkloric significance is immense.

Entrance to Tara is free and the site is always open. There are good explanatory panels by the entrance.

Regular Bus Éireann (www.buseireann. ie) services link Dublin to within 1km of the site (€10, one hour, hourly). Ask the driver to drop you off at Tara Cross, where you take a left turn off the main road.

Battle of the Boyne

More than 60,000 soldiers of the armies of King James II and King William III fought in 1690 on this patch of farmland on the border of Counties Meath and Louth. William ultimately prevailed and James sailed off to France.

The **battle site** (☏041-980 9950; www. battleoftheboyne.ie; Drybridge; adult/child €5/3; ⊙9am-5pm May-Sep, to 4pm Oct-Apr) has an informative visitor centre and parkland walks. It's 6km west of Drogheda's town centre along Rathmullan Rd (follow the river). Buses run to/from Drogheda (€4.80, 20 minutes, two daily).

At the visitor centre you can watch a short film about the battle, see original and replica weaponry of the time, and explore a laser battlefield model. Self-guided walks through the parkland and battle site allow time to ponder the events that saw Protestant interests remain in Ireland. Costumed reenactments take place in summer.

Drogheda & Around

Only 48km north of Dublin, Drogheda is a historic fortified town straddling the River Boyne. Stately old buildings, a handsome cathedral and a riveting museum provide plenty of cultural interest, while atmospheric pubs, fine restaurants, numerous sleeping options and good transport links make it a handy base for exploring the region.

A number of historic sites lie close to Drogheda, but you'll need your own transport to explore them.

⊙ SIGHTS

Monasterboice   Historic Site
(⊙sunrise-sunset) FREE Crowing ravens lend an eerie atmosphere to Monasterboice, an intriguing monastic site down a leafy lane in sweeping farmland, which contains a cemetery, two ancient church ruins, one of the finest and tallest round towers in Ireland, and two of the most important high crosses.

Come early or late in the day to avoid the crowds. It's just off the M1 motorway, about 8km north of Drogheda.

Old Mellifont Abbey   Ruins
(☏041-982 6459; www.heritageireland.ie; Tullyallen; site admission free, visitor centre adult/ student €5/3; ⊙site 24hr year-round, visitor centre 10am-6pm Jun-early Sep) In its Anglo-Norman prime, this abbey, 1.5km off the main Drogheda–Collon road (R168), was the Cistercians' first and most magnificent centre in Ireland. Highly evocative and well worth exploring, the ruins still reflect the site's former splendour.

Mellifont's most recognisable building and one of the country's finest examples of Cistercian architecture is the 13th-century lavabo, the monks' octagonal washing room.

High cross at Monasterboice

🍴 EATING & DRINKING

Kitchen   Mediterranean €€

(📞041-983 4630; www.facebook.com/thekitch-enrestaurantdrogheda; 2 South Quay; mains lunch €13-17, dinner €19-27; ☺11am-9pm Wed, to 10pm Thu-Sat, noon-9pm Sun Mar-Oct, noon-7pm Wed & Sun, from 11am Thu, 11am-9pm Fri & Sat Nov-Feb; 🛜) Fronted by a sage-green facade, Droghe-da's best restaurant is aptly named for its shiny open kitchen. Organic local produce is used along with worldly ingredients such as Cypriot halloumi and Serrano ham. Breads are made on-site and there's an excellent choice of wine by the glass. Don't miss the salted-caramel baked Alaska for dessert.

Grey Goose   Bar

(www.facebook.com/Thegreygoosewestst; 89 West St; ☺10.30am-11.30pm Mon-Thu, to 12.30am Fri & Sat, 12.30-11pm Sun; 🛜) Grey Goose has a vast downstairs bar with herringbone floors, stained glass and leather sofas, and a grand piano in its upstairs cocktail lounge, the Birdcage, where DJs spin on Friday and Saturday, bands play on Sunday and trad sessions take place on Monday. Alongside Irish and international craft beers, local spir-its include Listoke gin and Slane whiskey.

Gastropub fare (mains €8 to €13), spanning house-speciality wood-fired pizzas to burgers, smoky ribs and salads, is served until 9pm.

ℹ️ GETTING THERE & AWAY

The **bus station** (cnr Donore Rd & George's St) is on the south side of the river.

Bus Éireann (www.buseireann.ie) links Drogheda with Dublin (€9, 1½ hours, half-hourly Monday to Saturday, hourly Sunday) and Dun-dalk (€8, 55 minutes, hourly).

Matthews (www.matthews.ie) also serves Dublin (€10, 45 minutes, half-hourly Monday to Friday, hourly Saturday and Sunday) and Dundalk (€10, 30 minutes, half-hourly Monday to Friday, hourly Saturday and Sunday).

The **train station** (www.irishrail.ie; off Dublin Rd) is just south of the river and east of the town centre. Drogheda is on the main Belfast–Dublin line (Dublin €12.90, one hour; Belfast €14.50, 1½ hours) with hourly (or more frequent) trains.

KILKENNY CITY

Kilkenny City

Kilkenny is the Ireland of many visitors' imaginations. Built from dark-grey limestone flecked with fossil seashells, Kilkenny (from the Irish 'Cill Chainnigh', meaning the Church of St Canice) is also known as 'the marble city'. Its picturesque 'Medieval Mile' of narrow lanes and historic buildings strung between castle and cathedral along the bank of the River Nore is one of the southeast's biggest tourist draws. It's worth braving the crowds to soak up the atmosphere of this creative crucible – Kilkenny is a centre for arts and crafts, and home to a host of fine restaurants, cafes, pubs and shops.

One Day in Kilkenny

Spend the morning wandering the aristocratic halls of **Kilkenny Castle** (p112), then cross the road for shopping and lunch at **Kilkenny Design Centre** (p117). In the afternoon explore the **Medieval Mile Museum** (p114) and the historical delights of **St Canice's Cathedral** (p114) before sitting down to a Michelin-starred dinner at **Campagne** (p119).

Two Days in Kilkenny

On day two visit the **Rothe House & Garden** (p116) museum in the morning, then (if you have a car) pick up a copy of the **Made in Kilkenny** craft trail booklet from the tourist office and spend the rest of the day travelling the back roads of County Kilkenny, discovering a cornucopia of potteries, crafts studios and glass-blowers workshops.

Previous page: Saint Canice's Cathedral (p114), Kilkenny

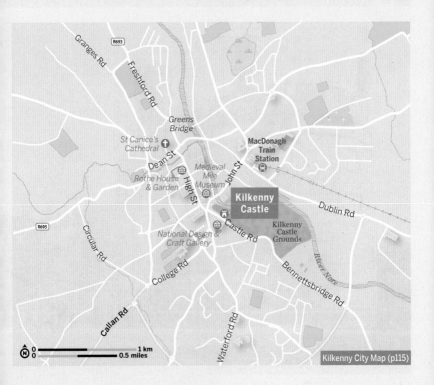

Arriving in Kilkenny

Kilkenny city has frequent train and bus links to Dublin and Waterford; for Cork, bus is the only choice.

Kilkenny MacDonagh train station is a 10-minute walk northeast of the town centre.

Bus Éireann (www.buseireann.ie) and **Dublin Coach** (www.dublincoach.ie) services run to the bus stop at the train station and the stop on Ormonde Rd (nearer the town centre). **Kavanagh Coaches** (www.bernardkavanagh coaches.ie) going to Dublin Airport stop at Ormonde Rd only.

Where to Stay

Kilkenny city has a wide range of accommodation, from camping grounds and backpacker hostels to luxury hotels. Elsewhere in the county there's a more than ample choice of rural B&Bs and country-house hotels.

Book well ahead at weekends, in summer and during festivals.

ROBINSONBECQUART/GETTY IMAGES ©

Kilkenny Castle

Rising above the River Nore, Kilkenny Castle is one of Ireland's most visited heritage sites. Stronghold of the powerful Butler family, it has a history dating back to the 12th century, though much of its present look dates from Victorian times.

Great For...

☑ **Don't Miss**

The superbly sculpted Carrara marble fireplace in the Long Gallery.

History

Kilkenny Castle has a rich – and lengthy – past. The first structure on this strategic site was a wooden tower built in 1172 by Richard de Clare, the Anglo-Norman conqueror of Ireland better known as Strongbow. In 1192 Strongbow's son-in-law, William Marshall, erected a stone castle with four towers, three of which survive. The castle was bought by the powerful Butler family (later earls and dukes of Ormonde) in 1391, and their descendants continued to live here until 1935. Maintaining the castle became such a financial strain that most of the furnishings were sold at auction. The property was handed over to the city in 1967 for the princely sum of £50.

Long Gallery

BOULENGER XAVIER/SHUTTERSTOCK ©

ⓘ Need to Know

☑056-770 4100; www.kilkennycastle.ie; The Parade; adult/child €8/4; ⊘9am-5.30pm Jun-Aug, 9.30am-5.30pm Apr, May & Sep, 9.30am-5pm Mar, 9.30am-4.30pm Oct-Feb

✕ Take A Break

The **Kilkenny Design Centre Restaurant** (www.kilkennydesign.com; Castle Yard; mains €7-15; ⊘10am-6pm; ☎) is right across the street from the castle.

★ Top Tip

A path from the castle grounds leads down to the riverside, along which you can walk back into town.

Visiting the Castle

For most visitors, the focal point of a visit is the **Long Gallery**, which showcases portraits of Butler family members, the oldest dating from the 17th century. It is an impressive hall with a 19th-century timber roof vividly painted with Celtic, medieval and Pre-Raphaelite motifs by John Hungerford Pollen (1820–1902), who also created the magnificent Carrara marble fireplace, delicately carved with scenes from Butler family history. During the winter months (November to January) visits are by 40-minute guided tours only, which shift to self-guided tours from February to October. Highlights include the Long Gallery with its painted roof and carved marble fireplace. There's an excellent tearoom in the former castle kitchens, all white marble and gleaming copper.

The basement **Butler Gallery** (☑056-776 1106; www.butlergallery.com; Kilkenny Castle; ⊘10am-5.30pm May-Nov, 10am-1pm & 2-4.30pm Dec-Feb, 10am-1pm & 2-5pm Mar & Apr) **FREE**, featuring contemporary artwork in temporary exhibitions, is expected to relocate to its new Barrack Lane premises in 2020.

About 20 hectares of **public parkland** (www.kilkennycastle.ie; Castle Rd; ⊘8.30am-8.30pm May-Aug, to 7pm Apr & Sep, shorter hours Oct-Mar) extend to the southeast of Kilkenny Castle, framing a fine view of Mt Leinster, while a Celtic-cross-shaped rose garden lies northwest of the castle.

Kilkenny City

In the Middle Ages Kilkenny was intermittently the unofficial capital of Ireland, with its own Anglo-Norman parliament. In 1366 the parliament passed the Statutes of Kilkenny, aimed at preventing the adoption of Irish culture and language by the Anglo-Norman aristocracy – they were prohibited from marrying the native Irish, taking part in Irish sports, speaking or dressing like the Irish or playing any Irish music. Although the laws remained on the books for more than 200 years, they were never enforced with any great effect and did little to halt the absorption of the Anglo-Normans into Irish culture.

During the 1640s Kilkenny sided with the Catholic royalists in the English Civil War. The 1641 Confederation of Kilkenny, an uneasy alliance of native Irish and Anglo-Normans, aimed to bring about the return of land and power to Catholics. After Charles I's execution, Cromwell besieged Kilkenny for five days, destroying much of the southern wall of the castle before the ruling Ormonde family surrendered. The defeat signalled a permanent end to Kilkenny's political influence over Irish affairs.

Today tourism is Kilkenny's main economic focus, but the city is also the regional centre for more traditional pursuits such as agriculture – you'll see farmers on tractors stoically dodging tour buses.

◎ SIGHTS

Medieval Mile Museum   Museum

(☑056-781 7022; www.medievalmilemuseum. ie; 2 St Mary's Lane; adult/child self-guided tour €6.80/3, 45min guided tour €12/5; ☉10am-6pm Apr-Oct, 11am-4.30pm Nov-Mar) Dating from the early 13th century, St Mary's Church has been converted into a fascinating modern museum that charts the history of Kilkenny in medieval times. Highlights include the Rothe Chapel, lined with ornate 16th- and 17th-century tombs carved from local limestone, remnants of the 17th-century timber roof above the crossing, and a selection of 13th- and 14th-century grave slabs. A huge interactive map of Kilkenny allows you to explore maps and documents relating to the medieval city.

St Canice's Cathedral   Cathedral

(☑056-776 4971; www.stcanicescathedral. ie; Coach Rd; cathedral/round tower/combined adult €4.50/4/7, child €3.50/4/6.50; ☉9am-6pm Mon-Sat, 1-6pm Sun Jun-Aug, shorter hours Sep-May) Ireland's second-largest medieval cathedral (after St Patrick's in Dublin) has a long and fascinating history. The first monastery was built here in the 6th century by St Canice, Kilkenny's patron saint. The present structure dates from the 13th to 16th centuries, with extensive 19th-century reconstruction, its interior housing ancient grave slabs and the tombs of Kilkenny Castle's Butler dynasty. Outside stands a 30m-high round tower, one of only two in Ireland that you can climb.

Records show that a wooden church on the site was burned down in 1087. The existing structure was raised between 1202 and 1285, but then endured a series of catastrophes and resurrections. The first disaster, the collapse of the church tower in 1332, was associated with Dame Alice Kyteler's conviction for witchcraft. Her maid Petronella was also convicted, and her nephew, William Outlawe, was implicated. The unfortunate maid was burned at the stake, but Dame Alice escaped to London and William saved himself by offering to reroof part of St Canice's Cathedral with lead tiles. His new roof proved too heavy, however, and brought the church tower down with it.

In 1650 Cromwell's forces defaced and damaged the church, using it to stable their horses. Repairs began in 1661; the beautiful roof in the nave was completed in 1863.

Inside, highly polished ancient grave slabs are set on the walls and the floor. On the northern wall, a slab inscribed in Norman French commemorates Jose de Keteller, who died in 1280; despite the difference in spelling he was probably the father of Alice Kyteler. The stone chair of St Kieran embedded in the wall dates from

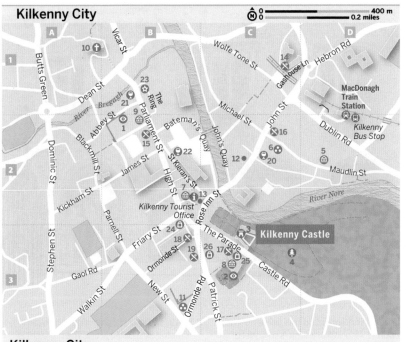

Kilkenny City

the 13th century. The fine 1596 monument to Honorina Grace at the western end of the southern aisle is made of beautiful local black limestone. In the southern transept is the handsome black tomb of Piers Butler, who died in 1539, and his wife, Margaret Fitzgerald. Tombs and monuments (listed on a board in the southern aisle) to other

Rothe House

notable Butlers crowd this corner of the church. Also worth a look is a model of Kilkenny as it was in 1642.

Apart from missing its crown, the 9th-century round tower is in excellent condition. Inside is a tight squeeze and you'll need both hands to climb the 100 steps up steep ladders (under 12s not admitted).

Walking to the cathedral from Parliament St leads you over Irishtown Bridge and up St Canice's Steps, which date from 1614; the wall at the top contains fragments of medieval carvings. The leaning tombstones scattered about the grounds prompt you to look, at the very least, for a black cat.

Rothe House & Garden   Museum
(🖉056-772 2893; www.rothehouse.com; 16 Parliament St; house & garden adult/child €7.50/4.50, garden only €4/2; ⏰10.30am-5pm Mon-Sat, noon-5pm Sun) Dating from 1594, this is Ireland's finest example of a Tudor merchant house, complete with a restored medieval garden. Built around a series of courtyards, it now houses a museum with a rather sparse display of local artefacts, including a rusted

Viking sword and a grinning stone head sculpted by a Celtic artist. The highlight is the delightful walled garden, divided into fruit, vegetable and herb sections and an orchard as it would have been in the 17th century. There's also a genealogy centre.

In the 1640s the wealthy Rothe family played a part in the Confederation of Kilkenny, and Peter Rothe, son of the original builder, had all his property confiscated. His sister was able to reclaim it, but just before the Battle of the Boyne (1690) the family supported James II and so lost the house permanently. In 1850 a Confederation banner was discovered in the house; it's now in the National Museum in Dublin.

National Design & Craft Gallery   Gallery
(🖉056-779 6147; www.ndcg.ie; Castle Yard; ⏰10am-5.30pm Tue-Sat, from 11am Sun) FREE Contemporary Irish crafts are showcased at the imaginative National Design & Craft Gallery, set in former stables across the road from Kilkenny Castle, next to the shops of the Kilkenny Design Centre.

Ceramics dominate, but exhibits often feature furniture, jewellery and weaving from the members of the Crafts Council of Ireland. Family days are held the second Saturday of every month, with a tour of the gallery and free hands-on workshops for children. Check the website for additional workshops and events.

Butler House Gardens   Gardens
(www.butler.ie; The Parade; ⏰10am-5pm Mon-Fri, to noon Sat & Sun except during private events) **FREE** The beautiful Butler House gardens are home to an unusual water feature constructed from remnants of the British-built Nelson's Pillar, blown up by nationalists in Dublin's O'Connell St in 1966. Access is via a gate at the back of the courtyard behind the National Design & Craft Gallery. Access is restricted during weddings and other private events.

Kilkenny Arts & Crafts

At least 130 full-time craftspeople and artists work commercially in County Kilkenny – one of the highest concentrations in Ireland – thanks to its fine raw materials and inspirational scenery.

Recommended studios and galleries:

Rudolf Heltzel Goldsmith (📞056-772 1497; www.rudolfheltzel.com; 10 Patrick St; ⏰9.30am-1pm & 2-5.30pm Mon-Sat) Fine-art jewellery.

Jerpoint Glass Studio (www.jerpoint glass.com; Glenmore, Stoneyford; ⏰10am-5.30pm Mon-Sat, noon-5pm Sun Apr-Sep, 10am-5pm Mon-Sat Oct-Mar) **FREE** Watch skilled glass-blowers at work.

Moth to a Flame (📞056-772 7826; www.mothtoaflame.ie; Kilkenny Rd; ⏰9am-6pm Mon-Sat) Handmade art candles.

Nicholas Mosse Irish Country Shop (📞056-772 7505; www.nicholasmosse.com; Annamult Rd; ⏰10am-6pm Mon-Sat, 1.30-5pm Sun) Brightly coloured ceramics and tableware.

Bridge Pottery (📞056-772 9156; www.thebridgepottery.com; off N76, Burnchurch; ⏰10am-6pm Mon-Sat) Small studio creating gorgeous ceramics.

Clay Creations (📞087 257 0735; www.bridlyonsceramics.com; Low St; ⏰10am-5.30pm Wed, Thu & Sat, 10am-1pm & 3.30-5.30pm Fri, by appointment Tue) Gallery of original and unusual ceramic pieces.

Pick up a copy of the *Made in Kilkenny* craft trail (www.madeinkilkenny.ie) for a comprehensive list.

Nicholas Mosse ceramics
JACKIE ELLIS / ALAMY STOCK PHOTO ©

⊙ TOURS

Pat Tynan Walking Tours   Walking
(📞087 265 1745; www.kilkennywalkingtours.ie; adult/child €10/8; ⏰11am & 2pm Mon-Sat, 11.15am & 12.30pm Sun Apr-Oct, by appointment Nov-Mar) Entertaining, informative 70-minute walking tours through Kilkenny's narrow lanes, steps and pedestrian passageways. Meet at the tourist office (p121).

Kilkenny Cycling Tours   Cycling
(📞086 895 4961; www.kilkennycyclingtours.com; 16 John St; adult/child tours from €25/12.50, bike hire €20/10; ⏰10am-6pm) Explore the city and surrounds on a bike during a two-hour guided tour that includes an optional lunch. Prebooking is essential, at least 48 hours in advance. Bikes are also available to hire.

🔒 SHOPPING

Kilkenny Design Centre   Arts & Crafts
(📞056-772 2118; www.kilkennydesign.com; Castle Yard; ⏰9am-6pm) Top-end Irish crafts and artworks from artisans county-wide are sold at this design centre. Look for John Hanly wool blankets, Cushendale woollen goods, Foxford scarves and Bunbury cutting boards.

Kilkenny's City Walls

Parts of Kilkenny's medieval city walls, mostly dating from the 14th and 15th centuries, can still be seen in several places, notably at **Talbot's Tower** (cnr Ormonde Rd & New St), **Maudlin Tower** (Maudlin St) and the **Black Freren Gate** (Abbey St) – the only surviving city gate. **Maudlin Castle** (Maudlin St), dating from around 1500, is a more substantial tower house and once protected the eastern approach to the city.

Black Freren Gate
DOUGLAS PFEIFFER/SHUTTERSTOCK ©

Kilkenny Book Centre   Books

(☎056-776 2117; www.thebookcentre.ie; 10 High St; ☻9am-6pm Mon-Sat, 1-5pm Sun) Kilkenny's largest bookshop stocks plenty of Irish-interest fiction and nonfiction, periodicals and a good range of maps. There's a cafe upstairs.

EATING

The Cutting Vedge   Vegetarian, Vegan €

(☎087 243 6754; www.facebook.com/helen costelloes; 4 Ormonde St; dishes €5-11; ☻9am-5pm Mon-Fri, 10am-5pm Sat; ✎) ✦ At the cutting edge of the worldwide trend for vegetarian and vegan cuisine, this brilliant cafe, opened in 2018, kicks off at breakfast with dishes such as tofu burritos, followed at lunch by white bean goulash; cauliflower and leek crumble; potato and basil Wellington; almond-crusted courgette and daily soups such as parsnip and watercress. Sandwiches are served on organic oatmeal bread.

Everything is made from scratch, with a zero-waste policy.

Kilkenny Book Centre

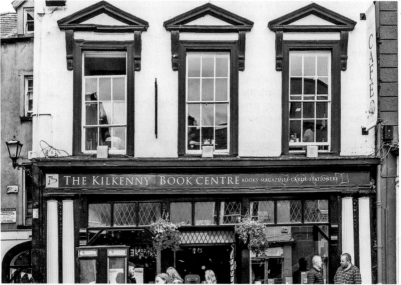

BEN/OE2001/SHUTTERSTOCK ©

Foodworks
Bistro, Cafe €€

(☑056-777 7696; www.foodworks.ie; 7 Parliament St; mains €17.50-26.50, 3-course dinner menus €26-29; ☺noon-9pm Wed & Thu, to 9.30pm Fri & Sat, to 5pm Sun; 🛜🐾) 🍴 The owners of this cool and casual bistro keep their own pigs and grow their own salad leaves, so it would be churlish not to try their pork loin stuffed with black pudding, or pressed pig's trotter – and you'll be glad you did. Delicious food, excellent coffee and friendly service make this a justifiably popular venue; it's best to book a table.

Its excellent kids menu (mains €7 to €9.50) includes grilled cod and chips, stone-baked pizzas, and local sausages with gravy and mash.

Zuni
Irish €€

(☑056-772 3999; www.zuni.ie; 26 Patrick St; mains breakfast & lunch €8-15, dinner €19.50-28.50; ☺8-11.15am, 12.30-2.30pm & 6-9.30pm; 🛜) 🍴 Among Kilkenny's most stylish and busiest restaurants, Zuni is sophisticated yet informal, with a kitchen that elevates humble comfort food such as black pudding scotch eggs, confit duck terrine, spinach-wrapped cod and parsnip parcels and savoury beetroot cheesecake.

Hungry Moose
Burgers €€

(☑056-775 1469; www.facebook.com/the hungrymoosekilkenny; 60 John St; burgers €15-20; ☺noon-9.30pm Sun-Thu, to 10pm Fri & Sat; 🛜🐾) Winner of Ireland's Best Burger 2018 for its house speciality Hungry Moose (smoked bacon, dill pickles, aged Canadian Moose cheddar and beer-battered onion rings), this Kilkenny hotspot has another seven beef varieties on offer. There are also fish, veggie and vegan burgers, all served with chunky, skinny or curly fries. Reclaimed timbers kit out the stripped-back dining space (no takeaways).

Sides include corn on the cob with chilli-infused butter, kimchi slaw and fried jalapeño poppers; craft beers come from around the country and as far afield as Hawaii.

Kids burgers can be made to order.

Kilkenny's World-Class Festivals

Kilkenny hosts several world-class events throughout the year, attracting thousands of revellers.

Cat Laughs Comedy Festival (www.the catlaughs.com; ☺May-Jun) World-famous comedians, including Irish stars such as Dara Ó Briain and Aisling Bea, perform in Kilkenny's hotels and pubs over a long weekend in late May/early June.

Kilkenny Arts Festival (www.kilkenny arts.ie; ☺Aug) In early to mid-August the city comes alive for 10 action-packed days of theatre, cinema, music, literature, visual arts, children's events and street spectacles.

Kilkenny Rhythm & Roots (www. kilkennyroots.com; ☺Apr-May) More than 30 pubs and other venues participate in hosting this major music festival over three days in late April/early May. Its emphasis is on country and 'old time' American roots music.

Kilkenny Arts Festival
BOULENGER XAVIER/SHUTTERSTOCK ©

Campagne
Gastronomy €€€

(☑056-777 2858; www.campagne.ie; 5 Gashouse Lane; 3-course lunch & early-bird menu €38, 3-course dinner menu €60; ☺6-10pm Wed & Thu, 12.30-2.30pm & 6-10pm Fri & Sat, 12.30-2.30pm Sun, closed late Jun–early Jul & mid-Jan–early Feb) 🍴 Chef Garrett Byrne was awarded a Michelin star for this bold, stylish restaurant in his native Kilkenny. He's passionate about supporting local and artisan producers, and adds a French accent to memorable culinary creations such as black-pudding-stuffed pigs trotters or rhubarb-crumble souffle. The early-bird menu (to 9pm Wednesday to Friday, to 6pm Saturday) is a serious bargain.

🍷 DRINKING & NIGHTLIFE

John St and Parliament St are nightlife hubs, with numerous pubs, many hosting live music.

Kyteler's Inn   Pub
(☎056-772 1064; www.kytelersinn.com; 27 St Kieran's St; ⊙11am-11.30pm Mon-Thu, to 2am Fri & Sat, 12.15pm-midnight Sun) Dame Alice Kyteler's old house was built back in 1224 and has seen its share of history: she was charged with witchcraft in 1323. Today the rambling bar incorporates the original building, vaulted ceiling and arches. There's a beer garden and a large upstairs room for live music (nightly from March to October), ranging from trad to blues.

O'Hara's Brewery Corner   Pub
(☎056-780 5081; www.carlowbrewing.com/our-pub; 29 Parliament St; ⊙1-11.30pm Mon-Thu, to 12.30am Fri & Sat, to 11pm Sun) Kilkenny's best venue for craft brews is a long, narrow beer hall of a place owned by Carlow Brewing Company, with a wide selection of ciders and ales, including Carlow's own IPA.

John Cleere's   Pub
(☎056-776 2573; www.cleeres.com; 28 Parliament St; ⊙noon-12.30am) One of Kilkenny's finest venues for live music, theatre and comedy, this long bar has blues, jazz and rock, as well as trad-music sessions on Monday and Wednesday. Food such as Irish stew is served throughout the day.

Bridie's General Store   Pub
(☎056-776 5133; www.facebook.com/bridiesbar; 72 John St; ⊙11am-10pm Sun-Wed, 6pm-2am Thu-Sat) Top design talent was employed by the Langton's empire to create this reproduction trad grocery-pub. The front is a beguiling retail potpourri of souvenirs, jokes, toys, preserves and deli items. Step through the swinging doors to the pub with polished timber and beautiful tiles. Out back is a classy, partly covered beer garden.

Kyteler's Inn

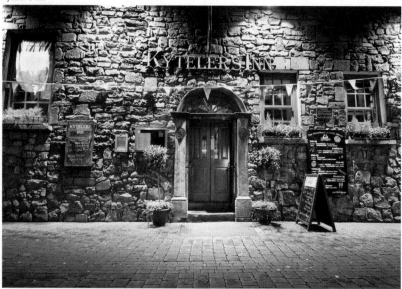

LITTLENYSTOCK/SHUTTERSTOCK ©

John Cleere's

⭐ ENTERTAINMENT

Watergate Theatre　　　　　Theatre
(☎ box office 056-776 1674; www.watergate
theatre.com; Parliament St) Kilkenny's top
theatre venue hosts drama, comedy and
musical performances. If you're wondering
why intermission lasts 18 minutes, it's so
patrons can nip across to John Cleere's pub
for a pint.

ℹ️ INFORMATION

Kilkenny Tourist Office (☎ 056-775 1500; www.
visitkilkenny.ie; Rose Inn St; ⊙ 9am-5pm Mon-Sat,
10am-4pm Sun) Stocks guides and walking maps.

ℹ️ GETTING THERE & AWAY

BUS

Bus Éireann (www.buseireann.ie) and Dublin
Coach (www.dublincoach.ie) services run to the
bus stop (Dublin Rd) at the train station and the
stop on Ormonde Rd (nearer the town centre).

Bernard Kavanagh Coaches (www.bernard
kavanaghcoaches.ie) going to Dublin Airport
stop at Ormonde Rd only.

Carlow (€10, 35 minutes, two daily Monday to
Saturday, one Sunday) Bus Éireann.

Cork (€15, 2½ hours, every two hours) Dublin
Coach M9 Express.

Dublin (€10, 1½ hours, every two hours) Dublin
Coach M9 Express.

Dublin Airport (€20, 2½ hours, every two hours)
Bernard Kavanagh Coaches.

Waterford (€5, 40 minutes, every two hours)
Dublin Coach M9 Express.

TRAIN

Kilkenny's **MacDonagh Train Station** (Dublin
Rd) is a 10-minute walk (800m) northeast of the
town centre. Trains run to Dublin Heuston (€13,
1½ hours, seven daily) and Waterford (€7.50, 35
minutes, seven daily).

COUNTY
TIPPERARY

County Tipperary

Landlocked Tipperary boasts the sort of fertile soil that farmers dream of. The central area of the county is low-lying, but rolling hills spill over from adjoining counties. An upper-crust gloss still clings to traditions here, with fox hunts in full legal cry during the winter season.

Walking and cycling opportunities abound, especially in the Glen of Aherlow near Tipperary town. But the real crowd pleasers are the iconic Rock of Cashel and Cahir Castle. In between, you'll find bucolic charm along pretty much any country road you choose.

One Day in County Tipperary

You'll need two hours to properly explore the **Rock of Cashel** (p126), so devote the morning to that followed by a slap-up lunch at **Cafe Hans** (p131).

In the afternoon visit the **Brú Ború** (p130) and **Cashel Folk Village** (p130) museums in town, then take a walk out to the atmospheric ruins of **Hore Abbey** (p130).

Two Days in County Tipperary

On day two head to Cahir for a visit to impressive **Cahir Castle** (p132), followed by a pleasant walk along the wooded banks of the River Suir to the delightful and unexpected **Swiss Cottage** (p133). If you're continuing west to County Clare, then make the most of the afternoon with a scenic drive through the lovely **Glen of Aherlow** (p132).

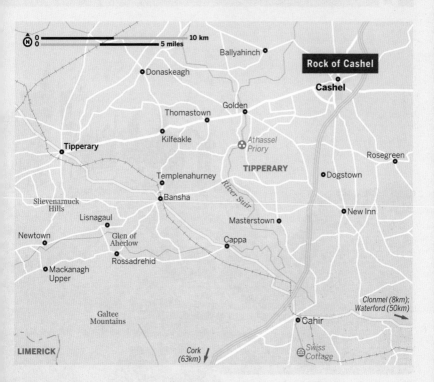

Rock of Cashel

Cashel

Ballyahinch

Donaskeagh

Golden

Thomastown

Kilfeakle

Athassel Priory

Rosegreen

Tipperary

TIPPERARY

Dogstown

Templenahurney

River Suir

Bansha

New Inn

Slievenamuck Hills

Lisnagaul

Masterstown

Newtown

Glen of Aherlow

Cappa

Mackanagh Upper

Rossadrehid

Galtee Mountains

Clonmel (8km);
Waterford (50km)

Cahir

LIMERICK

Cork (63km)

Swiss Cottage

Arriving in County Tipperary

The M8 motorway links Dublin to Cashel, Cahir and Mitchelstown. There are good bus links from Dublin and Cork to Clonmel and the main towns, while rail is really only useful for travelling from Waterford to Clonmel, Cahir and Tipperary town. Bus Éireann runs eight buses daily between Cashel and Cork.

Where to Stay

The best choice of accommodation is to be found in Tipperary's larger towns such as Clonmel, Cashel and Cahir, but there are some good country inns and lots of rural B&Bs scattered across the county. The best campsites are around Clonmel, and in the Glen of Aherlow to the west.

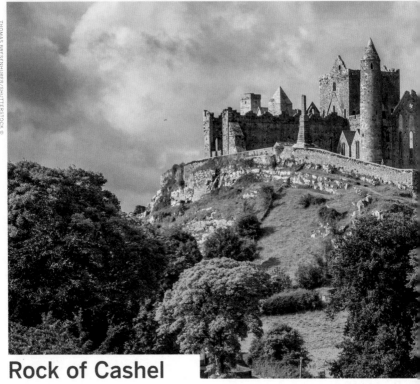

THOMAS BRESENHUBER/SHUTTERSTOCK ©

Rock of Cashel

For more than 1000 years the Rock of Cashel was a symbol of power and the seat of kings and priests. Exploring this monumental complex offers a fascinating insight into Ireland's past.

The Rock of Cashel is one of Ireland's most spectacular historic sites: a prominent green hill, banded with limestone outcrops, rising from a grassy plain and bristling with ancient fortifications. Sturdy walls circle an enclosure containing a complete round tower, a 13th-century Gothic cathedral and the finest 12th-century Romanesque chapel in Ireland, home to some of the land's oldest frescoes.

It's a five-minute stroll from the town centre up to the Rock, from where fantastic views range over the Tipperary countryside.

History

The word 'cashel' is an Anglicised version of the Irish word *caiseal,* meaning 'fortress' (related to the English 'castle', from the Latin *castellum*). In the 4th century the Rock of Cashel was chosen as a base by

Great For...

☑ **Don't Miss**

The carving of a centaur firing an arrow at a rampaging lion, on Cormac's Chapel.

Rock of Cashel ⊚
○ Cashel

❶ Need to Know

📞062-61437; www.heritageireland.ie; adult/
child €8/4, incl Cormac's Chapel €11/7;
🕘9am-7pm early Jun–mid-Sep, to 5.30pm
mid-Mar–early Jun & mid-Sep–mid-Oct, to
4.30pm mid-Oct–mid-Mar; P

✕ Take a Break

Head for Cafe Hans (p131) in the village,
immediately below the rock.

★ Top Tip

Download a free audio-guided tour of
the town from the tourist office website
(www.cashel.ie).

Buildings

Numerous buildings must have occupied the cold and exposed Rock over the
years, but it is the ecclesiastical relics that
have survived even the depredations of
the Cromwellian army in 1647. The vast
medieval **cathedral** was used for worship
until the mid-1700s. Among the graves are
a 19th-century high cross and mausoleum
for local landowners the Scully family;
the top of the Scully Cross was razed by
lightning in 1976.

But the undoubted highlight of the Rock
is the early 12th-century Cormac's Chapel,
an exquisite gem of Romanesque architecture with beautifully carved doorways
and the precious remains of colourful wall
paintings. Access is by 45-minute guided
tour only (€3 extra, book at entrance).

the Eóghanachta clan from Wales, who
went on to conquer much of Munster and
become kings of the region. For some 400
years it rivalled Tara as a centre of power
in Ireland. The clan was associated with St
Patrick, hence the Rock's alternative name
of St Patrick's Rock. In the 10th century the
Eóghanachta lost possession of the rock to
the O'Brien (Dál gCais) tribe under Brian
Ború's leadership. In 1101 King Muircheart-
ach O'Brien presented the Rock to the
Church to curry favour with the powerful
bishops and to end secular rivalry over possession of the Rock with the Eóghanachta,
by now known as the MacCarthys.

Rock of Cashel

A TOUR OF THE COMPLEX

For more than 1000 years the Rock of Cashel was a symbol of power and the seat of kings and clergymen who ruled over the region. Exploring this monumental complex offers a fascinating insight into Ireland's past.

Enter via the 15th-century **1 Hall of the Vicars Choral**, built to house the male choristers who sang in the cathedral. Exhibits in its undercroft include rare silverware, stone reliefs and the original St Patrick's Cross. In the courtyard you'll see the replica of **2 St Patrick's Cross**. A small porch leads into the 13th-century Gothic **3 cathedral**. To the west of the nave are the remains of the **4 Archbishop's Residence**. From the cathedral's north transept on the northeastern corner is the Rock's earliest building, an 11th- or 12th-century **5 Round Tower**. Nestled in the southeast corner of the cathedral is the compelling **6 Cormac's Chapel**, Ireland's earliest surviving Romanesque church. It dates from 1127 and the medieval integrity of its trans-European architecture survives. Inside the main door on the left is the sarcophagus said to house King Cormac, dating from between 1125 and 1150. Before leaving, take time for a close-up look at the Rock's **7 enclosing walls and corner tower**.

Hall of the Vicars Choral
Head upstairs from the ticket office to see the restored choristers' kitchen and dining hall, complete with period furniture, tapestries and paintings beneath a fine carved-oak roof and gallery.

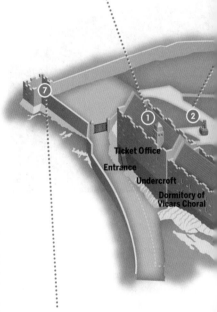

Ticket Office

Entrance

Undercroft

Dormitory of Vicars Choral

Enclosing Walls & Corner Tower
Constructed from lime mortar around the 15th century, and originally incorporating five gates, stone walls enclose the entire site. It's thought the surviving corner tower was used as a watchtower.

TOP TIPS

➡ Good photographic vantage points for framing the mighty Rock are on the road into Cashel from the Dublin Rd roundabout or from the little roads just west of the centre.

➡ The best photo opportunities, however, are from inside the atmospheric ruins of Hore Abbey, 1km to the west.

St Patrick's Cross
In the castle courtyard, this cross replicates the eroded Hall of the Vicars Choral original – an impressive 12th-century crutched cross depicting a crucifixion scene on one face and animals on the other.

Archbishop's Residence
The west side of the cathedral is taken up by the Archbishop's Residence, a 15th-century, four-storey castle, which had its great hall built over the nave, reducing its length. It was last inhabited in the mid-1700s.

Cathedral
A huge square tower with a turret on the southwestern corner soars above the cathedral. Scattered throughout are monuments, a 16th-century altar tomb, coats of arms panels, and stone heads on capitals and corbels.

Turret

④

③

⑤

⑥

Choir

Scully Cross

Round Tower
Standing 28m tall, the doorway to this ancient edifice is 3.5m above the ground – perhaps for structural rather than defensive reasons. Its exact age is unknown but may be as early as 1101.

Cormac's Chapel
Look closely at the exquisite doorway arches, the grand chancel arch and ribbed barrel vault, and carved vignettes, including a trefoil-tailed grotesque and a Norman-helmeted centaur firing an arrow at a rampaging lion.

Cashel

It's little wonder that Cashel (Caiseal Mumhan) is such a fabulous draw (the Queen included it on her historic visit in 2011). The iconic religious buildings that crown the blustery summit of the Rock of Cashel (p126) seem to emerge from the craggy landscape itself and the neighbouring market town of Cashel rewards rambles around its charming streets.

⊙ SIGHTS

Hore Abbey   Ruins
(⊙dawn-dusk) FREE The formidable ruin of 13th-century Hore Abbey (also known as Hoare Abbey or St Mary's) stands in flat farmland 1km west of the Rock of Cashel. Originally Benedictine and settled by monks from Glastonbury in England at the end of the 12th century, it later became a Cistercian house. Now an enjoyably gloomy, jackdaw-haunted ruin, the abbey was gifted to the order by a 13th-century archbishop who expelled the Benedictine monks after dreaming that they planned to murder him.

Brú Ború   Museum
(☎062-61122; www.bruboru.ie; The Kiln; adult/child €5/3; ⊙9am-5pm Mon-Fri, longer hours Jul–mid-Aug) This privately run cultural centre is next to the car park below the Rock of Cashel, and offers absorbing insights into Irish traditional music, dance and song. The centre's main attraction, the Sounds of History exhibition, relates the story of Ireland and its music through imaginative audio displays; various other musical events take place in summer.

Cashel Folk Village   Museum
(☎087 915 1316; www.cashelfolkvillage.ie; St Dominic St; adult/child €7/4; ⊙10.15am-7.30pm Mon-Sat, 11am-5.30pm Sun mid-Mar–mid-Oct, by appointment mid-Oct–mid-Mar) An engaging exhibition of old buildings, shopfronts and memorabilia from around the town. It's all a bit amateurish and slipshod, but in a charming, heart warming way.

Cashel Heritage Centre   Museum
(☎062-61333; www.cashel.ie; Main St; ⊙9.30am-5.30pm Mon-Sat mid-Mar–mid-Oct, Mon-Fri only rest of year) FREE Located in the town hall

Mikey Ryan's

alongside the tourist office, the displays here include a scale model of Cashel in the 1640s with an audio commentary.

EATING

Apart from the Rock, Cashel is best-known in Ireland and beyond for award-winning Cashel Blue farmhouse cheese, Ireland's first-ever blue cheese, still handmade locally.

Mikey Ryan's   Gastropub €€

(☑062-62007; www.mikeyryans.ie; 76 Main St; mains lunch €9-16, dinner €17-30; ⊙food served noon-3pm & 6-9.30pm; 🛜🐾) This long-established bar has been given a glitzy gastropub makeover, with a bright, sun-drenched dining room at the back, and a gorgeous garden complete with barbecue and horse-box bar. The delicious farmhouse-style food is sourced from local farmers and artisan producers, and Cashel Blue cheese makes several appearances on the menu – in pesto, on pizza and topping a burger.

Cafe Hans   Cafe €€

(☑062-63660; Dominic St; mains €15-26; ⊙noon-5.30pm Tue-Sat; 🐾) Competition for the 32 seats is fierce at this gourmet cafe run by the family behind Chez Hans along the street. There are fantastic salads, open sandwiches (including succulent prawns with tangy Marie Rose sauce) and filling fish, shellfish, lamb and vegetarian dishes, accompanied by a discerning wine selection and mouth-watering desserts. No credit cards. Enter via Moor Lane.

Arrive before or after the lunchtime rush or plan on waiting for a table.

Chez Hans   Irish €€€

(☑062-61177; www.chezhans.net; Dominic St; mains €28-39, 2-/3-course Sun lunch €28/35; ⊙6-10pm Wed-Sat, 12.30-3.30pm Sun) Since 1968 this former church has been a place of worship for foodies from Ireland and beyond. Still as fresh and inventive as ever, the restaurant has a regularly

🏛 The Ruins of Athassel Priory

Reached over a stile and across grassy (sometimes muddy) fields, the atmospheric ruins of **Athassel Priory** (Golden; ⊙dawn-dusk) sit in the shallow and verdant River Suir Valley, 7km southwest of Cashel. The original buildings date from 1205, and Athassel was once one of the richest and most important monasteries in Ireland. What survives is substantial: the gatehouse and portcullis gateway, the cloister (ruined but recognisable) and large stretches of walled enclosure, as well as some medieval tomb effigies.

To get here, take the N74 to the village of Golden, then head 2km south along the narrow L4304 road signed 'Athassel Abbey'. Roadside parking is limited and quite tight.

Nave of Athassel Priory
TRAVELPIXPRO/GETTY IMAGES ©

changing menu and gives its blessing to all manner of Irish produce, including steamed Galway mussels, beetroot risotto with deep-fried goat's cheese and steamed halibut with fennel puree. No credit cards.

ℹ INFORMATION

Tourist Office (☑062-61333; www.cashel.ie; Town Hall, Main St; ⊙9.30am-5.30pm Mon-Sat mid-Mar–mid-Oct, Mon-Fri only mid-Oct–mid-Mar) Helpful office with reams of info on the area.

 Glen of Aherlow

The broad, fertile valley of the Glen of Aherlow, slung between the wooded Slievenamuck Hills and the shapely Galtee Mountains, is the most scenic part of County Tipperary and one of Ireland's hidden delights.

A beautiful and leisurely 25km scenic drive through the Glen is signposted from Tipperary town. At the eastern end of the Glen, between Tipperary and Cahir, the village of Bansha (An Bháinseach) marks the start of a 20km trip west to Galbally, an easy bike ride or scenic drive along the R663 that takes in the best of the glen's landscapes.

The R663 from Bansha and the R664 south from Tipperary converge at Newtown at the Coach Road Inn, a fine old pub that's popular with walkers. Hidden around the back of the pub, the enthusiastically staffed Glen of Aherlow **tourist office** ([☎]062-56331; www.aherlow. com; Coach Rd, Newtown; ⊙9am-5pm Mon-Fri, 10am-4pm Sat May-Sep) is an excellent source of information on the area, including hiking trails.

S. MUELLER/SHUTTERSTOCK ©

ℹ️ GETTING THERE & AWAY

Bus Éireann (www.buseireann.ie) runs eight buses daily between Cashel and Cork (€16, 1¾ hours) via Cahir (€6, 20 minutes, six daily). The bus stop for Cork is at the northeast end of Main St. The Dublin stop (€16, 2½ hours, six daily) is opposite.

Not-for-profit service **Local Link Tipperary** ([☎]076 106 6140; www.locallinktipperary.ie) runs buses twice daily Monday to Friday, linking Cashel with Cahir (€3, 20 minutes) and Tipperary town (€3, 35 minutes).

Parking in town is cheaper and less crowded than the car park below the Rock.

Cahir

At the eastern tip of the Galtee Mountains, 15km south of Cashel, Cahir (An Cathair; pronounced 'care') is a compact and attractive town that encircles a sublime castle. Walking paths follow the verdant banks of the River Suir, one of Ireland's finest trout-fishing streams.

◉ SIGHTS

Cahir Castle   Historic Site
([☎]052-744 1011; www.heritageireland.ie; Castle St; adult/child €5/3; ⊙9am-6.30pm mid-Jun–Aug, 9.30am-5.30pm Mar–mid-Jun & Sep–mid-Oct, to 4.30pm mid-Oct–Feb) Cahir's castle enjoys a river-island site with massive walls, towers and keep, mullioned windows, original fireplaces and a dungeon. Founded by Conor O'Brien in 1142, and passed to the Butler family in 1375, it's one of Ireland's largest castles. In 1599 the Earl of Essex shattered its walls with cannon fire, an event illustrated by a large model. The impressive Banqueting Hall has a huge set of antlers pinned to its white walls, and you can climb the Keep.

The castle, originally built to protect a salmon fishery and important river crossing, eventually surrendered to Cromwell in 1650 without a struggle; its future usefulness may have discouraged the usual Cromwellian 'deconstruction' – it is largely intact and still formidable. It was restored in the 1840s and again in the 1960s when it came under state ownership.

A 15-minute audiovisual presentation puts Cahir in context with other Irish castles. The buildings within the castle walls are sparsely furnished, although there are good displays, including an exhibition on 'Women in Medieval Ireland'. There are frequent guided tours.

Swiss Cottage Historic Building

(☑052-744 1144; www.heritageireland.ie; Cahir Park; adult/child €5/3; ☺10am-6pm mid-Mar–Oct) A 30-minute walk along a riverside path from Cahir Castle (p132) car park leads to this thatched cottage, surrounded by roses, lavender and honeysuckle. A lavish example of Regency Picturesque, the cottage was built in 1810 as a retreat for Richard Butler, 12th Baron Caher, and his wife, and was designed by London architect John Nash, creator of the Royal Pavilion at Brighton. The 30-minute (compulsory) guided tours are thoroughly enjoyable.

The *cottage-orné* style emerged during the late 18th and early 19th centuries in England in response to the prevailing taste for the picturesque. Thatched roofs, natural wood and carved weatherboarding were characteristics of the style and most examples were built as ornamental features on estates. The cottage was restored in the 1980s under the direction of Irish designer Sybil Connolly.

✖ EATING

Don't miss the **farmers market** (www.face book.com/cahirfarmersmarket; Castle car park; ☺9am-1pm Sat) ✿ on Saturday mornings, where you can browse some of the county's finest produce.

Lazy Bean Cafe Cafe €

(☑052-744 2038; www.thelazybeancafe.com; The Square; mains €7-10; ☺9am-6pm; 🛜👪) The most popular place in town for a bite to eat, this bustling old-fashioned cafe serves all-day breakfasts, choose-your-own sandwiches, wraps, bagels and panini, and rounds it off with top-notch coffee, hot chocolate and cake.

Galileo Italian €€

(☑052-744 5689; www.galileocafe.com; Church St; mains €12-25; ☺noon-10pm Mon-Sat, 1-9pm Sun) Serving excellent pizza and pasta to Cahir locals for more than a decade, Galileo is a smart and stylish Italian restaurant, with modern decor and efficient, friendly service. The restaurant has no licence, so BYO.

ℹ️ INFORMATION

Tourist Office (☑052-744 1453; www.tipperary. com; Castle car park; ☺9.30am-1pm & 1.45-5.30pm Tue-Sat Apr-Oct) Provides information about the town and region.

ℹ️ GETTING THERE & AWAY

BUS

Cahir is a hub for several Bus Éireann (www. buseireann.ie) routes, including Dublin–Cork, Limerick–Waterford, Galway–Waterford, Kilkenny–Cork and Cork–Athlone.

There are six buses per day to Cashel (€6, 20 minutes). Buses stop in the car park beside the castle.

TRAIN

From Monday to Saturday, the train from Waterford to Limerick Junction stops in Clonmel and Cahir (€16.50, one hour, twice daily).

COUNTY CORK

County Cork

Everything good about Ireland can be found in County Cork. Surrounding the country's second city – a thriving metropolis made glorious by location and its almost Rabelaisian devotion to the finer things of life – is a lush landscape dotted with villages that offer days of languor and idyll. The city's understated confidence is grounded in its plethora of food markets and ever-evolving cast of creative eateries, and in its selection of pubs, entertainment and cultural pursuits. Further afield, you'll pass inlets along eroded coastlines and a multitude of perfectly charming fishing towns and villages.

Two Days in County Cork

Visit **Blarney Castle** (p140) first thing, then explore Cork city, taking in **Cork City Gaol** (p143) and making sure not to miss the **English Market** (p138). Lunch at the **Farmgate Cafe** (p138) is a must, as is dinner at one of Cork's many restaurants. Day two is for a boat trip from nearby Cobh to fascinating **Spike Island** (p152).

Four Days in County Cork

Head to the coast at Kinsale (p149), and spend a day exploring its sea-scented streets, including a walk out to **Charles Fort** (p149), followed by dinner at one of its fine seafood restaurants. On day four take a drive along the scenic Cork coast to visit **Bantry House** (p152). Enjoy fine food at **Manning's Emporium** (p153) before continuing on the road to Killarney.

Cork city (p142)
SLONGY/GETTY IMAGES ©

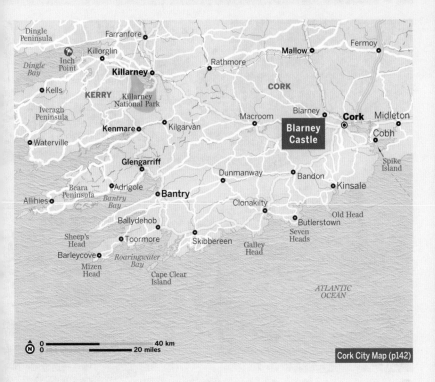

Cork City Map (p142)

Arriving in County Cork

Cork Airport is 8km south of the city centre. Buses shuttle between the airport, the train station and bus station every half hour between 6am and 10pm (€5.60 return, 30 minutes).

Kent Train Station is north of the River Lee, a 10- to 15-minute walk from the city centre.

Cork Bus Station is on Parnell Pl in the city centre.

Where to Stay

Cork city offers the full range of accommodation, from backpacker hostels and budget chain hotels to suburban B&Bs, boutique guesthouses and luxury hotels. The Cork coast has long been a holiday playground and is well endowed with farmhouse B&Bs, camping grounds and seaside hotels but, especially in the more remote areas, many places close down for the winter.

English Market

Gourmet Cork

Ireland's largest county can fairly lay claim to being the foodie capital of Ireland. Farmers markets and fine dining are the highlights of a visit.

Great For...

☑ **Don't Miss**

The farmhouse cheeses and Irish charcuterie at On the Pig's Back in the English Market.

English Market   Market

(www.englishmarket.ie; main entrance Princes St; ⊙8am-6pm Mon-Sat) It could just as easily be called the Victorian Market for its ornate vaulted ceilings and columns, but the English Market is a true gem, no matter what you name it. Scores of vendors sell some of the region's very best local produce, meats, cheeses and takeaway food. On a sunny day, take your lunch to nearby Bishop Lucey Park, a popular alfresco eating spot.

Farmgate Cafe   Cafe €

(☑021-427 8134; www.farmgatecork.ie; Princes St, English Market; mains €8-14; ⊙8.30am-5pm Mon-Sat) ✐ An unmissable experience at the heart of the English Market, the Farmgate is perched on a balcony overlooking the food stalls below, the source of all that fresh local produce on your plate –

Farmgate Cafe

ⓘ Need to Know

www.goodfoodireland.com lists hotels, restaurants and shops selling local artisanal produce, many located in County Cork.

✕ Take a Break

Buy picnic food in the English Market and take your lunch to nearby Bishop Lucey Park, a popular alfresco eating spot.

★ Top Tip

Cork city is also famous for its boutique coffee shops – try Cork Coffee Roasters (p145) or Filter (p145).

---

everything from crab and oysters to the lamb for an Irish stew. Up the stairs and turn left for table service, right for counter service.

On the Pig's Back   Deli

(☏021-427 0232; www.onthepigsback.ie; Unit 11, English Market; ⊗8am-5.30pm Mon-Sat) ✿ This famous deli stall in the English Market groans beneath serried ranks of French and Irish cheeses, charcuterie, homemade pâtés and pastries.

Midleton Farmers Market   Market

(Main St; ⊗9am-1pm Sat) ✿ Midleton's farmers market is one of Cork's best, with bushels of local produce on offer and producers who are happy to chat. It's behind the big roundabout at the north end of Main St.

Farmgate Restaurant   Irish €€

(☏021-463 2771; www.farmgate.ie; Broderick St; mains lunch €13-20, dinner €20-30; ⊗9am-5pm Tue-Sat, 5.30-9.30pm Thu-Sat) ✿ The original, sister establishment to Cork city's Farmgate Cafe, the Midleton restaurant offers the same superb blend of traditional and modern Irish cuisine. Squeeze through the deli selling amazing baked goods and local produce to the subtly lit, art-clad, 'farmhouse shed' cafe-restaurant, where you'll eat as well as you would anywhere in Ireland.

Ballymaloe Cookery School   Cooking

(☏021-464 6785; www.ballymaloecookery school.com; Shanagarry) TV personality Darina Allen (daughter-in-law of Myrtle Allen of Ballymaloe House; p148) runs this famous cookery school. Darina's own daughter-in-law, Rachel Allen, is also a high-profile TV chef and author, and regularly teaches at the school. Demonstrations cost €75; lessons, from half-day sessions (€95 to €135) to 12-week certificate courses (€10,995), are often booked out well in advance. For overnight students there are pretty cottages amid the 100 acres of grounds. It's 3km east of Ballymaloe House.

MIKROMAN6/SHUTTERSTOCK ©

Blarney Castle

If you need proof of the power of a good yarn, then join the queue to get into this 15th-century castle, one of Ireland's most popular tourist attractions.

The crowds are here, of course, to plant their lips on the Blarney Stone, which supposedly gives one the gift of the gab – a cliché that has entered every lexicon and tour route.

The Blarney Stone is perched at the top of a steep climb up claustrophobic spiral staircases within the castle. On the battlements, you bend backwards over a long, long drop (with safety grill and attendant to prevent tragedy) to kiss the stone; as your shirt rides up, coach loads of onlookers stare up your nose. Once you're upright again, don't forget to admire the stunning views before descending. Try not to think of the local lore about all the fluids that drench the stone other than saliva. Better yet, just don't kiss it.

The custom of kissing the stone is a relatively modern one, but Blarney's

Great For...

☑ **Don't Miss**

Stunning Poison Garden and Rock Close.

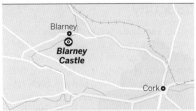

❶ Need to Know

📞021-438 5252; www.blarneycastle.ie; Blarney; adult/child €18/8; ⊗9am-7pm Mon-Sat, to 6pm Sun Jun-Aug, shorter hours Sep-May; 🅿

✖ Take a Break

Cafe next to the castle's stable yard; also, **Square Table** (📞021-438 2825; www. thesquaretable.ie; 5 The Square, Blarney; mains €20-30; ⊗6-9pm Wed & Thu, to 10pm Fri & Sat, 12.30-4pm Sun), 700m away serves superb Irish cuisine.

★ Top Tip

Book discounted tickets online to avoid queueing.

association with smooth talking goes back a long time. Queen Elizabeth I is said to have invented the term 'to talk blarney' out of exasperation with Lord Blarney's ability to talk endlessly without ever actually agreeing to her demands.

The famous stone aside, Blarney Castle itself is an impressive 16th-century tower set in gorgeous grounds. Escape the crowds on a walk around the Arboretum, which showcases specimen trees from around the world (including yews and Spanish chestnuts up to 600 years old), and the Fern Garden, an atmospheric jungle of 2m-tall tree ferns.

The Harry-Potterish Poison Garden is tucked beneath the castle battlements, and is home to a collection of the world's most toxic plants, including deadly nightshade, hemlock, and mandrake which, as any Harry Potter fan will know, is said to scream when its human-shaped root is ripped from the soil (the specimen here is kept behind bars to protect visitors from its narcotic and hallucinogenic effects).

You can also explore the landscaped nooks and crannies of the Rock Close, where trails laid out in the 18th century wend their way among ancient trees and manmade features that include standing stones, the Wishing Steps, the Fairy Glade and a bog garden.

Blarney is 8km northwest of Cork and buses run hourly from Cork bus station (€5.60 return, 20 minutes).

Cork City

Ireland's second city is first in every important respect – at least according to the locals, who cheerfully refer to it as the 'real capital of Ireland'. It's a liberal, youthful and cosmopolitan place that was badly hit by economic recession but is now busily reinventing itself with spruced-up streets, revitalised stretches of waterfront and – seemingly – an artisanal coffee bar on every corner. There's a bit of a hipster scene, but the best of the city is still happily traditional – snug pubs with live-music sessions, restaurants dishing up top-quality local produce, and a genuinely proud welcome from the locals.

◎ SIGHTS

The best sight in Cork is the city itself – soak it up as you wander the streets. A new

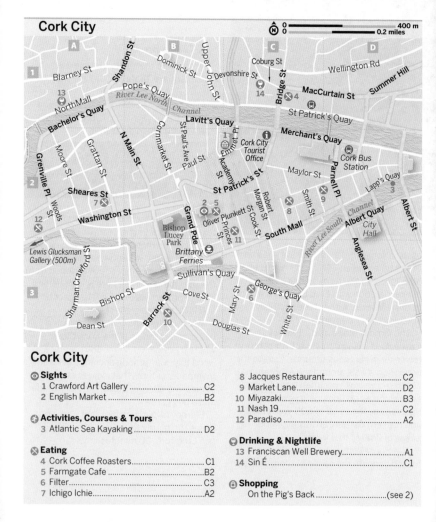

Cork City

◎ Sights

ANDREI NEKRASSOV/SHUTTERSTOCK ©

Cork City Gaol

conference and events centre, complete with 6000-seat concert venue, tourist centre, restaurants, shops, galleries and apartments, was scheduled to open in 2019, but the project has been delayed by financial problems. It will eventually be the focus of the new Brewery Quarter (the former Beamish & Crawford brewery site, fronted by the landmark mock Tudor 'counting house'), a block west of the English Market.

Shandon, perched on a hillside overlooking the city centre to the north, is a great spot for the views alone, but you'll also find galleries, antique shops and cafes along its old lanes and squares. Those tiny old row houses, where generations of workers raised huge families in very basic conditions, are now sought-after urban pieds-à-terre. Pick up a copy of the *Cork Walks – Shandon* leaflet from the tourist office (p147) for a self-guided tour of the district.

Cork City Gaol   Museum

(☑021-430 5022; www.corkcitygaol.com; Convent Ave; adult/child €10/6; ⊘9.30am-5pm Apr-Sep, 10am-4pm Oct-Mar) This imposing former prison is well worth a visit, if only to get a sense of how awful life was for prisoners a century ago. An audio tour (€2 extra) guides you around the restored cells, which feature models of suffering prisoners and sadistic-looking guards. Take a bus to University College Cork (UCC), and from there walk north along Mardyke Walk, cross the river and follow the signs uphill (10 minutes).

The tour is very moving, bringing home the harshness of the 19th-century penal system. The most common crime was that of poverty; many of the inmates were sentenced to hard labour for stealing loaves of bread. Atmospheric evening tours take place every weekday at 5.45pm (€12, booking required).

The prison closed in 1923, reopening in 1927 as a radio station that operated until the 1950s. The on-site Governor's House has been converted into a **Radio Museum** (☑021-430 5022; www.corkcitygaol.com/radio-museum; Cork City Gaol, Convent Ave; incl Cork City Gaol adult/child €10/6; ⊘9.30am-5pm Apr-Sep, 10am-4pm Oct-Mar; ▣) where, alongside collections of beautiful old radios, you can hear the story of radio pioneer Guglielmo Marconi's conquest of the airwaves.

Crawford Art Gallery Gallery

(📞021-480 5042; www.crawfordartgallery.ie; Emmet Pl; ⊙10am-5pm Mon-Wed, Fri & Sat, to 8pm Thu, 11am-4pm Sun) **FREE** Cork's public gallery houses a small but excellent permanent collection covering the 17th century through to the modern day, though the works on display change from year to year. Highlights include paintings by Sir John Lavery, Jack B Yeats and Nathaniel Hone, and Irish women artists Mainie Jellett and Evie Hone.

Lewis Glucksman Gallery Gallery

(📞021-490 1844; www.glucksman.org; University College Cork, Western Rd; suggested donation €5; ⊙10am-5pm Tue-Sat, 2-5pm Sun; 👬) This award-winning building is a startling construction of limestone, steel and timber, built in 2004 by Dublin architects O'Donnell and Tuomey. Three floors of galleries display the best in both national and international contemporary art and installation. The on-site **Bobo cafe** (📞021-490 1848; www.glucksman.org/visit/cafe; mains €6-13; ⊙10am-5pm Tue-Sat, noon-5pm Sun; 👬) is excellent.

🎯 TOURS

Cork Culinary Tour Food

(📞087 706 8391; www.bonner-travel.com/itinerary/cork-culinary-tour; per person €65) A four-hour tour of Cork's food markets and eating places; includes tasting sessions with food and drink sellers and ends with lunch in one of the city's many restaurants.

Atlantic Sea Kayaking Kayaking

(📞028-21058; www.atlanticseakayaking.com; Lapp's Quay; per person €50; ⊙Mar-Sep) Offers guided 'urban kayaking' trips around Cork's waterways from 6.30pm to 9pm (book in advance, minimum two people). It also offers a full-day expedition in two-seater kayaks to Cobh and Spike Island (p152; per person €100).

Cork City Tour Bus

(📞021-430 9090; www.corkcitytour.com; adult/child €15/5; ⊙Mar-Nov) A hop-on, hop-off open-top bus linking the city's main points of interest. Longer tours (€25 per adult) head to the Jameson Experience (p148) in Midleton.

Lewis Glucksman Gallery

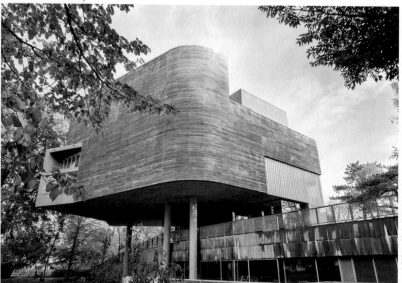

CHRISTOPHER HILL PHOTOGRAPHIC/ALAMY STOCK PHOTO ©

⊗ EATING

Cork Coffee Roasters
Cafe €

(📞021-731 9158; www.facebook.com/CorkCoffee; 2 Bridge St; mains €3-6; ⏰7.30am-6.30pm Mon-Fri, 8am-6.30pm Sat, 9am-5pm Sun; 🛜) In this foodiest of foodie towns it's not surprising to find a cafe run by artisan coffee roasters. The brew on offer in this cute and often crowded corner is some of the best in Cork, guaranteed to jump start your morning along with a buttery pastry, scone or tart.

Filter
Cafe €

(📞021-455 0050; filtercork@gmail.com; 19 George's Quay; mains €4-7; ⏰8am-6pm Mon-Fri, 9am-5pm Sat, 10am-3pm Sun; 🛜) 🍽 The quintessential Cork espresso bar, Filter is a carefully curated shrine to coffee nerdery, from the rough-and-ready retro decor to the highly knowledgable baristas serving up expertly brewed shots made with single-origin, locally roasted beans. The sandwich menu is a class act too, offering a choice of fillings that includes pastrami, chorizo and ham hock on artisan breads.

Nash 19
International €€

(📞021-427 0880; www.nash19.com; Princes St; mains €12-22; ⏰7.30am-4pm Mon-Fri, from 8.30am Sat) 🍽 A superb bistro and deli where locally sourced food is honoured at breakfast and lunch, either sit-in or take away. Fresh scones draw crowds early; daily lunch specials (soups, salads, desserts etc), free-range chicken pie and platters of smoked fish from Frank Hederman keep them coming for lunch – the Producers Plate (€22), a sampler of local produce, is sensational.

Market Lane
Irish €€

(📞021-427 4710; www.marketlane.ie; 5 Oliver Plunkett St; mains €14-25; ⏰noon-9.30pm Mon-Wed, to 10pm Thu, to 10.30pm Fri & Sat, 1-9.30pm Sun; 🛜👪) 🍽 It's always hopping at this bright corner bistro. The menu is broad and hearty, changing to reflect what's fresh at the English Market: perhaps roast hake with wild garlic velouté, or beetroot, walnut and feta cakes? No reservations for fewer than six diners; sip a drink at the bar till a table is free. Lots of wines by the glass.

🍽 Smokin' County Cork

No trip to Cork is complete without a visit to an artisan food producer, and the effervescent Frank Hederman is more than happy to show you around **Belvelly Smokehouse** (📞021-481 1089; www.frank hederman.com; Belvelly; free for individuals, charge for groups; ⏰by reservation 10am-5pm Mon-Fri) 🍽, the oldest traditional smokehouse in Ireland – indeed, the only surviving one. The smokehouse is 19km east of Cork on the R624 towards Cobh; call ahead to arrange a visit.

Alternatively, stop by Frank's stall at the **Cobh** (📞086 199 7643; www.facebook. com/cobhfarmers; The Promenade; ⏰10am-2pm Fri) 🍽 or Midleton (p139) farmers markets; you can also buy his produce at Cork's English Market (p138).

Seafood and cheese are smoked here – even butter – but the speciality is fish, particularly salmon. In a traditional process that takes 24 hours from start to finish, the fish is filleted and cured before being hung to smoke over beech woodchips. The result is subtle and delectable.

Smoked mackerel at Belvelly Smokehouse
ROS DRINKWATER / ALAMY STOCK PHOTO ©

Paradiso
Vegetarian €€

(📞021-427 7939; www.paradiso.restaurant; 16 Lancaster Quay; 2-/3-course menus €39/47; ⏰5.30-10pm Mon-Sat; 🚲) 🍽 A contender for best restaurant in town, Paradiso serves contemporary vegetarian dishes, including vegan fare: how about corn pancakes filled with leek, parsnip and Dunmanus cheese with fennel-caper salsa and smoked tomato? Reservations are essential.

DE KAM/SHUTTERSTOCK ©

Rates for dinner, bed and breakfast, staying in the funky upstairs rooms, start from €180/220 per single/double.

Jacques Restaurant Modern Irish €€
(☑021-427 7387; www.jacquesrestaurant.ie; 23 Oliver Plunkett St; mains lunch €8-15, dinner €23-29; ⊙10am-4pm Mon, to 10pm Tue-Sat) ✔ The Barry sisters draw on a terrific network of local suppliers built up over three decades to help them provide the freshest Cork food cooked simply, without frills. The menu changes daily: roast venison with turnip and parmesan gratin, perhaps, or West Cork scallops with almond and raisin salsa. Two-course dinners (€28) served Tuesday to Thursday, and pre-6.30pm Friday and Saturday.

Ichigo Ichie Japanese €€€
(☑021-427 9997; www.ichigoichie.ie; 5 Fenns Quay, Sheares St; per person €120-135; ⊙6-10.30pm Tue-Sat) More theatre than restaurant, this bold venture by chef Takashi Miyazaki immerses diners in the art and craft of Japanese *kappou* cuisine – an elaborate multicourse meal prepared and plated by the chef as you watch; expect a

dozen courses spread over three hours or so. The restaurant was awarded a Michelin star in 2019. Miyazaki also has a **takeaway restaurant** (☑021-431 2716; www.facebook. com/miyazakicork; 1A Evergreen St; mains €12-15; ⊙1-3.30pm & 5-9pm Tue-Sun).

🍸 DRINKING & NIGHTLIFE

Franciscan Well Brewery Pub
(☑021-439 3434; www.franciscanwellbrewery. com; 14 North Mall; ⊙1-11.30pm Mon-Thu, to 12.30am Fri & Sat, to 11pm Sun; 🛜) The copper vats gleaming behind the bar give the game away: the Franciscan Well brews its own beer (and has done since 1998). The best place to enjoy it is in the enormous beer garden at the back. The pub holds regular beer festivals together with other small independent Irish breweries.

Sin É Pub
(☑021-450 2266; www.facebook.com/sinecork; 8 Coburg St; ⊙12.30-11.30pm Mon-Thu, to 12.30am Fri & Sat, to 11pm Sun) You could easily spend an entire day at this place, which is everything a craic-filled pub should be –

long on atmosphere and short on pretension (Sin É means 'that's it!'). There's music every night from 6.30pm May to September, and regular sessions Tuesday, Friday and Sunday the rest of the year, most of them traditional but with the odd surprise.

INFORMATION

Cork City Tourist Office (☏1850 230 330; www. purecork.ie; 125 St Patrick's St; ☺9am-5pm Mon-Sat; 📶) Information desk; free city maps and self-guided walk leaflets.

GETTING THERE & AWAY

AIR

Cork Airport (p304) is 8km south of the city on the N27. Airlines servicing the airport include Aer Lingus, Ryanair and Jet2.com.

BOAT

Brittany Ferries (p304) sails to Roscoff (France) weekly from the end of March to October. The crossing takes 14 hours; fares vary widely. The ferry terminal is at Ringaskiddy, 15 minutes by car southeast of the city centre along the N28.

BUS

Bus Éireann (☏1850 836 611; www.bus eireann.ie) operates from the **bus station** (cnr Merchant's Quay & Parnell Pl), while **Aircoach** (☏01-844 7118; www.aircoach.ie), **Dublin Coach** (☏01-465 9972; www.dublincoach.ie), **GoBus** (☏091-564 600; www.gobus.ie; 📶) and **Citylink** (☏091-564 164; www.citylink.ie; 📶) services depart from St Patrick's Quay, across the river.

Dublin Bus Éireann; €16.50, 3¾ hours, six daily

Dublin Aircoach; €17, three hours, hourly

Dublin GoBus; €18, three hours, six to nine daily

Dublin Airport Aircoach; €20, 3½ hours, hourly

Dublin Airport GoBus; €28, 3¼ hours, six to nine daily

Galway Citylink; €20, three hours, five daily

Kilkenny Dublin Coach; €15, 2½ hours, eight daily

Killarney Bus Eireann; €19, 1½ hours, hourly

Limerick Citylink; €16, 1½ hours, five daily

Waterford Dublin Coach; €10, 2 hours, 9 daily

TRAIN

Kent Train Station (☏021-450 6766) is north of the River Lee on Lower Glanmire Rd, a 10- to 15-minute walk from the city centre. Bus 205 runs into the city centre (€2.20, five minutes, every 15 minutes).

Dublin €59, 2¼ hours, eight daily

Galway €57, four to six hours, seven daily, two or three changes

Killarney €25, 1½ to two hours, nine daily

Waterford €33, three to five hours, five daily, one or two changes

GETTING THERE & AROUND

TO/FROM THE AIRPORT

Bus Éireann service 226A shuttles between the train station, bus station and Cork Airport every half hour between 6am and 10pm (€2.80/5.60 one way/return, 30 minutes). A taxi to/from town costs €22 to €26.

BUS

Most places are within easy walking distance of the centre. Single bus tickets costs €2.20 each; a day pass is €5.40. Buy all tickets on the bus.

CAR

You can avoid city centre parking problems by using **Black Ash Park & Ride** on the South City Link Rd, on the way to the airport. Parking costs €5 a day, with buses into the city centre at least every 15 minutes (10-minute journey time).

Taxi

Cork Taxi Co-op (☏021-427 22 22; www.corktaxi.ie)

Yellow Cabs Cork (☏021-427 22 55; www.yellowcabscork.com)

Midleton

Aficionados of a particularly fine Irish whiskey will recognise the name Midleton, and the main reason to linger in this bustling market town is to visit the old Jameson

County Cork Food Festivals

If you're in town in mid-September, don't miss **Taste of West Cork Food Festival** (www.atasteofwestcork.com; ⊙Sep). This foodie extravaganza includes a lively farmers market, cookery demonstrations, competitions, food tastings, talks, exhibitions and children's events.

Seafood is king at **Cork Oyster & Seafood Festival** (www.corkoysterfestival. com; ⊙Sep). This three-day event includes cooking demos, tastings, a Gourmet Trail, an oyster-shucking contest and live music at venues across town.

At the **Kinsale Gourmet Festival** (www.kinsalerestaurants.com; ⊙Oct) three days of tastings, cookery demonstrations and competitions kick off with the Cork Heat of the All-Ireland seafood chowder cook-off (the final takes place in Kinsale in April).

Taste of West Cork Food Festival
APHPERSPECTIVE/ALAMY STOCK PHOTO ©

whiskey distillery, along with a meal at one of the town's famously good restaurants. The surrounding region is full of pretty villages, craggy coastlines and heavenly rural hotels such as **Ballymaloe House** (☎021-465 2531; www.ballymaloe.ie; Shanagarry; r from €280; P 🛜 ✻ ✻).

◎ SIGHTS

Jameson Experience   Museum
(☎021-461 3594; www.jamesonwhiskey.com; Old Distillery Walk; tours adult/child €22/11; ⊙shop 10am-6pm; P) Coachloads pour in to tour this restored 200-year-old distillery

building. Exhibits and 75-minute tours (run between 10am and 4pm) explain the process of taking barley and creating whiskey (Jameson is today made in a modern factory in Cork). There's a well-stocked gift shop, and the **Malt House Restaurant** (open noon to 3pm) has live music on Sunday.

ℹ️ GETTING THERE & AWAY

Midleton is 20km east of Cork. The train station is 1.5km (20 minutes' walk) north of the Jameson Experience. There are frequent trains from Cork (€6, 25 minutes, at least hourly).

There are also frequent buses from Cork bus station (€7.70, 30 minutes, every 15 to 45 minutes). You'll need a car to explore the surrounding area.

Cobh

Cobh (pronounced 'cove') is a charming waterfront town on a glittering estuary, dotted with brightly coloured houses and overlooked by a splendid cathedral. It's a far cry from the harrowing Famine years when more than 70,000 people left Ireland through the port in order to escape the ravages of starvation (from 1848 to 1950, no fewer than 2.5 million emigrants passed through). Cobh was also the final port of call for the *Titanic;* a poignant museum commemorates the fatal voyage's point of departure.

◎ SIGHTS

Cobh, The Queenstown Story   Museum
(☎021-481 3591; www.cobhheritage.com; Lower Rd; adult/child €10/6; ⊙9.30am-6pm mid-Apr–mid-Oct, 9.30am-5pm Mon-Sat, 11am-5pm Sun mid-Oct–mid-Apr) The howl of the storm almost knocks you off balance, there's a bit of fake vomit on the deck, and the people in the pictures all look pretty miserable – that's just one room at Cobh Heritage Centre. Housed in the old train station (next to the current station), this interactive museum is way above average, chronicling

Irish emigrations across the Atlantic in the wake of the Great Famine.

Titanic Experience Cobh   Museum

(📞021-481 4412; www.titanicexperiencecobh.ie; 20 Casement Sq; adult/child €10/7; ⏱9am-6pm Apr-Sep, 10am-5.30pm Oct-Mar; 👶) The original White Star Line offices, where 123 passengers embarked on (and one lucky soul absconded from) the RMS *Titanic*, now house this powerful insight into the ill-fated liner's final voyage in 1912. Admission is by tour, which is partly guided and partly interactive, with holograms, audiovisual presentations and exhibits; allow at least an hour. The technical wizardry is impressive but what's most memorable is standing on the spot from where passengers were ferried to the waiting ship offshore, never to return.

ⓘ GETTING THERE & AWAY

BUS

CobhConnect (www.cobhconnect.ie) buses run hourly from St Patrick's Quay in Cork to Park Rd

in Cobh (uphill from St Colman's Cathedral (€4, 30 minutes).

TRAIN

Hourly trains connect Cobh with Cork (€6, 25 minutes) via Fota.

Kinsale

The picturesque yachting harbour of Kinsale (Cionn tSáile) is one of many colourful gems strung along the coastline of County Cork. Narrow, winding streets lined with galleries and gift shops, lively bars and superb restaurants, and a handsome natural harbour filled with yachts and guarded by a huge 17th-century fortress, make it an engrossing place to spend a day or two.

⊙ SIGHTS

Charles Fort   Fort

(📞021-477 2263; www.heritageireland.ie; Summercove; adult/child €5/3; ⏱10am-6pm mid-Mar–Oct, to 5pm Nov–mid-Mar; 🅿) One of Europe's best-preserved star-shaped artillery forts,

Cobh

🔭 Fastnet Rock: Ireland's Teardrop

Named 'Ireland's Teardrop' because it was the last sight of the 'ould country' for emigrants sailing to America, the Fastnet Rock is the most southerly point of Ireland.

This isolated fang of rock, topped by a spectacular lighthouse, stands 6.5km southwest of Cape Clear Island, and in good weather is visible from many places on the coastline from Baltimore to Mizen Head. Its image – usually with huge waves crashing around it – graces a thousand postcards, coffee-table books and framed art photographs.

The Fastnet lighthouse, widely considered the most perfectly engineered lighthouse in the world, was built in 1904 from ingeniously interlocked blocks of Cornish granite – there are exhibits about its construction at **Mizen Head Visitor Centre** (☏028-35115; www.mizen head.ie; Mizen Head; adult/child €7.50/4.50; ⊙10am-6pm Jun-Aug, 10.30am-5pm mid-Mar–May, Sep & Oct, 11am-4pm Sat & Sun Nov–mid-Mar; 🅿♿) and **Cape Clear Heritage Centre** (☏028-39100; www.capeclear museum.ie; adult/child €2/1; ⊙11am-1pm & 2-6pm Jul & Aug, shorter hours Jun & Sep).

From May to August, **Fastnet Tour** (☏028-39159; www.fastnettour.com; adult/family €40/90; ⊙May-Aug) operates boat trips to the rock (no landing), departing from Schull and Baltimore and travelling via Cape Clear Island. Tours are weather-dependent and last from 11am to 5pm.

this vast 17th-century fortification would be worth a visit for its spectacular views alone. But there's much more here: the 18th- and 19th-century ruins inside the walls make for some fascinating wandering. It's 3km southeast of Kinsale along the minor road through Scilly; if you have time, hike there along the lovely coastal Scilly Walk.

Old Head Signal Tower & Lusitania Museum   Museum

(☏021-419 1285; www.oldheadofkinsale.com; Signal Tower, Old Head of Kinsale; adult/concession €5/3.50; ⊙10am-6pm daily Easter-Oct, Sat & Sun only Mar-Easter; 🅿) This 200-year-old signal tower houses a museum dedicated to the RMS *Lusitania*, which was torpedoed by a German U-boat in 1915 with the loss of 1200 lives. You can walk to the nearby clifftops for impressive views south towards the Old Head, the nearest point of land to the disaster; a privately owned **golf club** (☏021-477 8444; www.oldhead.com; green fees €200-350) prevents you from reaching the lighthouse at the tip of the headland. The tower is 13km south of town via the R604.

✖ EATING

OHK Cafe   Cafe €

(O'Herlihy's; ☏087 950 2411; www.oherlihys kinsale.com; The Glen; mains €6-12; ⊙9am-3.30pm Tue-Sat, 10am-4pm Sun; 🗯♿) The black sheep of Kinsale's cafe family, OHK occupies an artfully distressed dining room and serves a Mediterranean-inspired menu that includes off-the-beaten-track breakfast options such as Portuguese sardines, or Serrano ham and Manchego cheese on sourdough toast. Lunchtime salad plates are both hearty and healthy, with sides of hummus and pomegranate seed garnishes.

Black Pig Wine Bar   Irish €€

(☏021-477 4101; www.facebook.com/theblack pigwinebar; 66 Lower O'Connell St; mains €10-19; ⊙5.30-11pm Wed, Thu & Sun, to 11.30pm Fri & Sat) ✐ This candlelit hideaway is set in an 18th-century coach house with a charming cobbled courtyard out the back, and offers a mouth-watering menu of gourmet nibbles, charcuterie platters and cheese boards sourced from artisan local suppliers. The award-winning wine list offers no fewer than 200 wines by the bottle and 100 by the glass, including many organic varieties. Reservations recommended.

Bastion   Modern Irish €€€

(☎021-470 9696; www.bastionkinsale.com; cnr Main & Market Sts; mains €18-35; ☺5-10pm Wed-Sun; ☝) ❧ Holder of a Michelin Bib Gourmand since 2016, this place offers diners a relaxed and informal entry into the world of haute cuisine. Waitstaff will guide you through the concise à la carte menu of local oysters, beef, fish and venison, but it's best to go for the seven-course tasting menu (€78) or the five-course early-bird menu (pre-6pm; €58).

Finn's Table   Modern Irish €€€

(☎021-470 9636; www.finnstable.com; 6 Main St; mains €30-40; ☺6-10pm Mon, Tue & Thu-Sat) ❧ Owning a gourmet restaurant in Kinsale means plenty of competition, but John and Julie Finn's venture is more than up to the challenge. Elegant but unstuffy, Finn's Table

offers a warm welcome, and its menu of seasonal, locally sourced produce rarely fails to please. Seafood (including lobster when in season) is from West Cork, while meat is from the Finn family's butchers.

INFORMATION

Tourist Office (☎021-477 2234; www.kinsale.ie; cnr Pier Rd & Emmet Pl; ☺9.15am-5pm Tue-Sat year-round, 9.15am-5pm Mon Apr-Oct, 10am-5pm Sun Jul & Aug) **Has a good map detailing walks in and around Kinsale.**

ⓘ GETTING THERE & AWAY

Bus Éireann (☎021-450 8188; www.buseireann. ie) service 226 connects Kinsale with Cork bus station (€9.50, one hour, hourly) via Cork Airport, and continues to Cork train station. The **bus stop** is on Pier Rd, near the tourist office.

Bantry

Framed by the Sheep's Head hills and the craggy Caha Mountains, magnificent,

Charles Fort (p149)

MARTIN DUNLEA/SHUTTERSTOCK ©

 Spike Island Prison

This low-lying green **island** (021-237 3455; www.spikeislandcork.com; Cork Harbour; adult/child incl ferry €20/10; ferry departures 10am-3pm Jun-Aug, noon & 2pm May & Sep, Sat & Sun only Feb-Apr & Oct) in Cork Harbour was once an important part of the port's defences, topped by an 18th-century artillery fort. In the second half of the 19th century, during the Irish War of Independence, and from 1984 to 2004 it served as a prison, gaining the nickname 'Ireland's Alcatraz'. Today you can enjoy a guided walking tour of the former prison buildings, then go off and explore on your own; the ferry departs from Kennedy Pier, Cobh.

The guided tour takes in the modern prison, the old punishment block, the shell store (once used as a children's prison) and No 2 bastion with its massive 6in gun. Other highlights include the Gun Park, with a good display of mostly 20th-century artillery; the Mitchell Hall, with an exhibit on the Aud, a WWI German gun-running ship that was sunk in the entrance to Cork Harbour; and the Glacis Walk, a 1.5km trail that leads around the walls of the fortress, with great views of Cobh town and the harbour entrance. You'll need around four hours to make the most of a visit. There's a cafe and toilets on the island.

sprawling Bantry Bay is one of the country's most attractive seascapes. Sheltered by islands at the head of the bay, Bantry town is neat and respectable, with narrow streets of old-fashioned, one-off shops and a picturesque waterfront.

Pride of place goes to Bantry House, the former home of one Richard White, who earned his place in history when, in 1798, he warned authorities of the imminent landing of Irish patriot Wolfe Tone and his French fleet, in support of the United Irishmen's rebellion. In the end storms prevented the fleet from landing and the course of Irish history was definitively altered – all Wolfe Tone got for his troubles was a square and a statue bearing his name.

⊙ SIGHTS

Bantry House & Garden   Historic Building

(027-50047; www.bantryhouse.com; Bantry Bay; house & garden adult/child €11/3, garden only €6/free; 10am-5pm daily Jun-Aug, Tue-Sun mid-Apr–May, Sep & Oct; P) With its melancholic air of faded gentility, 18th-century Bantry House makes for an intriguing visit. From the Gobelin tapestries in the drawing room to the columned splendour of the library, it conjures up a lost world of aristocratic excess. But the gardens are its greatest glory, with lawns sweeping down towards the sea, and the magnificent Italian garden, with its staircase of 100 steps, at the back, offering spectacular views. The entrance is 1km southwest of the town centre on the N71.

The house has belonged to the White family since 1729 and every room brims with treasures brought back from each generation's travels. The entrance hall is paved with mosaics from Pompeii, French and Flemish tapestries adorn the walls, and Japanese chests sit next to Russian shrines. Upstairs, worn bedrooms look out wanly over an astounding view of the bay. Experienced pianists are invited to tinkle the ivories of the ancient grand piano in the library.

If it looks like the sort of place you can imagine staying in, you're in luck – the owners offer **B&B accommodation** (027-50047; www.bantryhouse.com; Bantry Bay; d from €189; Apr-Oct; P) in one of the wings.

Bantry House & Garden

🍴 EATING

Manning's Emporium
Cafe €

(☎027-50456; www.manningsemporium.ie; N71, Ballylickey; mains €8-13; ⊙10am-5pm Sun-Thu, to 9pm Fri & Sat; P🖥) ✎ This gourmet deli and cafe is an Aladdin's cave of West Cork's finest food. Grab a menu, choose a table, and order at the counter – tasting plates are the best way to sample the local artisan produce and farmhouse cheeses on offer. Foodie events take place regularly. It's on the N71 in Ballylickey (on the right approaching from Bantry).

Wood-fired pizza is available Friday to Sunday.

Organico
Cafe €

(☎027-55905; www.organico.ie; 2 Glengarriff Rd; mains €7-11; ⊙9am-6pm Mon-Sat; 🖥) ✎ This bright and lively wholefood shop and cafe serves tinglingly fresh salads, sandwiches and soups, and lunch specials such as falafel platters with hummus and tahini. Great coffee and cakes too.

Fish Kitchen
Seafood €€

(☎027-56651; http://thefishkitchen.ie; New St; mains lunch €10-14, dinner €16-28; ⊙noon-3pm & 5.30-9pm Tue-Sat) This outstanding little restaurant above a fishmonger's shop does seafood to perfection, from the live-tank local oysters (served with lemon and Tabasco sauce) to Bantry Bay mussels in white wine. If you don't fancy seafood, it does a juicy steak too. Friendly, unfussy and absolutely delicious.

ℹ️ INFORMATION

Tourist Office (☎027-50229; www.visitbantry.ie; Wolfe Tone Sq; ⊙10am-6pm Mon-Sat Apr-Oct) Staffed by volunteers, so hours may vary.

ℹ️ GETTING THERE & AWAY

Bus Éireann (www.buseireann.ie) runs four to six buses daily between Bantry and Cork (€22, two hours).

COUNTY KERRY

County Kerry

County Kerry contains some of Ireland's most iconic scenery: surf-pounded sea cliffs and soft golden strands, emerald-green farmland criss-crossed by tumbledown stone walls, mist-shrouded bogs and cloud-torn mountain peaks. With one of the country's finest national parks as its backyard, the lively tourism hub of Killarney spills over with colourful shops and pubs loud with spirited trad music. The town is the jumping-off point for Kerry's two famed loop drives: the larger Ring of Kerry skirts the mountainous, island-fringed Iveragh Peninsula; the more compact Dingle Peninsula is like a condensed version of its southern neighbour.

Two Days in County Kerry

Begin with a wander around Killarney town then take a **jaunting car ride** (p166) out to **Muckross House** (p163), followed by a boat trip on Lough Leane. On day two embark on a driving tour of the **Ring of Kerry** (p158), stopping for something to eat either at **Quinlan & Cooke** (p170) in Cahersiveen or the **Boathouse** (p170) in Kenmare.

Four Days in County Kerry

On day three you have a choice. If the weather is kind (May to September), make the once-in-a-lifetime boat trip to magnificent **Skellig Michael** (p160). Otherwise, enjoy a more leisurely boat-and-bike (or bus and jaunting car) trip to the scenic **Gap of Dunloe** (p167). On day four head to **Dingle town** (p171) for lunch, and an afternoon drive around Slea Head.

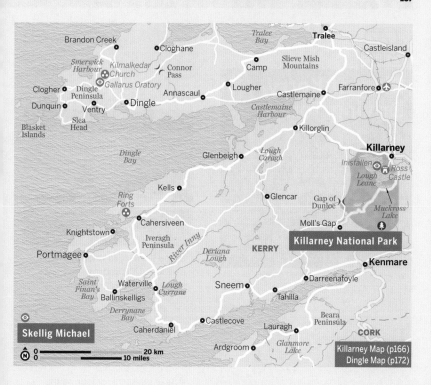

Skellig Michael

Killarney National Park

Killarney Map (p166)
Dingle Map (p172)

Arriving in County Kerry

Kerry Airport (p168) is at Farranfore, about 17km north of Killarney on the N22.

Killarney train station is behind the Malton Hotel, just east of the centre.

Bus Éireann runs one or two services a day to Killarney and Dingle town from Dublin and Cork. Citylink also runs a service to Killarney from Galway.

Where to Stay

Killarney makes an excellent base for exploring the county and has a wealth of accommodation options, from camping grounds to hostels, B&Bs and large hotels. Dingle town also has plenty of choices. Be sure to book ahead in summer and during festivals. Elsewhere, you'll find some charming rural B&Bs, inns and pub accommodation, although some close during the winter months.

Ring of Kerry Driving Tour

Windswept beaches, waves crashing against rugged cliffs, medieval ruins, soaring mountains and glinting loughs are some of the stunning distractions along the Ring of Kerry circle drive.

Start Killorglin
Distance 179km
Duration One to two days

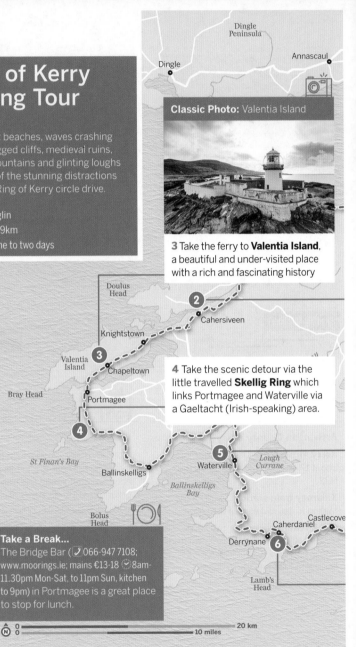

Classic Photo: Valentia Island

3 Take the ferry to **Valentia Island**, a beautiful and under-visited place with a rich and fascinating history

4 Take the scenic detour via the little travelled **Skellig Ring** which links Portmagee and Waterville via a Gaeltacht (Irish-speaking) area.

Dingle Peninsula
Annascaul
Dingle

Doulus Head
②
Cahersiveen
Knightstown
Valentia Island ③
Chapeltown
Bray Head
Portmagee
④
St Finan's Bay
⑤ Waterville Lough Currane
Ballinskelligs
Ballinskelligs Bay
Skellig Michael
Bolus Head
Castlecove
Caherdaniel
Derrynane ⑥
Lamb's Head

Take a Break...
The Bridge Bar (📞 066-947 7108; www.moorings.ie; mains €13-18 ⏰ 8am-11.30pm Mon-Sat, to 11pm Sun, kitchen to 9pm) in Portmagee is a great place to stop for lunch.

Ⓝ 0 _____ 20 km
0 _____ 10 miles

1 On the N70 between Killorglin and Glenbeigh, the **Kerry Bog Village Museum** (www.kerrybog village.ie; Ballincleave, Glenbeigh; adult/child €6.50/4.50; ☺9am-6pm) recreates a 19th-century bog village.

START

Killarney ●

★ **Top Tip**
Drivers – start early or late, or travel clockwise, to avoid tour-bus crowds.

2 The former barracks at Caher-siveen is now a the **Old Barracks Heritage Centre** (p169) and the surrounding countryside is a delight to explore.

● Moll's Gap

5 Continue to **Waterville**, an old-fashioned seaside resort known for golf and fishing. Silent-movie star Charlie Chaplin holidayed here in the 1960s.

FINISH
7
● Kenmare

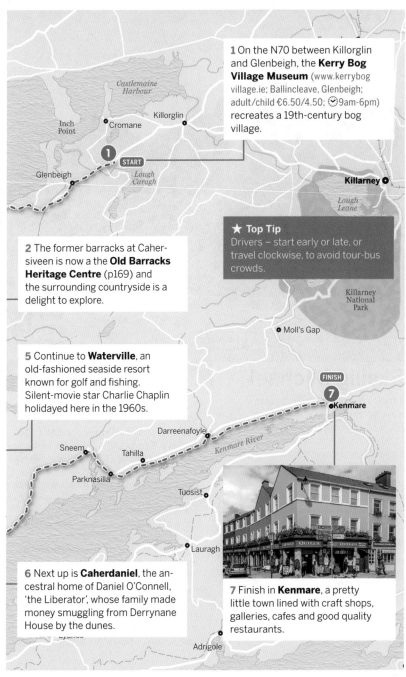

6 Next up is **Caherdaniel**, the an-cestral home of Daniel O'Connell, 'the Liberator', whose family made money smuggling from Derrynane House by the dunes.

7 Finish in **Kenmare**, a pretty little town lined with craft shops, galleries, cafes and good quality restaurants.

IVA PHOTOS/SHUTTERSTOCK ©

Skellig Michael

A trip to the Skellig Islands, two wave-battered pinnacles of rock 12km off the coast, and the site of Ireland's most remote and spectacular ancient monastery, is an unforgettable experience.

Great For...

☑ **Don't Miss**

The 6th-century, stone-built beehive cells at the very summit of Skellig Michael.

The jagged, 217m-high rock of Skellig Michael (Archangel Michael's Rock; like St Michael's Mount in Cornwall and Mont St Michel in Normandy) is the larger of the two Skellig Islands and a Unesco World Heritage Site. Early Christian monks established a community and survived here from the 6th until the 12th or 13th century. The monastic buildings perch on a saddle in the rock, some 150m above sea level, reached by 600 steep steps cut into the rock face.

The astounding 6th-century oratories and beehive cells vary in size; the largest cell has a floor space of 4.5m by 3.6m. You can see the monks' south-facing vegetable garden and their cistern for collecting rainwater. The most impressive structural achievements are the settlement's foundations – platforms built on the steep

Stone cross

BASTIAN BODYL/SHUTTERSTOCK ©

Portmagee

Ballinskelligs

*Skellig
Michael* Small
Skellig

❶ Need to Know

www.heritageireland.ie; ⊙mid-May–Sep
FREE

✕ Take A Break

There are no facilities on Skellig Michael
– take a packed lunch with you.

★ Top Tip

To see the islands up close without
landing, consider a cruise with **Skellig
Experience** (☎066-947 6306; www.skellig
experience.com; adult/child €5/3, incl cruise
€35/20; ⊙10am-7pm Jul & Aug, to 6pm May,
Jun & Sep, to 4.30pm Fri-Wed Mar, Apr, Oct &
Nov; ℗) from Valentia Island.

slope using nothing more than earth and
drystone walls.

Influenced by the Coptic Church
(founded by St Anthony in the deserts of
Egypt and Libya), the monks' determined
quest for ultimate solitude led them to this
remote, windblown edge of Europe. Not
much is known about the life of the monastery, but there are records of Viking raids
in AD 812 and 823. Monks were kidnapped
or killed, but the community recovered
and carried on. In the 11th century a
rectangular oratory was added to the site,
but although it was expanded in the 12th
century, the monks abandoned the rock
around this time.

After the introduction of the Gregorian
calendar in 1582, Skellig Michael became a
popular spot for weddings. Marriages were
forbidden during Lent, but since Skellig

used the old Julian calendar, a trip to the
islands allowed those unable to wait for
Easter to tie the knot.

Skellig Michael famously featured as
Luke Skywalker's Jedi temple in *Star Wars:
The Force Awakens* (2015) and *Star Wars:
The Last Jedi* (2017), attracting a whole
new audience to the island's dramatic
beauty.

While Skellig Michael looks like two
triangles linked by a spur, Small Skellig is
longer, lower and much craggier. From a
distance it looks as if someone battered
it with a feather pillow that burst. Close
up you realise you're looking at a colony
of over 20,000 pairs of breeding gannets,
the second-largest breeding colony in
the world. Most boats circle the island so
you can see the gannets and you may see
basking seals as well. Small Skellig is a bird
sanctuary; no landing is permitted.

PETER ZELEI IMAGES/GETTY IMAGES ©

Killarney National Park

Any cynicism engendered by Killarney's shamrock-filled souvenir stores evaporates when you begin to explore the lakes and woods of sublime Killarney National Park.

Great For...

☑ **Don't Miss**

A boat tour of the Killarney lakes.

The core of the national park is the Muckross Estate, donated to the state by Arthur Bourn Vincent in 1932; the park was designated a Unesco Biosphere Reserve in 1982. The Killarney Lakes – Lough Leane (the Lower Lake, or 'Lake of Learning'), Muckross (or Middle) Lake and the Upper Lake – make up about a quarter of the park, surrounded by natural oak and yew woodland, and overlooked by the high crags and moors of Purple Mountain (832m) to the west and Knockrower (552m) to the south.

The park is rich in wildlife as well as scenic beauty: deer swim out to graze on the lake islands, red squirrels and pine martens scamper in the woods, and salmon and brown trout thrive in the clean waters. Fifteen white-tailed eagles were reintroduced here in 2007; by 2015 at least four nesting pairs were established in County

Muckross House

ANNETTE GREGORY/SHUTTERSTOCK ©

www.killarneynationalpark.ie `FREE`

✕ Take A Break

There's a good cafe in the visitor centre near Muckross House.

★ Top Tip

Take binoculars, and look out for rare white-tailed eagles circling above the Middle Lake.

Kerry, with one pair breeding successfully in the national park.

Killarney House & Gardens   Historic Building

(Map p166; www.facebook.com/killarney nationalpark; Muckross Rd; ◷8.30am-7.30pm May-Sep, 9am-5.30pm Oct-Apr) `FREE` Dating from the early 18th century, Killarney House was once part of a much larger residence that was later demolished; it was restored in 2016 and now houses the Killarney National Park visitor centre. There are free guided tours of the house every half-hour, and seasonal guided walks in the vast gardens, which sweep majestically towards a gorgeous view of the Kerry mountains.

Ross Castle   Castle

(☏064-663 5851; www.heritageireland.ie; Ross Rd; adult/child €5/3; ◷9.30am-5.45pm early

Mar-Oct; P) Lakeside Ross Castle dates back to the 15th century, when it was a residence of the O'Donoghue family. It was the last place in Munster to succumb to Cromwell's forces, thanks partly to its cunning spiral staircase, every step of which is a different height in order to break an attacker's stride. The castle is a lovely 3km walk or bike ride from the pedestrian park entrance; you may well spot deer along the way.

Muckross House   Historic Building

(☏064-667 0144; www.muckross-house.ie; Muckross Estate; adult/child €9.25/6.25, incl Muckross Traditional Farms €15.50/10.50; ◷9am-7pm Jul & Aug, to 6pm Apr-Jun, Sep & Oct, to 5pm Nov-Mar; P) This impressive Victorian mansion is crammed with fascinating objects (70% of the contents are original). Portraits by John Singer Sargent adorn the walls alongside trophy stags heads and giant stuffed trout, while antique Killarney furniture, with its distinctive inlaid scenes of local beauty spots, graces the grand apartments along with tapestries, Persian rugs, sliverware and china specially commissioned for Queen Victoria's visit in 1861. It's 5km south of Killarney, signposted from the N71.

Muckross Traditional Farms
Museum

(☑064-663 0804; www.muckross-house.ie; Muckross Estate; adult/child €9.25/6.25, incl Muckross House €15.50/10.50; ⊙10am-6pm Jun-Aug, from 1pm Apr, May & Sep, from 1pm Sat & Sun Mar & Oct) These re-creations of 1930s farms evoke the sights, sounds and smells of real farming – cow dung, hay, wet earth and peat smoke, plus a cacophony of chickens, ducks, pigs and donkeys. Costumed guides bring the traditional farm buildings to life, and the petting area allows kids to get up close and personal with piglets, lambs, ducklings and chicks. The farms are immediately east of Muckross House; you'll need at least two hours to do justice to the self-guided tour.

Muckross Abbey
Ruins

(Muckross Estate; ⊙24hr) **FREE** This well-preserved ruin (actually a friary, though everyone calls it an abbey) was founded in 1448 and burned by Cromwell's troops in 1652. There's a square-towered church and a small, atmospheric cloister with a giant yew tree in the centre (legend has it that the tree is as old as the abbey). In the chancel is the tomb of the McCarthy Mòr chieftains, and an elaborate 19th-century memorial to local philanthropist Lucy Gallwey. The abbey is 1.5km north of Muckross House (signposted).

Inisfallen
Island

The first monastery on Inisfallen (the largest of the lake's islands) was founded by St Finian the Leper in the 7th century. The extensive ruins of a 12th-century

Muckross Abbey

Augustinian priory and an oratory with a carved Romanesque doorway stand on the site of St Finian's original. You can hire a motor boat with boatman (around €10) from Ross Castle for the 10-minute trip to the island. In calm weather you can hire a rowing boat (€5 per hour; allow 30 minutes each way).

Knockreer House & Gardens
Gardens

FREE Killarney House, built for the Earl of Kenmare in the 1870s, burned down in 1913; the present Knockreer House was built on the same site in 1958 and is now home to a national park education centre. It isn't open to the public, but its gardens are, featuring a terraced lawn and a summerhouse, have magnificent views across the lakes to the mountains.

From the park entrance opposite St Mary's Cathedral, follow the path to your right for about 500m.

Killarney Lake Tours
Cruise

(MV Pride of the Lakes; ☏064-663 2638; www.killarneylaketours.ie; Ross Castle Pier; adult/child €10/5; ☺Apr-Oct) One-hour tours of Lough Leane in a comfortable, enclosed cruise boat depart four times daily from the pier beside Ross Castle, taking in the island of Inisfallen (no landing) and O'Sullivan's Cascade (a waterfall on the west shore).

Getting Around

Walking, cycling and boat trips are the best ways to explore the park.

From the cathedral entrance it's 2.5km (a 30-minute walk) to Ross Castle; to reach Muckross Estate on foot or by bike you have to follow the cycle path beside the N71 south for 3km where it veers off towards the lake (it's 5km all up to Muckross House, p163).

Jaunting cars depart from Kenmare Pl in Killarney town centre, and from the Jaunting Car Entrance to Muckross Estate, at a car park 3km south of town on the N71. Expect to pay around €15 to €20 per person for a tour from Killarney to Ross Castle and back. There are no set prices; haggle for longer tours.

> **ⓘ Need to Know**
>
> Killarney tourist office stocks walking guides and maps of the national park.

JIRICASTKA/SHUTTERSTOCK ©

Muckross Lake Loop Trail

This hiking trail takes in some of the best scenery in the park, including the Meeting of the Waters where channels from all three of Killarney's lakes merge.

Killarney

A town that's been in the business of welcoming visitors for more than 250 years, Killarney is a well-oiled tourism machine fuelled by the sublime scenery of its namesake national park. It's set amid sublime scenery that spans lakes, waterfalls and woodland beneath a skyline of 1000m-plus peaks. Competition keeps standards high and visitors on all budgets can expect to find good restaurants, great pubs and comfortable accommodation.

TOURS

Jaunting Car Tours   Tours

(Map p166; ☎064-663 3358; www.killarney jauntingcars.ie; Kenmare Pl; per jaunting car €40-80) Killarney's traditional horse-drawn jaunting cars provide tours from the town to Ross Castle and Muckross Estate, complete with amusing commentary from the driver (known as a 'jarvey'). The cost varies depending on distance; cars can fit up to four people. The pickup point, nicknamed 'the Ha Ha' or 'the Block', is on Kenmare Pl.

Killarney

Killarney

Killarney Guided Walks Walking
(Map p166; ☑087 639 4362; www.killarney
guidedwalks.com; adult/child €12/6) Guided
two-hour walks through the national-park
woodlands leave at 11am daily from opposite
St Mary's Cathedral (Map p166; www.killarney
parish.com; Cathedral Pl; ☺8am-6.30pm) at the
western end of New St; advance bookings
are required from November to April. Tours
meander through Knockreer gardens, then
to spots where Charles de Gaulle holidayed,
David Lean filmed *Ryan's Daughter* and
Brother Cudda slept for 200 years.

Tours are available at other times on
request.

Killarney Golf & Fishing Club Golf
(☑064-663 1034; www.killarneygolfclub.com;
Mahony's Point; green fees €60-125) This historic club, which has hosted the Irish Open
on several occasions, has three championship golf courses with lakeside settings and
mountain views. It's 3.4km west of Killarney
on the N72.

EATING
Curious Cat Café Cafe €
(Map p166; ☑087 663 5540; www.facebook.com/
curiouscatcafe; 4 New Market Lane; mains €9-15;
☺9am-9pm Fri & Sat, to 4pm Sun & Mon) Tucked
away on New Market Lane, with cable-drum
tables out the front, this quirky little cafe
serves a varied menu that ranges from
breakfast smoothies with banana-
chocolate bread, to sweet and savoury pancakes, to homemade soups and lunch dishes
such as chicken wings with blue-cheese dip
or steak sandwiches. Good coffee too.

Look out for its feisty sangria in the
warmer months.

Murphy Brownes International €€
(Map p166; ☑064-667 1446; www.facebook.
com/murphybrownesrestaurant; 8 High St; mains
€14-25; ☺5-9.30pm Mar-early Jan) Elegant and
candlelit, but pleasantly informal, this place
is ideal for a relaxing dinner. Service is smil-
ing and attentive without being overbearing,
and the crowd-pleasing menu is a mix of
Irish and international favourites, with local

 Gap of Dunloe

The Gap of Dunloe is a wild and scenic
mountain pass – studded with crags
and bejewelled with lakes and waterfalls – that lies to the west of Killarney
National Park, squeezed between Purple
Mountain and the high summits of
Macgillycuddy's Reeks (Ireland's highest
mountain range).

A boat trip through the lakes followed
by a bike ride through the Gap of Dunloe
is the classic Killarney region experience. Your hostel, hotel or campsite can
arrange it for you (boat €20 per person,
plus bike hire €12 to €15 per day).

Gap of Dunloe Tours (Map p166; ☑064-
663 0200; www.gapofdunloetours.com; 7 High
St; ☺Mar-Oct) can arrange a walking tour
(€17.50), highly recommended bike-and-
boat circuit (€20), or bus-and-boat tour
(€35) taking in the Gap. Buses depart
from O'Connor's pub (p168).

River Loe in the Gap of Dunloe
JOE DUNCKLEY/SHUTTERSTOCK ©

mussels, Kerry lamb shank and fish and
chips sitting alongside beef lasagne, chick-
en curry and Caesar salad.

Treyvaud's Irish €€
(Map p166; ☑064-663 3062; www.treyvauds
restaurant.com; 62 High St; mains €10-30; ☺5-
10pm Mon, from noon Tue-Thu & Sun, to 10.30pm
Fri & Sat) Mustard-fronted Treyvaud's has
a strong reputation for subtle dishes that
merge trad Irish with European influences.
The seafood chowder – a velvet stew of
mussels, prawns and Irish salmon – makes
a filling lunch; dinner mains incorporating

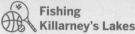

Fishing
Killarney's Lakes

Trout Fishing for brown trout in the lakes of Killarney National Park is free (no permit needed). The season runs from 15 February to 12 October. Fishing from the bank is allowed, but the best sport is to be had from a boat, which you can hire at **Ross Castle** (☏085 174 2997; Ross Castle Pier; ☺9.30am-5pm Apr-Oct, by reservation Nov-Mar) or at **Sweeney's** (☏064-664 4207; www.theinvicta.com; Invicta B&B, Tomies, Beaufort), at the west end of Lough Leane, for €40 a day (including outboard motor, up to three people).

Salmon The River Laune, which flows from Lough Leane to the sea, is one of Ireland's best salmon rivers. The season runs from 17 January to 30 September, with the best fishing from late July onward. Both a permit (one day €20) and a state rod licence (one day/three weeks €20/40) are required. You can also fish for salmon in the Killarney lakes (no permit needed, but state rod licence is still required).

O'Neill's (Map p166; ☏064-663 1970; www.facebook.com/oneillsofkillarney; 6 Plunkett St; ☺9.30am-10pm Mon-Fri, to 9pm Sat, 10.30am-8pm Sun) angling centre in Killarney provides information, rents rods and tackle, and sells permits and licences.

Fishing in Killarney National Park
GABRIEL12/SHUTTERSTOCK ©

local ingredients include roast cod with horseradish mash and tomato-and-caper salsa, and a hearty beef and Guinness stew.

🍷 DRINKING & NIGHTLIFE

O'Connor's   Pub

(Map p166; www.oconnorstraditionalpub.ie; 7 High St; ☺noon-11.30pm Sun-Thu, to 12.30am Fri & Sat; 🛜) Live music plays every night at this tiny traditional pub with leaded-glass doors, one of Killarney's most popular haunts. There are more tables upstairs, and in warmer weather the crowds spill out onto the adjacent lane.

Celtic Whiskey Bar & Larder   Bar

(Map p166; ☏064-663 5700; www.celticwhiskey bar.com; 93 New St; ☺10.30am-11.30pm Mon-Thu, to 12.30am Fri & Sat, to 11pm Sun; 🛜) Of the thousand-plus whiskeys stocked at this stunning contemporary bar, over 500 are Irish, including 1945 Willie Napier from County Offaly and 12-year-old Writers' Tears from County Carlow. One-hour tasting sessions and masterclasses (from €15) provide an introduction to the world of Irish whiskey. A dozen Irish craft beers are on tap; sensational **food** (mains €9-27; ☺served noon-9.45pm) is available too.

ℹ️ INFORMATION

Killarney's **tourist office** (Map p166; ☏064-663 1633; www.killarney.ie; Beech Rd; ☺9am-5pm Mon-Sat; 🛜) can handle most queries and is especially good with transport intricacies.

ℹ️ GETTING THERE & AWAY

AIR

The nearest airport to Killarney is **Kerry Airport** (KIR; ☏066-976 4644; www.kerryairport.ie; Farranfore), at Farranfore, 17km north of Killarney on the N22. There are daily flights to Dublin and London's Luton and Stansted airports, and less frequent services to Berlin and Frankfurt in Germany.

BUS

Bus Éireann operates from the **bus station** (Map p166) on Park Rd. For Dublin you need to change at Cork – the train is much faster.

Cork €18.05, two hours, hourly

TRAIN

Killarney's **train station** (📞064-663 1067; Fair Hill) is behind the bus station, just east of the centre.

There are one or two direct services per day to Cork and Dublin; otherwise you'll have to change at Mallow.

Cork €25, 1½ hours

Dublin €62, 3¼ hours

ⓘ GETTING AROUND

BICYCLE

Bicycles are ideal for exploring the scattered sights of the Killarney region, many of which are accessible only by bike or on foot.

Many of Killarney's hostels and hotels offer bike rental. Alternatively, try **O'Sullivan's Bike Hire** (Map p166; 📞064-663 1282; www.killarneyrenta bike.com; Beech Rd; per day/week from €15/85).

BUS

The **Killarney Shuttle Bus** (Map p166; 📞087 138 4384; www.killarneyshuttlebus.com; single €2-5, day pass €10; ☉Mar-Oct) runs daily from the tourist office (p168) to all the main tourist spots, including Gap of Dunloe, Ross Castle, Muckross House, Torc Waterfall and Ladies' View. Buy tickets from the driver. A day pass giving unlimited travel on the shuttle bus offers the best value.

Cahersiveen

The main town of the Iveragh Peninsula, Cahersiveen (pronounced caar-suh-*veen;* from *cathair saidhbhín,* Little Sarah's Ring Fort) is indelibly linked with the fight for Irish independence – it was the birthplace of Daniel O'Connell, 'the Great Liberator', and was where the first shots of the 1867 Fenian Rising were fired.

⦿ SIGHTS

Ring Forts   Ruins

(Ballycarbery) FREE Some 3km northwest of Cahersiveen, two extraordinary stone ring forts situated 600m apart are reached

Viewpoint: Aghadoe

On a hilltop 5km west of town, Aghadoe offers sweeping views of the Killarney lakes, mountains and Inisfallen Island that have made jaws drop for centuries. At the eastern end of the hilltop meadow are the ruins of a Romanesque church and 13th-century Parkavonear Castle. Parkavonear's keep, still standing, is one of the few cylindrical keeps built by the Normans in Ireland.

There's no public transport, but several tour buses stop here.

Doorway of the cathedral at Aghadoe
COLLPICTO/ALAMY STOCK PHOTO ©

from a shared parking area. Cahergal, the larger and more impressive, dates from the 10th century and has stairways on the inside walls, a *clochán* (circular stone building, shaped like an old-fashioned beehive), and the remains of a roundhouse. The smaller, 9th-century Leacanabuile contains the outlines of four houses. Both have a commanding position overlooking **Ballycarbery Castle** (Ballycarbery) FREE and Valentia Harbour, with superb views of the Kerry mountains.

Old Barracks Heritage Centre   Museum

(📞066-401 0430; www.theoldbarracks cahersiveen.com; Bridge St; adult/child €4/2; ☉10am-5pm Mon-Sat, 11am-4pm Sun Mar-Nov; 🅿) Established in response to the Fenian Rising of 1867, the Royal Irish Constabulary barracks at Cahersiveen were built in an eccentric Bavarian-Schloss style, complete with pointy turret and stepped gables.

Dingle Town

Burnt down in 1922 by anti-Treaty forces, the imposing building has been restored and now houses fascinating exhibitions on the Fenian Rising and the life and works of local hero Daniel O'Connell.

🍴 EATING

Quinlan & Cooke   Seafood €€

(🖉066-947 2244; www.qc.ie; 3 Main St; mains €18-27; ⏱food served 6-9pm, bar 3-10pm Thu-Mon Easter-Sep, shorter hours Oct-Easter; 📶🚗) 🍃 This is a modern take on a trad pub, so you can drop in for pints and craic in the afternoon, and stay for dinner. Some of the finest food on the Ring pours forth, particularly locally sourced seafood from the owner's fishing fleet, including fish and chips, and crab and prawn bisque. Hours can vary, so call to confirm.

Kenmare

Kenmare (pronounced 'ken-*mair*') is the thinking person's Killarney. Ideally positioned for exploring the Ring of Kerry (and the Beara Peninsula), but without the coach-tour crowds of its more famous neighbour, Kenmare (Neidín, meaning 'little nest' in Irish) is a pretty spot with a neat triangle of streets lined with craft shops, galleries, cafes and good-quality restaurants.

🍴 EATING

Boathouse Bistro   Bistro €€

(🖉064-664 2889; www.dromquinnamanor.com; Dromquinna Manor, Sneem Rd; mains €15-28; ⏱12.30-9pm daily mid-Mar–Sep, Fri-Sun only Oct–mid-Mar; 🅿) 🍃 At the water's edge, this blue-and-white 1870s boathouse 4.5km west of Kenmare has been stunningly converted to a beach-house-style bistro specialising in local seafood delivered daily to its own wharf. Expertly cooked dishes (Kenmare Bay crab claws in chilli and garlic butter, beer-battered fish and chips) are accompanied by a great selection of by-the-glass wines and craft gins.

Tom Crean Fish & Wine   Irish €€

(🖉064-664 1589; www.tomcrean.ie; Main St; mains €17-31; ⏱5-9.30pm Thu-Mon Sep-Jun,

DOMINICK CORRADO/SHUTTERSTOCK ©

daily Jul & Aug; 🛜) 🍴 Named for Kerry's pioneering Antarctic explorer, and run by his granddaughter, this venerable restaurant uses only the best of local organic produce, cheeses and fresh seafood. Sneem lobster is available in season, the oysters *au naturel* capture the scent of the sea, and the seafood gratin served in a scallop shell is divine.

Upstairs, the 19th-century townhouse has boutique rooms with king-size beds (doubles from €75).

ℹ️ GETTING THERE & AWAY

Bus Éireann (www.buseireann.ie) runs between Kenmare and Killarney (€12.40, 45 minutes, one to three daily), and runs a daily Ring of Kerry loop service from late June to late August.

Dingle Peninsula

One of the highlights of the Wild Atlantic Way, the Dingle Peninsula (Corca Dhuibhne) culminates in the Irish mainland's westernmost point. In the shadow of sacred Mt Brandon, a maze of fuchsia-fringed *boreens* (country lanes) weaves together an ancient landscape of prehistoric ring forts and beehive huts, early Christian chapels, crosses and holy wells, picturesque hamlets and abandoned villages.

Dingle Town

Framed by its fishing port, the Dingle peninsula's charming little 'capital' manages to be quaint without even trying. Some pubs double as shops, so you can enjoy Guinness and a singalong among hats and hardware, horseshoes and wellies. It has long drawn runaways from across the world, making it a cosmopolitan and creative place.

◎ SIGHTS & ACTIVITIES

Dingle Oceanworld   Aquarium
(Map p172; 📞066-915 2111; www.dingle-oceanworld.ie; The Wood; adult/child/family €15.50/10.75/47; ⏲10am-7pm Jul & Aug, to 6pm

 ### 👓 Moll's Gap

Built in the 1820s to replace an older track to the east (the Old Kenmare Rd, now followed by the Kerry Way hiking trail), the vista-crazy N71 Killarney to Kenmare road (32km) winds between rock and lake, with plenty of lay-bys to stop and admire the views (and recover from the switchback bends). Watch out for the buses squeezing along the road.

About 17km south of Killarney is the panoramic viewpoint **Ladies' View** (N71).

A further 5km south is the summit of the pass at Moll's Gap, which is worth a stop for great views and refreshments at **Avoca Cafe** (📞064-663 4720; www.avocahandweavers.com; N71, Moll's Gap; mains €5-9; ⏲9.30am-5pm Mon-Fri, from 10am Sat & Sun Mar-Nov; 🛜♿).

LOUIELEA/SHUTTERSTOCK ©

Sep-Jun) Dingle's aquarium is a lot of fun, and includes a walk-through tunnel and a touch pool. Psychedelic fish glide through tanks that recreate such environments as Lake Malawi, the River Congo and the piranha-filled Amazon. Reef sharks and stingrays cruise the shark tank; water pumped from the harbour fills the Ocean Tunnel tank where you can spot native Irish species such as dogfish, mullet, plaice, conger eels and the spectacularly ugly wreckfish.

Dingle Distillery   Distillery
(📞066-402 9011; www.dingledistillery.ie; Ventry Rd; tour €15; ⏲tours noon-4pm Mar-Sep,

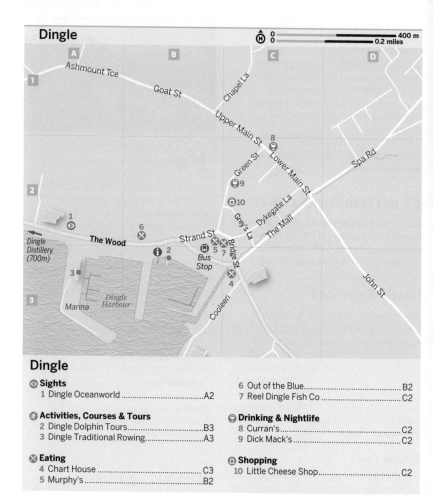

Dingle

from 2pm Oct-Feb) An offshoot of Dublin's Porterhouse microbrewery, this small-scale craft distillery went into operation in 2012, and began bottling its distinctive single malt whiskey in 2016. It also produces award-winning artisan gin and vodka.

Dingle Traditional Rowing Boating

(Naomhòg Experience; Map p172; ☎087 699 2925; www.dinglerowing.com; Dingle Marina; lessons €25) *Naomhòg* is the Kerry name for a *currach*, a traditional Irish boat made from a wooden frame covered with tarred canvas (originally animal hides). They were used by the Blasket islanders for fishing, and are now maintained and raced by local enthusiasts. You can book a one-hour session in Dingle Harbour (minimum two people) to learn how to row one.

It also runs harbour tours and sunset cruises (€25 per person per hour, minimum two people).

Dingle Dolphin Tours   Cruise

(Map p172; ☑066-915 2626; www.dingle
dolphin.com; The Pier; adult/child €16/8) Boats
run by the Dingle Boatmen's Association
cooperative leave the pier daily for one-hour
trips to see Dingle's most famous resident,
Fungie the dolphin. It's free if Fungie doesn't
show, but he usually does. The ticket office
is next to the tourist office (p174).

EATING

Reel Dingle Fish Co   Fish & Chips €

(Map p172; ☑066-915 1713; Bridge St; mains
€5-15; ⊘1-10pm) ✔ Locals queue along the
street to get hold of the freshly cooked local
haddock (or cod, or monkfish, or hake, or
mackerel...) and chips at this tiny outlet.
Reckoned to be one of the best chippies in
Kerry, if not in Ireland.

Murphy's   Ice Cream €

(Map p172; www.murphysicecream.ie; Strand St;
1/2/3 scoops €4.50/6.50/8.50; ⊘11.30am-10pm
May-Oct, to 8pm Nov-Apr; ☎) Made here in
Dingle, Murphy's sublime ice cream comes
in a daily changing range of flavours that
include brown bread, sea salt, Dingle gin
and whiskey-laced Irish coffee, along with
sorbets made with rainwater. In addition to
a second Dingle branch at the pier opposite
the tourist office (p174), its runaway success has seen it expand Ireland-wide.

Out of the Blue   Seafood €€€

(Map p172; ☑066-915 0811; www.outoftheblue.ie;
The Wood; mains €19-39; ⊘5-9.30pm Mon-Sat,
12.30-3pm & 5-9.30pm Sun) ✔ Occupying a
bright blue-and-yellow waterfront fishing
shack, this rustic spot is one of Dingle's top
restaurants, with an intense devotion to
fresh local seafood (and only seafood). If
staff don't like the catch, they don't open,
and they resolutely don't serve chips.
Highlights might include Dingle Bay prawn
bisque with lobster or chargrilled whole sea
bass flambéed in cognac.

Chart House   Irish €€€

(Map p172; ☑066-915 2255; www.
thecharthousedingle.com; The Mall; mains

Fungie the Dolphin

In 1983 a bottlenose dolphin swam into
Dingle Bay and local tourism hasn't
been quite the same since. Showing an
unusual affinity for human company,
he swam around with the local fishing
fleet. Eventually somebody got the idea
of charging tourists to go out on boats
to see the friendly dolphin (nicknamed
Fungie). Today up to 12 boats at a time
and more than 1000 tourists a day ply
the waters with Dingle's mascot, now
a cornerstone of the local economy;
there's even a bronze statue of him
outside the tourist office (p174).

In the wild, bottlenose dolphins live
for an average of 25 years, though they
have been known to live to over 40 in
captivity. As Fungie has been around
for more than 35 years (yes, it's still
the same dolphin, recognisable by his
distinctive markings), speculation is
rife about how long it will be before he
finally glides into the deep for the last
time. And what will Dingle do without its
dolphin?

PETRAKOSONEN/GETTY IMAGES ©

€22-32; ⊘6-10pm Jun-Sep, hours vary Oct-Dec
& mid-Feb–May) Window boxes frame this
free-standing stone cottage, while inside
dark-red walls, polished floorboards and
flickering candles create an intimate
atmosphere. Creative cooking uses Irish
produce: Cromane mussels and Dingle
Bay prawns, Annascaul black pudding and
Brandon Bay crab, fillet of Kerry beef and
Cashel Blue cheese. Book up to several
weeks ahead at busy times.

The Irish cheeseboard comes with a glass of vintage port.

Little Cheese Shop   Food
(Map p172; www.facebook.com/thelittlecheese shop; Grey's Lane; ⊙11am-6pm Mon-Fri, to 5pm Sat) The tiny shop of Swiss-trained cheese-maker Maja Binder overflows with aromatic cheeses from all over Ireland, including her own range of Dingle Peninsula Cheeses.

🍸 DRINKING & NIGHTLIFE

Dick Mack's   Pub
(Map p172; www.dickmackspub.com; Green St; ⊙11am-11.30pm Mon-Thu, to 12.30am Fri & Sat, noon-11pm Sun) Stars in the pavement bear the names of Dick Mack's celebrity customers. Ancient wood and snugs dominate the interior, while the courtyard out back hosts a warren of tables, chairs and characters, plus artisan food trucks in summer. In 2017 the adjacent 19th-century brewhouse was restored and now creates the pub's very own craft beers.

Curran's   Pub
(Map p172; Main St; ⊙10am-11pm) One of Dingle's most traditional shop-pubs, stocking everything from wellies to bags of potatoes, Curran's has nooks and crannies including original stained-glass snugs. Its Guinness is some of the best for miles around. Spontaneous trad sessions regularly take place.

ℹ️ INFORMATION

Busy but helpful, Dingle's **tourist office** (Map p172; ☑1850 230 330; www.dingle-peninsula.ie; The Pier; ⊙9am-5pm Mon-Sat) has maps, guides and plenty of information on the entire peninsula.

ℹ️ GETTING THERE & AWAY

Buses **stop** (Map p172; The Tracks) outside the car park behind the supermarket. Getting to Killarney by bus means a change in Tralee (€15.20, two hours, three daily).

Dingle Shuttle Bus (☑087 250 4767; www. dingleshuttlebus.com) runs a minibus service between Kerry airport and destinations on the

Gallarus Oratory

SHERI WAKE/SHUTTERSTOCK ©

Dingle peninsula (book in advance) and offers private Dingle Peninsula and Ring of Kerry tours.

Slea Head Drive

A host of superbly preserved structures from Dingle's ancient past including bee-hive huts, ring forts, inscribed stones and early Christian sites are a highlight of Slea Head, set against staggeringly beautiful coastal scenery. The landscape is especial-ly dramatic in shifting mist, although it's obliterated when thick sea fog rolls in.

The signposted Slea Head Drive is a 47km loop that passes through the villages of Ventry, Dunquin, Ballyferriter and Bally-david to the west of Dingle town, and takes in all the main sights.

 SIGHTS

Gallarus Oratory

Historic Site

(www.heritageireland.ie; Gallarus; P) FREE Gallarus Oratory is one of Ireland's most beautiful ancient buildings, its smoothly constructed dry-stone walls in the shape of an upturned boat. It has withstood the elements in this lonely spot beneath the brown hills for some 1200 years. There's a narrow doorway on the western side and a single, round-headed window on the east. Gallarus is clearly signposted off the R559, 8km northwest of Dingle town, and is 400m east of the (paid) **Gallarus Visitor Centre** (www.gallarusoratory.ie; Gallarus; €3; 9am-6pm Easter-Oct) car park.

Kilmalkedar Church

Ruins

(Kilmalkedar; 24hr) FREE The Dingle Peninsula's most important Christian site, Kilmalkedar has a beautiful setting with sweeping views over Smerwick Harbour. Built in the 12th century on the site of a 7th-century monastery founded by St Maolcethair, the roofless church is a superb example of Irish Romanesque architecture, its round-arched west door decorated with chevron patterns and a carved human head. In the graveyard you'll find an Ogham stone and a carved stone sundial. It's 2km northeast of Gallarus.

COUNTY CLARE

County Clare

Along the Wild Atlantic Way, the ocean relentlessly pounds Clare's coastline, eroding rock into fantastic formations, and fashioning sheer cliffs including those at the iconic Cliffs of Moher and ends-of-the-earth Loop Head. Along the coast, the waves are a magnet for surfers, and surf schools set up on many of Clare's beaches in summer.

If the land is hard, Clare's soul certainly isn't – traditional Irish culture and music flourish here. And it's not just a show for tourists, either. In larger towns and even the tiniest of villages you'll find pubs with trad music sessions year-round.

One Day in County Clare

Explore the town of **Ennis** (p184), taking in **Ennis Friary** (p184) and a hearty pub lunch in **Nora Culligans** (p184), then head west with camera in hand to view the magnificent **Cliffs of Moher** (p180). Plan to spend the night in nearby Doolin so you can see the sunset from the cliffs and take in a **trad music session** (p182) in one of its pubs.

Two Days in County Clare

Day two depends on which direction you're heading. If it's south towards Kerry, visit **Loop Head** (p187) for more spectacular coastal scenery before taking the ferry across the Shannon to Tarbert and the road to Dingle. If it's north towards Galway, book a day's **guided walk** (p188) exploring the beguiling limestone landscapes of the **Burren** (p188).

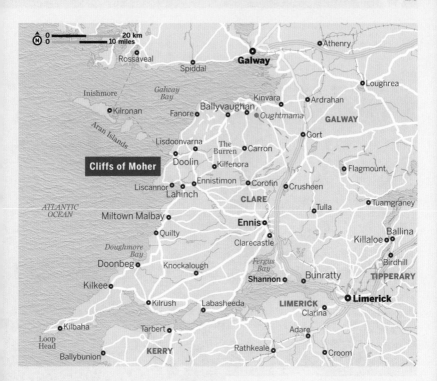

Arriving in County Clare

Exploring County Clare by public transport is difficult and time-consuming. If you don't have a car, it's best to base yourself in Galway city, and visit the Cliffs of Moher and Doolin as part of a guided coach tour such as **Burren Wild Tours** (p188).

Where to Stay

Ennis makes a central base for exploring Clare but you'll find camping grounds, hostels, B&Bs, pubs and hotels throughout the county, notably in and around Doolin and Lahinch. Many places only open from around Easter to October and fill quickly at weekends and during school holidays, when you'll need to book ahead.

Cliffs of Moher

In good visibility the Cliffs of Moher are staggeringly beautiful. Views stretch to the Aran Islands and the hills of Connemara. Sunsets here see the sky turn a kaleidoscope of amber, rose-pink and deep garnet-red.

Great For...

☑ **Don't Miss**

The view west along the cliffs around sunset, when the scenery is at its most spectacular.

The entirely vertical cliffs rise to a height of 203m, their edge falling away abruptly into the constantly churning sea. A series of heads, the dark layered sandstone seems to march in a rigid formation that amazes, no matter how many times you look. On a clear day views extend to the Aran Islands etched on the waters of Galway Bay, and beyond to the hills of Connemara in western Galway.

Its fame guarantees a steady stream of visitors which can surge to a swell almost as impressive as the raging ocean below, but the tireless Atlantic winds can drown out the chatter and you can shrug off the crowds, even though busloads arrive in summer. A vast visitor centre is set back into the side of a hill. As part of the development, however, the main walkways and viewing areas along the cliffs have been

O'Brien's Tower

MALLEY PHOTOGRAPHY/SHUTTERSTOCK ©

Doolin

Cliffs of Moher ⊙

Liscannor ●

❶ Need to Know

☎065-708 6141; www.cliffsofmoher.ie; R478; adult/child incl parking €8/free; ☺8am-9pm May-Aug, to 7pm Mar, Apr, Sep & Oct, 9am-5pm Nov-Feb

✕ Take A Break

Escape the overcrowded cafes in the visitor centre by taking a picnic and dining on the cliff tops.

★ Top Tip

Get a different perspective by taking a boat trip from nearby Doolin to view the cliffs from the sea.

surrounded by a 1.5m-high wall that's too high and set too far back from the edge.

Walking Trails

There are good rewards if you're willing to walk for 10 minutes. Past the end of the 'Moher Wall' south, a trail runs along the cliffs to Hag's Head (about 5.5km) – few venture this far, yet the views are uninhibited. From here you can continue on to Liscannor for a total walk of 12km (about 3½ hours). To the north, you can follow the Doolin Trail via O'Brien's Tower right to the village of Doolin (about 7km and 2½ hours). The entire Liscannor to Doolin walking path via the cliffs is now signposted; note that there are a lot of ups and downs and narrow, cliff-edge stretches.

Visitor Centre

The modern visitor centre contains numerous shops and a few cafes, plus a rewarding exhibition regarding the fauna, flora, geology and climate of the cliffs. There is also an audio-visual virtual reality experience called The Ledge, shown on a film-loop in an auditorium through the day. Free information booklets on the cliffs are available.

Boat Trips
Doolin Ferry Co   Cruise

(☎065-707 5555; www.doolinferry.com; Doolin Pier; €15; ☺mid-Mar–Oct) These unforgettable trips to the Cliffs of Moher's soaring rock faces set off from the pier at Doolin village, 6km to the northeast. The wildlife-spotting can be memorable; on late-afternoon cruises the slanting sunlight produces dramatic effects. Book.

Trad session in McGann's

CHRIS HOWES/WILD PLACES PHOTOGRAPHY/ALAMY STOCK PHOTO ©

Trad Music Sessions

From cosy, atmospheric pubs in tiny villages where non-instrument-playing patrons are a minority to rollicking urban boozers in Ennis, Clare is one of Ireland's best counties for traditional music.

Great For...

☑ Don't Miss

A session at Vaughan's in Kilfenora, one of Ireland's top trad music venues.

Ennis

You can bounce from one music-filled pub to another on most nights, especially in the summer. Musicians from around the county come here to show off and there are good venues for serious trad pursuits.

Brogan's   Pub

(☎065-684 4365; www.brogansbarand restaurant.com; 24 O'Connell St; ⊘noon-mid-night) On the corner of Cooke's Lane, Brogan's is a big pub that rambles from one room to the next with a fine bunch of musicians rattling even the stone floors from about 9pm Monday to Thursday (more nights in summer).

Doolin

There's a collection of pubs here with night-ly trad music sessions. However, tourist

Vaughan's Pub Pub

(☎065-708 8004; www.vaughanspub.ie; Main St; ⊙10.30am-11.30pm, hours can vary) A pub with a big reputation in Irish music circles; seafood, traditional foods and local produce feature on the menu. Have a pint under the big tree out front. There's music in the bar every night during the summer and on many nights at other times. The adjacent barn is the scene of terrific **s**et-dancing sessions on Thursday (10pm) and Sunday (9pm).

Ennistimon

A charming village inland from Doolin with a couple of ancient pubs attracting top local talent.

Eugene's Pub

(☎065-707 1777; Main St; ⊙10.30am-11.30pm Mon-Thu, to 12.30am Fri & Sat, 12.30-11pm Sun) With one of the most amazing pub frontages you'll ever see, Eugene's is a classic choice. Intimate and cosy, with a trademark collection of visiting cards covering its walls, it has a great whiskey collection and some fab stained glass.

crowds can be intense, so sensations of intimacy or enjoyment can evaporate.

McGann's Pub

(☎065-707 4133; www.mcgannspubdoolin.com; Roadford; ⊙10am-11.30pm Mon-Wed, to 12.30am Thu-Sat, to 11pm Sun; 🛜) McGann's has all the classic touches of a full-on Irish music pub, with action often spilling onto the street. The food here (mains €11 to €18) is the best of Doolin's three famous pubs. Inside you'll find locals playing darts in its warren of small rooms, some with peat fires.

Kilfenora

Small village with a big musical heritage on show at the great local pub Vaughan's.

Ennis

Clare's charming commercial hub, Ennis (Inis), lies on the banks of the fast-moving River Fergus. Sights are few, but the town centre, with its narrow, pedestrian-friendly streets, is enjoyable to wander. Handily situated 23km north of Shannon Airport (p304), it makes an ideal base for exploring the county: you can reach any part of Clare in under two hours from here.

◎ SIGHTS

Ennis Friary   Church
(☎065-682 9100; www.heritageireland.ie; Abbey St; adult/child €5/3; ☺10am-6pm Easter-Sep, to 5pm Oct) North of the Square, Ennis Friary was founded by Donnchadh Cairbreach O'Brien, a king of Thomond, between 1240 and 1249. A mix of structures dating between the 13th and 19th centuries, the friary has a graceful five-section window dating from the late 13th century, a McMahon tomb (1460) with alabaster panels depicting scenes from the Passion, and a particularly fine *Ecce Homo* panel portraying a stripped and bound Christ.

✖ EATING & DRINKING

Food Heaven   Cafe €
(☎065-682 2722; www.food-heaven.ie; 21 Market St; dishes €6-12; ☺8.30am-6pm Mon-Sat; 🛜) The aptly named Food Heaven rustles up creative, fresh fare right from the American-style breakfast pancakes, via lunchtime open crayfish sandwiches through to afternoon teas. Be ready to queue at lunch for its renowned handmade sausage rolls.

Nora Culligans   Pub
(☎065-682 4954; www.noraculligans.com; Abbey St; ☺4-11.30pm Mon-Thu, to 2am Fri, noon-2am Sat, noon-midnight Sun; 🛜) Magnificently restored, cavernous Nora Culligans retains original features including the front bar's ornate two-storey-high whiskey cabinets and timber panelling in the back bar. It's an atmospheric venue for live music across a diverse array of genres, from jazz and blues to acoustic singer-songwriters and reggae as well as trad.

Ennis Friary

Poet's Corner Bar   Pub

(☎065-682 8127; https://www.oldgroundhotel
ennis.com/poets-corner-bar.html; Old Ground
Hotel, O'Connell St; ☺11am-11.30pm Mon-Thu,
to 12.30am Fri & Sat, noon-11pm Sun) It's partly
the regular trad sessions (Wednesday to
Sunday, May to September; Friday and Saturday, October to April), partly the timber
panels and snugs, and partly the chatty,
welcoming vibe that help make the pub in
the **Old Ground Hotel** (www.oldgroundhotel
ennis.com; s €130, d €180-200, ste €230-275) a
favourite with locals and visitors.

 # INFORMATION

Ennis' **tourist office** (☎1850 230 330; www.
visitennis.com; Arthur's Row; ☺9.30am-5.30pm
Tue-Fri, 9am-5pm Sat) is housed in the same
building as the Clare Museum.

 # GETTING THERE & AWAY

The M18 bypass east of the city lets traffic
between Limerick and Galway zip right past.

BUS

Bus Éireann (www.buseireann.ie) services
operate from the **bus station** (Station Rd) beside
the train station. Connect in Galway or Limerick
for Dublin.

Destinations include the following:

Cork Bus 51; €19, three hours, hourly

Doolin Bus 350; €9.50, 50 minutes, five daily,
via Corofin, Ennistimon, Lahinch, Liscannor and
Cliffs of Moher

Galway Bus 51; €9.50, 1½ hours, hourly, via Gort

Limerick Bus 51; €7, one hour, hourly, via
Bunratty

Shannon Airport Bus 51; €8.50, 30 minutes,
hourly

TRAIN

Irish Rail (www.irishrail.ie) trains serve Limerick
(€6, 40 minutes, nine daily), where you can connect to trains to places further afield, including
Dublin.

 **Trad Music
Festivals**

Traditional music in venues across town
keeps the tunes flowing during **Ennis
Trad Festival** (www.ennistradfest.com;
☺early–mid-Nov), taking place over five
days in November.

Held on the last weekend in February,
the **Russell Memorial Weekend**
(☎065-707 4168; www.michorussellweekend.
ie; ☺Feb) festival celebrates the work of
legendary Doolin musician Micho Russell and his brothers. It features workshops, dancing classes and trad-music
sessions throughout town.

MICHAEL KEVIN DALY/FUSE/GETTY IMAGES ©

The line to Galway (€7.50, 1¼ hours, four to
five daily) takes in some superb Burren scenery.

Bunratty

Bunratty (Bun Raite) is home to a splendid
castle that abuts a theme park recreating
an Irish village of yore. It's a double act that
draws in countless visitors, particularly
given its proximity to Shannon Airport,
13km to the west.

 # SIGHTS

Bunratty Castle & Folk Park   Castle

(☎061-711 222; www.bunrattycastle.ie; adult/
child/family €16/12/45; ☺9am-5.30pm) Dating
from the 15th century, square, hulking
Bunratty Castle is only the latest of several
edifices to occupy its location beside the
River Ratty. Vikings founded a settlement

Clare's Best Music Festival

Willie Clancy Summer School (☑065-708 4148; www.scoilsamhraidhwillieclancy.com; ☺Jul) is Miltown Malbay's tribute to native son Willie Clancy, one of Ireland's greatest pipers; it's one of the best traditional-music festivals in the country. During the nine-day festival, which usually begins in the first or second week of July, impromptu sessions occur day and night and the town pubs are packed. Workshops and classes underpin the event.

Uileann pipes
STEVIE O'CUANA/SHUTTERSTOCK ©

here in the 10th century, and later occupants included the Norman Thomas de Clare in the 1250s. It's accessed via the folk park, a reconstructed traditional Irish village with smoke coiling from thatched-cottage chimneys, a forge and working blacksmith, weavers, post office, grocery-pub, small cafe and more. Tickets are 10% cheaper online.

⊗ EATING

Gallagher's of Bunratty — Seafood €€€

(☑061-363 363; www.gallaghersofbunratty.com; Old Bunratty Rd; mains €15-40; ☺5.30-9.30pm daily, plus 12.30-3pm Sun) Stone walls, exposed beams, timber panelling and a wood stove make this thatched cottage as enchanting inside as it is out. But the real reason to book is for some of Ireland's most magnificent seafood, such as saffron-infused John Dory with samphire, whole

Dover sole, or garlicky hot buttered crab claws. The set meals (two/three courses €32/37) are excellent value.

✪ ENTERTAINMENT

Irish Evening at Bunratty — Live Performance

(☑061-711 222; www.shannonheritage.com/IrishEvening; adult/child €43/35; ☺7-9.30pm Apr-Oct) High-spirited Irish nights lift the roof of a corn barn in the folk park adjacent to Bunratty Castle (p185). Waitstaff serve Irish classics (stews, poached salmon, apple pie) amid traditional storytelling, music and dancing, while wine gets you in the mood for the singalong.

Loop Head

A sliver of land between the Shannon Estuary and the pounding Atlantic, windblown Loop Head Peninsula has an ends-of-the-earth feel. As you approach along the R487, sea begins to appear on both flanks as land tapers to a narrow shelf. On a clear day, the lighthouse-capped headland at Loop Head (Ceann Léime), Clare's southernmost point, has staggering views to counties Kerry and Galway. The often-deserted wilds of the head are perfect for exploration, but be extra careful near the cliff edge.

On the northern side of the cliff near the point, a dramatic crevice has been cleaved into the coastal cliffs where you'll first hear and then see a teeming bird-breeding area. Guillemots, choughs and razorbills are among the squawkers nesting in the rocky niches.

A long hiking trail runs along the cliffs to the peninsula's main town, Kilkee. A handful of other tiny settlements dot the peninsula.

⊙ SIGHTS & ACTIVITIES

Loop Head Lighthouse — Lighthouse

(www.loophead.ie; Loop Head; adult/child €5/2; ☺10am-6pm mid-Mar–early Nov) On a 90m-high cliff, this 23m-tall working lighthouse, complete with a Fresnel lens, rises up above Loop Head. Guided tours (included in admission) take you up the tower and onto the balcony – in fine weather you can see as far as the Blasket Islands and Connemara. There's been a lighthouse here since 1670; the present structure dates from 1854. It was converted to electricity in 1871 and automated in 1991.

Dolphinwatch
Cruise

(☎065-905 8156; www.dolphinwatch.ie; The Square, Carrigaholt; tours adult/child €35/20; ☺Apr-Oct) Some 200 resident bottlenose dolphins frolic in the Shannon Estuary; they're best encountered on Dolphinwatch's two-hour cruises, on which you might also see minke and fin whales in autumn. Sailings depend on tides and weather conditions. Boats depart from Carrigaholt's Castle Pier; it's best to park by Dolphinwatch's booking office a few hundred metres away, as accessing the pier itself by car is tricky.

Miltown Malbay

Miltown Malbay has a thriving music scene and hosts the annual Willie Clancy Summer School, one of Ireland's great traditional music events. The town was a favoured resort for well-to-do Victorians, though it isn't actually on the sea: the beach is 2km southwest at Spanish Point.

🍷 DRINKING & NIGHTLIFE

Miltown Malbay's traditional Irish pubs have wonderful trad sessions throughout the year.

Hillery's
Pub

(☎065-708 4188; Main St; ☺3pm-1am) Opened in 1891, Miltown Malbay's oldest pub has stained-glass windows and framed photos on the walls. Live trad sessions take place every weekend year-round and most nights in summer. Its Facebook page features updates on upcoming gigs.

🔭 Clare's Other Cliffs

On the way to and from the southern tip of Loop Head, take in the jaw-dropping sea vistas and drama of the sensational cliffs along the coast roads.

Heading west, from Carrigaholt drive south down central Church St for around 2km till you reach a junction with brown Loop Head Drive signs pointing right. This scenic route is the Coast Rd (L2002). It bounces beside a rocky shore, past reed beds and alongside green fields, offering splendid panoramas of the sea. It runs through the village of Rhinevilla, eventually rejoining the R487 at Kilbaha before surging onto the lighthouse at Loop Head.

Heading east from Loop Head Lighthouse, drive back along the R487 for a few minutes until signs point left along another Coast Rd (L2000). From here you make your way to Kilkee. You'll rejoin the R487 but can head north again along small roads north from just after either Oughterard or Cross for stunning views of soaring coastal cliffs.

Cliffs of Loop Head
BARTKOWSKI/SHUTTERSTOCK ©

Friel's Bar
Pub

(Lynch's; ☎065-708 5883; Mullagh Rd; ☺6pm-midnight Mon-Thu, to 1am Fri & Sat, 2pm-midnight Sun) This old-style charmer has walls crammed with photos and books, and regular trad sessions most nights in summer and on Friday, Saturday and Sunday evenings in winter.

 Guided Walks

Burren Guided Walks & Hikes (☏065-707 6100, 087 244 6807; www.burrenguided walks.com; from €20; ⊙by reservation) Long-time guide Mary Howard leads groups on a variety of rambles, off-the-beaten-track hikes and rugged routes.

Burren Wild Tours (☏087 877 9565; www.burrenwalks.com; €35; ⊙by appointment) John Connolly offers a broad range of walks, from gentle to more strenuous. Themes include heritage, botany and folklore.

Heart of Burren Walks (☏087 292 5487; www.heartofburrenwalks.com; €30; ⊙by reservation Tue-Sat) Local Burren author Tony Kirby leads walks and archaeology hikes lasting 2½ hours. Cash only.

Karst rock at the Burren
PETER ZELEI IMAGES/GETTY IMAGES ©

Although the place is called Friel's, the sign for Lynch's, picked out in black text on a white background, is much bigger.

The Burren

Stretching across northern Clare, the rocky, windswept Burren region is a unique striated lunar-like landscape of barren grey limestone that was shaped beneath ancient seas, then forced high and dry by a great geological cataclysm. It covers 250 sq km of exposed limestone, and 560 sq km in total.

Wildflowers in spring give the Burren brilliant, if ephemeral, colour amid its stark beauty. Villages throughout the region include the music hub of Doolin on the west coast, Kilfenora inland and charming Ballyvaughan in the north, on the shores of Galway Bay.

🏃 ACTIVITIES

The Burren is a walker's paradise. The stark, beautiful landscape, plentiful trails and ancient sites are best explored on foot. 'Green roads' are the old highways of the Burren, crossing hills and valleys to some of the remotest corners of the region. Many of these unpaved ways were built during the Famine as part of relief work, while some may date back thousands of years. Now used mostly by hikers and the occasional farmer, some are signposted.

Beginning in Lahinch and ending in Corofin, the **Burren Way** is a 123km way-marked network of walking routes along a mix of roads, lanes and paths. There are also seven waymarked trails through the national park, taking from 30 minutes to three hours to hike.

Guided nature, history, archaeology and wilderness walks are great ways to appreciate this unique region. Typically the cost of the walks averages €10 to €35 and there are many options, including private trips. Operators include Burren Guided Walks & Hikes, Heart of Burren Walks and Burren Wild Tours.

The **Burren National Park** (www.burren nationalpark.ie) also runs free guided walks; its website lists dates and has a downloadable hiking map.

ℹ️ GETTING THERE & AWAY

On its Limerick–Galway route 350, which runs via Ennis, Bus Éireann (www.buseireann.ie) stops at key Burren destinations, including Ballyvaughan, Corofin, Doolin, Fanore and Lisdoonvarna.

Kilfenora has limited services to Ennis and some coastal Clare destinations, while New Quay has limited services to Galway city. For Carron, you'll need your own transport.

Loop Head Lighthouse (p186)

Doolin

Doolin is hugely popular as a centre of Irish traditional music, with year-round trad sessions at its famous trio of music pubs. Located 6km northeast of the Cliffs of Moher in a landscape riddled with caves and laced with walking paths, it's also a jumping-off point for cliff cruises and ferries out to the Aran Islands.

Without a centre, this scattered settlement consists of three smaller linked villages. Charming Fisherstreet has some picturesque traditional cottages; there are dramatic surf vistas at the harbour 1.5km west along the coast. Doolin itself is about 1km east on the little River Aille. Roadford is another 1km east. None of the villages has more than a handful of buildings.

While the music pubs give Doolin a lively vibe, the heavy concentration of visitors means standards don't always hold up to those in some of Clare's less-frequented villages.

🍷 DRINKING & NIGHTLIFE

Doolin's famed music pubs – Gus O'Connor's in Fisherstreet and McGann's (p183) and McDermott's (p190) in Roadford – have sessions throughout the year, as does Fitz's (p190). To experience trad music in the intimate surrounds of an Irish home, reserve ahead to visit the **Doolin Music House** (⏢086 824 1085; www.doolinmusic house.com; R478, Caherkinalla; €20; ⏲by reservation 7-8.30pm Mon, Wed & Fri).

Gus O'Connor's   Pub
(⏢065-707 4168; www.gusoconnorsdoolin. com; Fisherstreet; ⏲9am-midnight Mon-Thu, to 2am Fri-Sun) Right on the river where it runs into the sea, this sprawling place dating from 1832 has a rollicking atmosphere when the music is in full swing. On some summer nights you won't squeeze inside. Music plays from 9.30pm nightly from late February to November and at weekends year-round.

The breakfasts and classic pub food served at both lunch (mains €8 to €17) and dinner (€13 to €27) are well above average.

McDermott's Pub

(MacDiarmada's; ☎065-707 4328; www.
mcdermottspub.com; Roadford; ⏰10am-11pm
Sun-Wed, to 12.30am Thu-Sat) This red-and-
white traditional pub is a rowdy favourite. Picnic tables face the street; inside
renowned music sessions kick off at 9pm
nightly from Easter to October, and several
nights a week the rest of the year.

Bar food (mains €12 to €23) is served
daily from 1pm to 9pm.

Fitz's Pub

(☎065-707 4111; www.hoteldoolin.ie; Doolin;
⏰noon-11.30pm Mon-Thu, to 12.30am Fri &
Sat, to 11pm Sun) At **Hotel Doolin** (d/f/tr
€145/188/205; 🅿🛜) 🐾, relative newcomer
Fitz's has trad sessions twice nightly from
April to October and at least three times a
week from November to March. Sample its
superb whiskey selection, fine craft beers
and ciders, or own-brewed Dooliner beer.

Bar food (mains €9 to €24) is first rate.
Ingenious cocktails include MV Plassy on
the Rocks, named after the Aran Islands
shipwreck (p200), a Burren martini and

a Father Jack Espresso (in honour of the
cantankerous priest from *Father Ted*).

ℹ️ INFORMATION

The town's **tourist information point** (☎065-
707 5649; Doolin; ⏰8am-8pm Easter-Sep) is
alongside the central Hotel Doolin. The website
www.doolin.ie has comprehensive tourist
information.

ℹ️ GETTING THERE & AWAY

BOAT

From mid-March to October, **Doolin Pier** (off
R439) is one of two ferry departure points to
the Aran Islands (the other is **Rossaveal Ferry
Terminal** (Rossaveal), 37km west of Galway city,
where services are year-round). Sailings can
be affected if high seas or tides make the small
dock inaccessible.

Doolin 2 Aran Ferries (☎065-707 5949; www.
doolin2aranferries.com; Doolin Pier; ⏰mid-
Mar–Oct) and **Doolin Ferry Co** (O'Brien Line;
☎065-707 5555; www.doolinferry.com; Doolin

Gus O'Connor's (p189)

Ferry at Doolin Pier

Pier; ⊙mid-Mar–Oct) each have sailings to Inisheer (one way/return €10/20, 30 minutes, three to four daily), Inishmore (€15/25, 1¼ hours, two to three daily) and Inishmaan (€15/25, from 45 minutes, two to three daily). Interisland ferry tickets cost €10 to €15 per crossing.

There are various combination tickets and online discounts.

BUS

Bus Éireann (www.buseireann.ie) bus 350 runs to the following destinations:

Ballyvaughan €8, one hour, five daily

Cliffs of Moher €3.30, 15 minutes, two to five daily

Ennis €9.50, 50 minutes, five daily

Galway €19, two hours, five daily

ARAN ISLANDS

Aran Islands

Easily visible from the coast of counties Galway and Clare along the Wild Atlantic Way, the rocky, wind-buffeted Aran Islands have a desolate beauty that draws countless day trippers. Those who stay longer may feel that they're much further removed from the Irish mainland than the 45-minute ferry ride or 10-minute flight suggests.

An extension of the limestone outcrop that forms the Burren in Clare, the islands have shallow topsoil scattered with wildflowers, grass where livestock grazes, and jagged cliffs pounded by surf. Ancient forts here are some of Ireland's oldest archaeological remains.

One Day on the Aran Islands

It's pretty much impossible to visit more than one island per day, so if you have only one day plump for **Inishmore** (p198) and explore the spectacular prehistoric fort of **Dun Aengus** (p196), and its smaller cousins **Dún Eochla** (p196) and **Dún Eoghanachta** (p197). If time allows, sit down to a cosy pub lunch at **Tí Joe Watty's Bar** (p199).

Two Days on the Aran Islands

With two days, you have the choice of relaxing overnight on Inishmore and taking in a trad music session at **Tí Joe Watty's Bar** (p199), or heading back to the mainland, spending the night there, and using day two for a trip to Inisheer (p200) to see **O'Brien's Castle** (p200) and a Father Ted photo-op at the wreck of the **Plassy** (p200).

North
Sound

ATLANTIC
OCEAN

Dún Eoghanachta
Kilmurvey Beach
Port Chorrúch
Aran Goat Cheese
Teampall Chiaráin
Dún Eochla
Dun Aengus
Kilmurvey
Wormhole
Kilronan
Cill Éinne Bay
Inishmore
Aran Islands
Galway Bay
Dún Dúchathair
Teampall Bheanáin
St Enda's Monastery
Teach Synge
Inishmaan
O'Brien's Castle
Well of Enda
Inisheer
Plassy
South Sound

N
0 — 5 km
0 — 2.5 miles

Arriving in the Aran Islands

Flights depart from Connemara regional airport, about 35km west of Galway. **Aer Arann Islands** (www.aerarannislands. ie) offers flights to each of the islands several times daily (10 minutes, hourly in summer).

Aran Island Ferries (www.aranisland ferries.com) leave from Rossaveal, 40km west of Galway City. Buses from Queen St in Galway connect with the sailings. From mid-March to October there are also ferries from Doolin.

Where to Stay

After the last day trippers have left in summer, the islands assume a lovely serenity. All three islands have B&Bs and pub accommodation, and Inishmore and Inishmaan have inns. Inishmore has a great camping and glamping site and a hostel; there's also a hostel on Inisheer. Advance bookings in summer and during festivals are essential. Some places only accept cash. Closures are common during winter.

Aerial view of Inishmore

MNSTUDIO/SHUTTERSTOCK ©

Dun Aengus

Three spectacular prehistoric forts stand guard over Inishmore, each believed to be around 2000 years old. Chief among them is Dun Aengus, with three massive drystone walls that run right up to sheer drops to the ocean below.

Great For...

☑ **Don't Miss**

The stunning view along the clifftops to the west of Dun Aengus.

The fort is protected by remarkable *chevaux de frise*, fearsome and densely packed defensive limestone spikes. A small visitor centre has displays that put everything in context and a slightly strenuous 900m walkway wanders uphill to the fort itself. Dun Aengus is around 7km west of Kilronan.

Powerful swells pound the 60m-high cliff face. A complete lack of railings or other modern additions that would spoil this incredible site means that you can not only go right up to the cliff's edge but also potentially fall to your doom below – take care.

Nearby Historic Sites

Between Kilronan and Dun Aengus you'll find the small, perfectly circular fort **Dún**

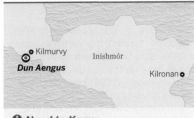

❶ Need to Know

Dún Aonghasa; Map p195; 📞099-61008; www.heritageireland.ie; adult/child €5/3; ⏱9.30am-6pm Apr-Oct, to 4pm Nov-Mar

✕ Take a Break

Refuel with a slap-up meal of fish and chips at Tí Joe Watty's Bar (p199).

★ Top Tip

Hiring a bike makes it easier to explore the myriad sites around the island.

Eochla (Map p195) **FREE**, which makes for a good walk from the main road.

The ruins of numerous stone churches identify the island's monastic history. The small **Teampall Chiaráin** (Church of St Kieran; Map p195), with a high cross in the churchyard, is near Kilronan.

West of Kilmurvey is the perfect Clochán na Carraige, an early Christian stone hut that stands 2.5m tall, and various small early Christian ruins known rather inaccurately as the **Na Seacht dTeampaill** (Seven Churches), comprising a couple of ruined churches, monastic houses and some fragments of a high cross from the 8th or 9th century. To the south of the ruins is **Dún Eoghanachta** (Map p195) **FREE**, another circular fort.

Along the low-lying northern coast, the sheltered little bay of Port Chorrúch is home to up to 50 grey seals, who sun themselves and feed in the shallows. Further on, Kilmurvey Beach gets an EU Blue Flag for its clean white-sand beach.

In the southeast, near Cill Éinne Bay, is the early Christian **Teampall Bheanáin** (Church of St Benen; Map p195). Near the airport are the sunken remains of a church; the spot is said to have been the site of **St Enda's Monastery** (Teaghlach Éinne; Map p195) in the 5th century, though what's visible dates from the 8th century onwards.

Dún Dúchathair (Black Fort; Map p195) **FREE** is an ancient fort dramatically perched on a south-facing clifftop promontory to the southwest of Kilronan.

Inishmore

Most visitors who venture out to the Aran Islands don't make it beyond the largest, and closest to Galway, Inishmore (Inis Mór) and its most spectacular prehistoric stone fort, Dun Aengus (p196), perched on the island's towering cliffs.

Inishmore is 14km long and 4km at its widest stretch. Boats arrive and depart from Inishmore's main settlement, **Kilronan** (Cill Rónáin), on the southeastern side of the island. The arid landscape to its west is dominated by stone walls, boulders, scattered buildings and the odd patch of deep-green grass and potato plants.

Today, tourism turns the wheels of the island's economy: from May to September tour vans greet each ferry and flight, offering a ride around the sights.

◉ SIGHTS

Aran Goat Cheese   Factory

(Map p195; ☑087 222 6776; www.arangoatcheese.com; Oughill; tours €15-30) You've encountered the produce on countless west Ireland menus; now meet the goats that make it all possible. Call ahead to join a tour of this tiny dairy where some 160 Nubian and Saanen goats produce 1000L of milk a week so you can sample delights like soft goat's cheese, a feta-like product and gouda.

Wormhole   Natural Pool

(Poll na bPeist; Map p195) Access to this extraordinary rectangular natural tidal pool is via a 750m clifftop walk southeast from Dun Aengus (p196), or via a 1km signposted walking path from the hamlet of Gort na gCapall. Dubbed 'Serpent's Lair', the pool is a regular on the Red Bull Cliff Diving World Series circuit, when daredevil divers plunge from nearly triple the height of an Olympic tower-dive platform. Take care as the area can be dangerous in wild weather and high seas.

⊗ EATING & DRINKING

Paudy's Ice Cream   Ice Cream €

(Kilmurvey; snacks from €3; ⊙11am-5pm Easter-Oct, winter hours vary) Award-winning crepes, waffles and, yep, ice cream.

Wormhole

STEFANO_VALERI/SHUTTERSTOCK ©

Bayview Restaurant International €€

(☎086 792 9925; www.bayviewrestaurant
inishmore.com; mains lunch €8-15, dinner €19-35;
☺noon-9pm; 🛜🚸) At Bayview there's local
art on the walls, and a deal of artistry on
the plates. Beautifully presented dishes
might feature Aran goat's cheese with
baked mushroom tapenade, whole lobster,
chargrilled steaks or the day's catch with
bursts of coriander or lime.

Teach Nan Phaidi Cafe €€

(☎099-20975; Kilmurvey; mains €5-12; ☺11am-
5pm) At tiny, thatched Nan Phaidi, picnic
tables and a riot of flowers sit in front of
whitewashed walls, and happy diners tuck
into award-winning treats. These might
range from zesty, home-baked orange cake
to fresh mackerel salad, or a flavourful beef
and Guinness stew.

Tí Joe Watty's Bar Pub

(☎086 049 4509; www.joewattys.ie; Kilronan;
☺noon-midnight Sun-Thu, 11.30am-12.30am Fri &
Sat Apr-Oct, 4pm-midnight Mon-Fri, noon-
midnight Sat & Sun Nov-Mar) Warmed by peat
fires, the island's oldest and most popular
pub has trad sessions every night in summer from 9pm or 10pm, and weekends the
rest of the year. Wednesday's darts night is
a local fixture. There's a large beer garden
and an extensive list of Irish gins, craft
beers and whiskeys.

Its seafood-focused menu (mains €14
to €25) is excellent; book for dinner in
summer.

The Bar Pub

(☎099-61130; www.inismorbar.com; Kilronan;
☺noon-11pm Sun-Thu, 11.30am-midnight
Fri & Sat) The buzzing Bar provided last
pints for those emigrating from Galway
to the USA, hence its former name, the
American Bar (and its photos of Elvis,
Bob Dylan et al). Live music plays nightly
from May to mid-October, and weekends
year-round.

Quality food (mains €8 to €24), spanning burgers and mussels steamed in wine,
is served from 10.30am to 9.30pm.

 **Shopping
on Inishmore**

You'll see local knitters handcrafting
traditional Aran sweaters at **Kilmurvey
Craft Village** (Kilmurvey; ☺hours vary),
a charming collection of traditional
thatched cottages. Woollens, Irish linen,
carved stonework and jewellery incorporating Celtic designs are among the
local arts and crafts for sale.

It tends to be open daily in the
summer; check with the tourist office if
you're making a special trip.

At Kilronan's main crossroads,
eclectic **Man of Aran Gift Shop** (☎085
710 5254; Kilronan; film per adult/child
€5/3; ☺9am-8pm Easter-Sep, winter hours
vary; 🛜) stocks souvenirs from T-shirts
to stained glass and Celtic-design
jewellery, and screens the iconic film
Man of Aran five times daily in its tiny
24-seat theatre. It also has wi-fi (free
with purchase) and a fine little coffee
bar serving Italian brews.

Kilmurvey Craft Village
MARIA_JANUS/SHUTTERSTOCK ©

 INFORMATION

The welcoming **tourist office** (☎099-61263;
www.aranislands.ie; Kilronan; ☺10am-5pm, to
6pm Jul & Aug) is on the waterfront 50m northwest of the ferry pier in Kilronan.

ⓘ GETTING AROUND

From May to September, minibuses offer
2½-hour tours of the island (€15) to ad hoc
groups. The drive – with commentary – between
Kilronan and Dun Aengus (p196) takes about

45 minutes each way. You can also negotiate for private and customised tours.

To see the island at a gentler pace, pony traps with a driver are available from Easter to September for trips between Kilronan and Dun Aengus; the return journey costs between €50 and €100 for up to four people.

Many places to stay have bicycles for use or rent; alternatively, **Aran Bike Hire** (099-61132; www.aranislandsbikehire.com; Inishmore Pier; mountain & road bike rental per day €10, electric bikes from €30, deposit €20-30; 10am-5pm) rents out road, mountain and electric bikes. They'll deliver your bicycles (or, if you prefer to cycle, deliver your bags) to accommodation anywhere on the island.

Inishmaan

The least visited of the islands, with the smallest population, Inishmaan (Inis Meáin) is a rocky respite, roughly 5km long by 3km wide. Early Christian monks seeking solitude were drawn to Inishmaan, as was the author JM Synge, who spent five summers here over a century ago.

The 300-year-old thatched cottage of **Teach Synge** (Map p179; 099-73036; €3; by appointment Apr–mid-Sep), now a small museum, is where Synge spent his summers between 1898 and 1902.

At the desolate western end of the island, **Synge's Chair** is a viewpoint at the edge of a sheer limestone cliff with the surf from Gregory's Sound booming below. The cliff ledge is often sheltered from the wind; do as Synge did and find a stone perch to take it all in.

Inisheer

Inisheer (Inis Oírr), the smallest of the Aran Islands at roughly 3km wide by 3km long, has a palpable sense of enchantment, heightened by the island's wild-flower-strewn landscapes, deep-rooted mythology and enduring traditional culture.

◎ SIGHTS

Well of Enda   Historic Site
(Tobar Éanna; Map p195) Some locals still carry out a pilgrimage known as the Turas to the Well of Enda (also known as Éinne or Endeus), a bubbling spring in a remote rocky expanse in the southwest. The ceremony involves, over the course of three consecutive Sundays, picking up seven stones from the ground nearby and walking around the small well seven times, putting one stone down each time, while saying the rosary until an elusive eel appears from the well's watery depths.

If, during this ritual, you're lucky enough to see the eel, it's said your tongue will be bestowed with healing powers, enabling you to literally lick wounds better.

O'Brien's Castle   Historic Building
(Caisleán Uí Bhriain; Map p195) FREE Built in the 14th century on the island's highest point, this tower house was constructed within the remains of a ring fort called Dún Formna, dating from as early as the 1st century AD. The 100m climb rewards with a sweeping panorama across clover-covered fields to the beach and harbour. The views are especially dramatic at sunset. You're free to walk around the ruins.

Plassy   Shipwreck
(Map p195) A steam trawler launched in 1940, the *Plassy* was thrown on to the rocks on 8 March 1960 and driven on to the island a couple of weeks later after another storm. Its cargo of whiskey was never recovered but miraculously, all on board were saved. The Tigh Ned pub has a collection of photographs and documents detailing the rescue. An aerial shot of the wreck was used in the opening sequence of the cult TV series *Father Ted*.

◎ EATING

Teach an Tae   Cafe €
(099-75092; www.cafearan.ie; dishes €5-12; 11am-5pm May-early Nov) Wild island raspberries and blackberries, home-grown

The *Plassy*

salads, eggs from the cafe's chickens and apples from its heritage orchard are used in dishes here. Treats include net-fresh local mackerel, a herby Aran goat's cheese tart and an Irish porter cake that's laced with Guinness. Cash only.

Tigh Ned Pub Food €
(099-75004; www.tighned.com; dishes €7-15; kitchen noon-4pm Apr-Oct, bar 10am-11.30pm Apr-Oct) That the daily seafood special is caught by the owner speaks volumes. Snug, welcoming Tigh Ned's has been here since 1897 dishing up inexpensive sandwiches, cottage pie and, of course, fish and chips. They're best enjoyed in Ned's harbour-view beer garden or inside listening to lively trad tunes (weekends, June to August).

COUNTY GALWAY

County Galway

County Galway's exuberant namesake city, the only major urban centre on the Wild Atlantic Way, is a swirl of colourful shop-lined streets filled with buskers and performance artists, enticing old pubs that hum with trad music sessions, and a sophisticated food scene.

Some of Ireland's most picturesque scenery fans out from Galway's city limits, particularly along breathtaking Connemara Peninsula. Tiny roads wander along a coastline studded with islands, dazzling white sandy beaches and picturesque villages, while its interior shelters heath-strewn bog lands, glassy lakes, looming mountains and isolated valleys.

Two Days in County Galway

Day one is for Galway city – be sure to visit the **City Museum** (p212) and fit in lunch at **Ard Bia cafe** (p214). If it's the weekend, **Galway Market** (p212) is a must. In the evening, gird your loins for a crawl around Galway's lively pubs and trad music sessions. On day two take a **cruise to Lough Corrib** (p214).

Four Days in County Galway

On day three follow our Connemara coastal drive (p206) and continue to the attractive village of Clifden, where you'll spend the night; prebook a table for dinner at **Mitchell's** (p218). On day four head back to Galway city via **Kylemore Abbey** (p219) and the wild bogs of **Connemara National Park** (p219).

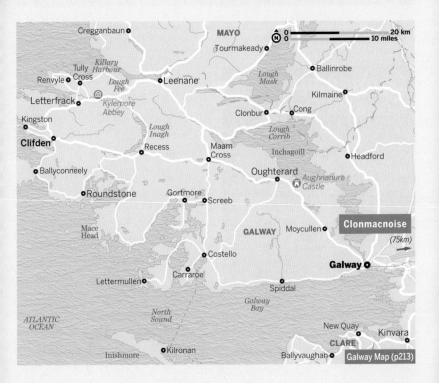

Arriving in County Galway

A car is the best option for exploring County Galway. If using public transport, base yourself in Galway city and take guided bus tours to the surrounding attractions.

There are up to nine fast, comfortable trains daily between Dublin's Heuston Station and Galway city (from €18, 2½ hours). Citylink coaches run between Galway and Cork (18, three hours, five to eight daily).

Where to Stay

It's possible to explore the entire county on day trips from Galway city, which has a wealth of options in all categories (book accommodation well in advance at peak times), but some wonderful hostels, B&Bs, inns and hotels county-wide allow more time for exploration. Properties in rural areas often close outside high season – check ahead.

Connemara Coastal Drive

With its shimmering black lakes, pale mountains, lonely valleys and more than the occasional rainbow, Connemara is one of the most gorgeous corners of Ireland. The lack of English signposting can be confusing at times, so a good road map is needed.

Start Barna Woods
Distance 90km
Duration Five to seven hours

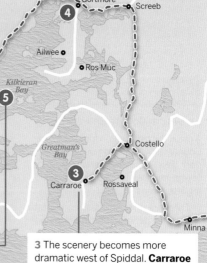

6 Carna is a small fishing village, with pleasant walks north to Moyrus and out to the wild headlands at Mace Head.

5 Kilkieran Bay is an intricate system of tidal marshes, bogs and tidal basins that contains an amazing diversity of wildlife.

3 The scenery becomes more dramatic west of Spiddal. **Carraroe** has fine beaches, including the Coral Strand, which is composed entirely of shell and coral fragments.

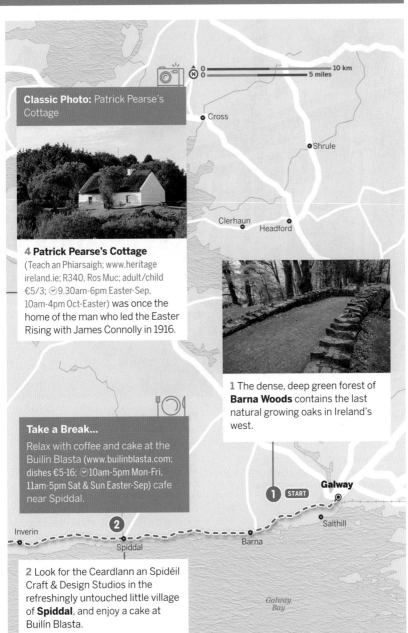

0 | 10 km
0 | 5 miles

Classic Photo: Patrick Pearse's Cottage

Cross

Shrule

Clerhaun   Headford

4 Patrick Pearse's Cottage

(Teach an Phiarsaigh; www.heritage ireland.ie; R340, Ros Muc; adult/child €5/3; ⊘9.30am-6pm Easter-Sep, 10am-4pm Oct-Easter) was once the home of the man who led the Easter Rising with James Connolly in 1916.

1 The dense, deep green forest of **Barna Woods** contains the last natural growing oaks in Ireland's west.

Take a Break...

Relax with coffee and cake at the Builín Blasta (www.builinblasta.com; dishes €5-16; ⊘10am-5pm Mon-Fri, 11am-5pm Sat & Sun Easter-Sep) cafe near Spiddal.

Galway

1 START

Salthill

Inverin

2

Spiddal

Barna

2 Look for the Ceardlann an Spidéil Craft & Design Studios in the refreshingly untouched little village of **Spiddal**, and enjoy a cake at Builín Blasta.

Galway Bay

New Quay

1 PAUL SHIELS/SHUTTERSTOCK © 4 DAVID ROBERTSON/ALAMY STOCK PHOTO ©

Tigh Neachtain

ANTON_IVANOV/SHUTTERSTOCK ©

Pub Crawl in Galway City

Galway's pub selection is second to none. The city is awash with traditional pubs offering live music, along with stylish wine and cocktail bars, which are thronged with revellers, especially on weekends.

Great For...

☑ **Don't Miss**

Taking in a live *céilidh* (trad music session) at the crowded traditional Irish pub, Tig Cóilí.

Tigh Neachtain   Pub

(www.tighneachtain.com; 17 Upper Cross St; ⊘11.30am-midnight Mon-Thu, to 1am Fri, 10.30am-1am Sat, 12.30-11.30pm Sun) Painted a bright cornflower blue, this 19th-century corner pub – known simply as Neách-tain's (*nock*-tans) or Naughtons – has a wraparound terrace for watching Galway's passing parade, and a timber-lined interior with a roaring open fire, snugs and atmosphere to spare. Along with perfectly pulled pints of Guinness and 130-plus whiskeys, it has its own range of beers brewed by Galway Hooker.

Crane Bar   Pub

(☏091-587 419; www.thecranebar.com; 2 Sea Rd; ⊘10.30am-11.30pm Mon-Thu, to 1am Fri, 12.30pm-1am Sat, to 11.30pm Sun) West of the Corrib, this atmospheric, always crammed two-storey pub is the best spot in Galway to

Tig Cóilí

HEMIS/ALAMY STOCK PHOTO ©

machines, fishing equipment, a stag's head and an almost life-size statue of John Wayne from *The Quiet Man*. Trad music and singalongs take place nightly.

Chalked blackboards feature quips including that the closest the pub gets to serving food is 'whiskey soup with ice croutons'.

catch an informal *céilidh*, with music nightly on both levels.

Tig Cóilí   Pub

(📞091-561 294; www.tigcoiligalway.com; Mainguard St; ⊙10.30am-11.30pm Mon-Thu, to 12.30am Fri & Sat, 12.30-11pm Sun) Two live *céilidh* a day (at 6pm and 9.30pm) draw the crowds to this authentic fire-engine-red pub just off High St. Decorated with photos of those who have played here, it's where musicians go to get drunk or drunks go to become musicians...or something like that. A gem.

O'Connor's   Pub

(📞091-523 468; www.oconnorsbar.com; Upper Salthill Rd, Salthill; ⊙7.30pm-late) Antiques fill every nook, cranny, wall and ceiling space of this 1942-established pub: clocks, crockery, farming implements, gas lights, sewing

Róisín Dubh   Pub

(📞091-586 540; www.roisindubh.net; 9 Upper Dominick St; ⊙5pm-2am Sun-Thu, to 2.30am Fri & Sat) From the rooftop terrace you can see sweeping views of Galway; inside emerging acts play here before they hit the big time. It's *the* place to hear bands but comedy's also on the menu.

Monroe's Tavern   Pub

(📞091-583 397; www.monroes.ie; 14 Upper Dominick St; ⊙10am-11.30pm Mon-Sat, noon-11.30pm Sun) Often photographed for its classic two-storey black-and-white facade, Monroe's has been at the heart of local nightlife for more than 50 years. Expect a buzzing vibe, live music nightly and an eclectic range of gigs.

ATTILA JANDI/SHUTTERSTOCK ©

Clonmacnoise

Gloriously situated overlooking the River Shannon, Clonmacnoise is one of Ireland's most important ancient monastic cities. Although it's located in neighbouring County Offaly, it's easily visited from Galway city.

Great For...

☑ Don't Miss

The Cross of the Scriptures, one of Ireland's finest carved stone high crosses.

When St Ciarán founded a monastery here in AD 548, it was the most important crossroads in the country, the intersection of the north–south River Shannon, and the east–west Esker Riada (Highway of the Kings).

The giant ecclesiastical city had a humble beginning and Ciarán died just seven months after building his first church. Over the years, however, Clonmacnoise grew to become an unrivalled bastion of Irish religion, literature and art and attracted a large lay population. Between the 7th and 12th centuries, monks from all over Europe came to study and pray here, helping to earn Ireland the title of the 'land of saints and scholars'.

The site is enclosed in a walled field and contains several early churches, high crosses, round towers and graves in astonishingly good condition. The surrounding marshy area is known as the Shannon Callows, home

The Cross of the Scriptures

CROM PHOTOGRAPHY/SHUTTERSTOCK ©

❶ Need to Know

www.heritageireland.ie; R444; adult/child
€8/4; ⊙9am-6.30pm Jun-Aug, 10am-6pm
mid-Mar–May, Sep & Oct, 10am-5.30pm
Nov–mid-Mar

✘ Take A Break

There's a coffee shop at the visitor centre, but no other source of refreshment nearby.

★ Top Tip

If you plan to visit more than three or four Heritage Ireland sites, save money with an OPW Heritage Card (€40).

mid-Mar–May, Sep & Oct, 10am-5.30pm Nov–mid-Mar, last admission 1hr before closing). A 20-minute audiovisual show provides an excellent introduction to the site.

The exhibition area contains the original high crosses (replicas have been put in their former locations outside) and various artefacts uncovered during excavation, including silver pins, beaded glass and an Ogham stone.

Cathedral

The largest building at Clonmacnoise, the cathedral was originally built in AD 909, but was significantly altered and remodelled over the centuries. Its most interesting feature is the intricate 15th-century Gothic doorway with carvings of Sts Francis, Patrick and Dominic. A whisper carries from one side of the door to the other and this feature was supposedly used by lepers to confess their sins without infecting the priests.

to many wild plants and one of the last refuges of the seriously endangered corncrake (a pastel-coloured relative of the coot).

Most of what you can see today dates from the 10th to 12th centuries. The monks would have lived in small huts surrounding the monastery. The site was burned and pillaged on numerous occasions by both the Vikings and the Irish. After the 12th century it fell into decline, and by the 15th century was home solely to an impoverished bishop. In 1552 the English garrison from Athlone reduced the site to a ruin.

Visitor Centre

Three connected conical huts, echoing the design of early monastic dwellings, house the **visitor centre museum** (☎090-967 4195; www.heritageireland.ie; R444; adult/child €8/4; ⊙9am-6.30pm Jun-Aug, 10am-6pm

Galway City

Arty, bohemian Galway (Gaillimh) is one of Ireland's most engaging cities. Brightly painted pubs heave with live music, while restaurants and cafes offer front-row seats for observing buskers and street theatre. Remnants of the medieval town walls lie between shops selling handcrafted Claddagh rings, books and musical instruments, bridges arch over the salmon-stuffed River Corrib, and a long promenade leads to the seaside suburb of Salthill, on Galway Bay, the source of the area's famous oysters.

While it's steeped in history, the city buzzes with a contemporary vibe, thanks in part to students, who make up around a fifth of the population. Its energy and creativity have seen it designated a European Capital of Culture for 2020.

◎ SIGHTS

Galway City Museum · Museum

(Map p179; 📞091-532 460; www.galwaycity museum.ie; Spanish Pde; ⏰10am-5pm Tue-Sat, plus noon-5pm Sun Easter-Sep) **FREE** Exhibits at this modern, three-floor museum engagingly convey the city's archaeological, political, cultural and social history. Look out for an iconic Galway hooker fishing boat, a collection of *currachs* (boats made of a framework of laths covered with tarred canvas) and sections covering Galway's role in the revolutionary events that shaped the Republic of Ireland.

Spanish Arch · Historic Site

(Map p179) The Spanish Arch is thought to be an extension of Galway's medieval city walls, designed to protect ships moored at the nearby quay while they unloaded goods from Spain. It was partially destroyed by the tsunami that followed the 1755 Lisbon earthquake. Today it reverberates with buskers and drummers, and the lawns and riverside form a gathering place for locals and visitors on sunny days, as kayakers negotiate the tidal rapids of the River Corrib.

Galway Market · Market

(Map p179; www.galwaymarket.com; Church Lane; ⏰8am-6pm Sat, noon-6pm Sun) Galway's bohemian spirit comes alive at its street market,

Spanish Arch

AMBEROS5/BUDGET TRAVEL ©

Galway

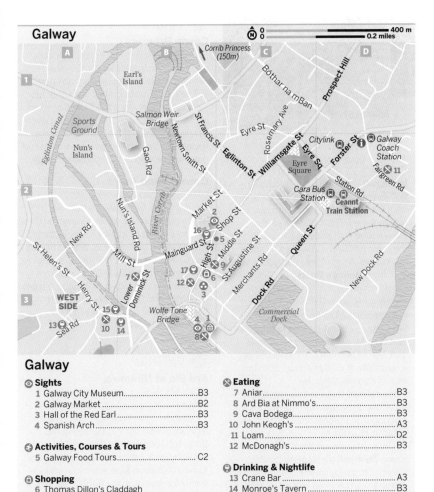

Galway

which has set up in this spot for centuries. Saturdays are the standout for food, when farmers sell fresh produce alongside stalls selling arts, crafts and ready-to-eat dishes. Additional markets take place from noon to 6pm on bank holidays, Fridays in July and August and every day during the Galway International Arts Festival (p217). Buskers add to the festive atmosphere.

Hall of the Red Earl
Archaeological Site

(Map p179; www.galwaycivictrust.ie; Druid Lane; ⊙9am-4.45pm Mon-Fri, 11am-3pm Sat) **FREE** In the 13th century, when the de Burgo family ruled Galway, Richard – the Red Earl – erected a large hall as a seat of power, where locals would arrive to curry favour. After the 14 tribes took over, the hall fell into ruin. It was

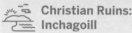
Christian Ruins: Inchagoill

Inchagoill The largest island on Lough Corrib, Inchagoill lies about 5km offshore from the lake's edge, some 8km north of Oughterard. The island is a lonely place dotted with ancient remains. In the summer Corrib Cruises (p217) runs day cruises. Alternatively, rent your own boat from **Molloy's Boats** (📞091-866 954; Baurisheen; motor/rowboat per day €70/40, motorboat with guide €150; ☺by appointment).

Inchagoill's most fascinating sight is a 6th-century obelisk called **Lia Luguaedon Mac Menueh** (Stone of Luguaedon, Son of Menueh), which identifies a burial site. It stands about 75cm tall, near the Saints' Church.

It's claimed that the Latin writing on the stone is the second-oldest Christian inscription in Europe, after those in the catacombs in Rome.

The prettiest church is the Romanesque **Teampall na Naoimh** (Saints' Church), probably built in the 9th or 10th century, with carvings around its arched doorway. **Teampall Phádraig** (St Patrick's Church) is a small oratory of a very early design, with some later additions.

Teampall na Naoimh
STEPHEN BARNES/SHUTTERSTOCK ©

lost until the 1990s, when expansion of the city's Custom House uncovered its foundations, along with more than 11,000 artefacts including clay pipes and gold cufflinks. The Custom House was built on stilts overhead, leaving the old foundations open.

🄶 TOURS

Corrib Princess
Cruise
(📞091-563 846; www.corribprincess.ie; Waterside, Woodquay; adult/child €17/8; ☺May-Sep) Ninety-minute cruises, aboard an open-top 157-seat boat, pass castles and other historic landmarks along the River Corrib en route to the Republic's largest lake, Lough Corrib. In season, there are two or three departures per day. Boats leave from Woodquay, just beyond the Salmon Weir Bridge.

Galway Food Tours
Food & Drink
(📞086 733 2885; www.galwayfoodtours.com; 21 Shop St; €50; ☺daily Wed-Sun) Galway's vibrant foodie scene shines through on these two-hour gourmet walking tours. Tastings include sushi, local cheeses, artisan breads and Galway Bay oysters. Booking is required. Tours leave from outside Griffin's Bakery.

Other tours include a six-hour pub trawl of Galway and Connemara, plus food-themed cycling and whiskey tours. All tours are also available in French.

🄓 EATING

Ard Bia at Nimmo's
Irish €€
(📞091-561 114; www.ardbia.com; Spanish Arch, Longwalk; cafe dishes €7-12, dinner mains €20-28; ☺cafe 10am-3.30pm Mon-Fri, to 3pm Sat & Sun, restaurant 6-9pm; 🗷) 🖉 Casually hip Ard Bia ('High Food' in Irish) is decorated with works by local artists and upcycled vintage furniture. Organic, local, seasonal produce (some foraged) features firmly – you might sample Cork monkfish, Burren smoked haddock or Galway goat's yoghurt. Opt for the upstairs restaurant or a street-level cafe serving flavour-packed breakfasts, brunches and lunches.

Cava Bodega
Tapas €€
(📞091-539 884; www.cavarestaurant.ie; 1 Middle St; tapas €7-14; ☺5-10pm Mon-Thu, 4-11pm Fri, noon-11.30pm Sat, noon-9.30pm Sun; 🗷) More than 50 regional Spanish tapas dishes are given a gourmet twist by star chef JP McMahon, whose other ventures include Michelin-starred Aniar. Showstoppers

include turf-smoked salmon, duck fritter with seaweed jam and a harissa-infused Connemara mountain lamb, along with over 100 Spanish wines.

On Friday and Saturday the bodega's bar stays open late.

John Keogh's Gastropub €€

(Lock Keeper; ☎091-449 431; www.johnkeoghs. ie; 22 Upper Dominick St; mains €11-24; ⏰kitchen 5-9pm Mon-Fri, 1-9pm Sat & Sun) Dark-wood panelling, snugs, stained glass, antique mirrors, book-lined shelves and blazing open fires set the scene for standout gastropub fare. John Keogh's doesn't take reservations, so arrive early to dine on mussels with home-baked soda bread and garlic aioli, or Irish oysters with a Guinness shot.

Loam Gastronomy €€€

(☎091-569 727; www.loamgalway.com; Fairgreen Rd; 2/3/7/9 courses €45/55/119/159; ⏰6-10pm Tue-Sat) 🍴 Enda McEvoy is one of the most groundbreaking chefs in Ireland today (with a Michelin star to prove it), producing inspired flavour combinations from home-grown, locally sourced or foraged ingredients: dried hay, fresh moss, edible flowers, wild oats, forest gooseberries, Salthill sea vegetables and hand-cut peat (which McEvoy uses in his extraordinary peat-smoked ice cream).

Aniar Irish €€€

(☎091-535 947; www.aniarrestaurant.ie; 53 Lower Dominick St; 6/8/10 courses €72/89/99, with wine pairings €107-169; ⏰6-9.30pm Tue-Thu, 5.30-9.30pm Fri & Sat) 🍴 Terroir specialist Aniar is passionate about the flavours and food producers of Galway and west Ireland. Owner and chef JP McMahon's multicourse tasting menus have earned him a Michelin star, yet the casual spring-green dining space remains refreshingly down to earth. The wine list favours small producers. Reserve at least a couple of weeks in advance.

🍷 DRINKING & NIGHTLIFE

Galway's nightlife is a blast; see Pub Crawl in Galway City (p208) for a top night out.

 Spoken Irish

One of the most important Gaeltacht (Irish-speaking areas) in Ireland begins around Spiddal, just east of Connemara, and stretches west to Cashel and north into County Mayo.

That the Irish language is enjoying a renaissance around the country can be credited in part to media outlets, including those based in Galway. Ireland's national Irish-language radio station, Radio na Gaeltachta (www.rte.ie/radio), first broadcast in 1972; its Irish-language TV station, TG4 (www.tg4.ie), launched in the 1990s – both continue to thrive.

Spiddal
LISANDRO LUIS TRARBACH/SHUTTERSTOCK ©

ℹ️ INFORMATION

Galway's large, efficient **tourist office** (☎1850 230 330; www.discoverireland.ie; Forster St; ⏰9am-5pm Mon-Sat) can help arrange tours and has plentiful information on the city and region.

ℹ️ GETTING THERE & AWAY

BUS

Bus Éireann (www.buseireann.ie; Cara Bus Station, Station Rd) operates daily services to all major cities in the Republic and the North from **Cara Bus Station** (☎091-562 000; Station Rd), near the train station. Hourly services include the following:

Cork bus 51, €20, 4½ hours

Dublin bus 20/X20, €16, 3½ hours

Citylink (www.citylink.ie; 17 Forster St; ⏱office 9am-6pm Mon-Sat, 10am-6pm Sun; 📶) services depart from **Galway Coach Station** (New Coach Station; Fairgreen Rd), northeast of Eyre Sq. Destinations include the following:

Clifden (Connemara) €14, 1½ hours, six daily

Cork €18, three hours, five to eight daily

GoBus (📞091-564600; www.gobus.ie; Galway Coach Station; 📶) also has frequent services from Galway Coach Station to Dublin (€13, 2½ hours) and Dublin Airport (€18, 2½ hours).

TRAIN

From the **train station** (www.irishrail.ie; Station Rd), just off Eyre Sq, there are six to nine direct trains daily to/from Dublin's Heuston Station (€18, 2½ hours), and three to five daily to Ennis (€8, 1¼ hours). Connections with other train routes can be made – some involve changing at Athlone (€11, one hour, four to 10 daily).

Connemara

The name Connemara (Conamara) translates as 'Inlets of the Sea' and the roads along the peninsula's filigreed shoreline bear this out as they wind around the coves of this breathtaking stretch of Ireland's jagged west coast.

Connemara's starkly beautiful interior, traversed by the N59, is a kaleidoscope of rusty bogs, lonely valleys and shimmering black lakes. At its heart are the Maumturk Mountains and the pewter-tinged quartzite peaks of the Twelve Bens mountain range, with a network of scenic hiking and biking trails. Everywhere the land is laced by stone walls.

★ Top Five Historic Sites – Galway

Clonmacnoise (p210)

Kylemore Abbey (p219)

Inchagoill (p214)

Hall of the Red Earl (p213)

Aughnanure Castle (p216)

ℹ️ INFORMATION

Galway city's tourist office (p215) has lots of information on the area.

Online, Connemara Tourism (www.connemara. ie) and Go Connemara (www.goconnemara.com) have region-wide info and links.

ℹ️ GETTING THERE & AROUND

BUS

Bus Éireann (www.buseireann.ie) serves most of Connemara. Services can be sporadic – a handful operate May to September only, or July and August only.

Citylink (www.citylink.ie) has several buses a day linking Galway city with Clifden via Oughterard and going on to Cleggan and Letterfrack.

For stop-offs between towns, you might be able to arrange a drop-off with the driver.

CAR

Your own wheels are the best way to get off this scenic region's beaten track. Watch out for the narrow roads' stone walls and meandering Connemara sheep.

Oughterard & Around

The charmingly down-to-earth village of Oughterard (Uachtar Árd) sits on the shore of the Republic's biggest lake, Lough Corrib. Some 64km long and covering around 175 sq km, the lake virtually cuts off western Galway from the rest of the country and encompasses more than 360 islands.

🎯 SIGHTS & ACTIVITIES

Aughnanure Castle   Castle

(📞091-552 214; www.heritageireland.ie; off N59; adult/child €5/3; ⏱9.30am-6pm Mar-Oct) The 'Fighting O'Flahertys' were based at this superbly preserved 16th-century fortress 4km east of Oughterard. The clan controlled the region for hundreds of years after they fought off the Normans. Today their six-storey tower house stands on a rocky outcrop overlooking Lough Corrib and has been extensively restored.

Surrounding the castle are the remains of an unusual double *bawn* (area surrounded by walls outside the main castle); there's also the remains of the banqueting hall and a small, now isolated watchtower with a conical roof. The River Drimneen once enclosed the castle on three sides, while today the waterway washes through a number of natural caverns and caves beneath the castle.

Corrib Cruises   Cruise

(🕿087 994 6380; www.corribcruises.com; Oughterard Pier; adult/child €28/14; ⊙noon Wed-Mon Jul & Aug) Cruises from Oughterard run to Inchagoill (p214) island and Ashford Castle near Cong (County Mayo) and back, taking a total of six hours. Check the website for seasonal sailing schedules.

 GETTING THERE & AWAY

Bus Éireann (www.buseireann.ie) bus 419 runs one to eight times daily to/from Galway city (€9, 35 minutes) and Clifden (€15.50, two hours). Three times a week it also runs to Roundstone (€14, 50 minutes).

Citylink (www.citylink.ie) has six services daily to/from Galway (€9, 35 minutes) and Clifden (€12, 55 minutes).

Roundstone

Clustered around a boat-filled harbour, picture-perfect Roundstone (Cloch na Rón) is the kind of Irish village you hoped to find. Colourful terrace houses and inviting pubs overlook the shimmering recess of Bertraghboy Bay, which is home to dramatic tidal flows, lobster trawlers and traditional *currach* boats with tarred canvas bottoms stretched over wicker frames.

 EATING

O'Dowd's   Seafood €€

(🕿095-35809; www.odowdsseafoodbar.com; Main St; mains €14-29; ⊙restaurant 5-9.30pm,

 **Top Galway Festivals**

Galway's packed calendar of festivals turns the city and surrounding communities into what feels like one nonstop party – streets overflow with revellers, and pubs often extend their opening hours.

Galway Food Festival (www.galwayfoodfestival.com; ⊙Easter) The area's sublime food and drink are celebrated for five days over the Easter weekend with food and foraging tours, talks, cookery demonstrations and a market.

Cúirt International Festival of Literature (www.cuirt.ie; ⊙Apr) Top-name authors converge on Galway over eight days in late April for one of Ireland's premier literary festivals, featuring poetry slams, theatrical performances and readings.

Galway Film Fleadh (www.galwayfilmfleadh.com; ⊙early Jul) Early July sees the six-day Galway Film Fleadh set screens alight with new, edgy works.

Galway International Arts Festival (www.giaf.ie; ⊙mid-late Jul) Catch performances and exhibits by top drama groups, musicians and bands, comedians, artists and much more during this two-week fiesta.

Galway International Oyster & Seafood Festival (www.galwayoysterfest.com; South Park; ⊙late Sep) Going strong since 1954, the world's oldest oyster festival draws thousands of visitors. Events include the World Oyster Opening Championships, live music, a masquerade carnival and family activities.

Galway International Arts Festival

Est. 1750.

Claddagh Rings

The fishing village of Claddagh has long been subsumed into Galway's city centre, but its namesake rings survive as a timeless reminder.

Popular with people of Irish descent everywhere, the rings depict a heart (symbolising love) between two out-stretched hands (friendship), topped by a crown (loyalty). Jewellery shops selling Claddagh rings include Ireland's oldest, **Thomas Dillon's Claddagh Gold** (091-566 365; www.claddaghring.ie; 1 Quay St; 10am-5pm Mon-Sat, noon-4pm Sun).

Thomas Dillon's jewellers
CHRISDORNEY/SHUTTERSTOCK ©

bar menu noon-9.30pm; 🛜) 🍴 Roundstone lobster, Aran Islands hake, plaice and sea bass, local crab and mackerel smoked in-house are sourced off the old stone dock directly opposite this wonderfully authentic old pub and restaurant, while produce comes from its garden. There's a strong list of Irish craft beers and ciders.

Its neighbouring summertime **cafe** (095-35809; www.odowdsseafoodbar.com; Main St; dishes €5.50-11.50; 9am-6pm Mar-Oct; 🛜) serves breakfast and lunch.

Clifden & Around

A definitive stop on any tour of Connemara, the region's 'capital', Clifden (An Clochán, meaning 'stepping stones'), is an appealing Victorian-era town presiding over the head of the narrow bay where the River Owenglin tumbles into the sea.

🚴 ACTIVITIES

Sky Road   Scenic Drive
Signposted from the N59 heading north out of Clifden, this aptly named 15km driving and cycling route traces a dizzying loop out to the township of Kingston and back, taking in rugged, stunningly beautiful coastal scenery en route. Set out clockwise from the southern side for the best views, which peak at sunset.

Errislannan Manor   Horse Riding
(095-21134; www.errislannanmanor.com; per hr from €35; by appointment Mon-Fri Mar-Oct) Guides provide lessons and lead treks along the beach and up into the hills on the iconic local ponies. All abilities are catered for and children's lessons are a speciality (per half hour €25).

It's 7.5km from Clifden: take the Bally-conneely Rd (the R341) south for 4km, turn northwest on to the Errislannan Peninsula and look out for the signs.

🍴 EATING

Mitchell's   Seafood €€
(095-21867; www.mitchellsrestaurantclifden. com; Market St; mains lunch €8-16, dinner €18-28; noon-9pm Mar-Oct) Seafood from the surrounding waters takes centre stage at this elegant spot, from velvety chowder and open crab sandwiches at lunchtime to intricate dinner mains. The highlight is a standout seafood platter (€26), piled high with Ros A Mhil prawns, Killary mussels, Oranmore oysters, Connemara smoked salmon and Cleggan crab. Strong wine list. Book ahead.

Letterfrack & Around

Founded by Quakers in the mid-19th century, Letterfrack (Leitir Fraic) is a crossroads with a few pubs and B&Bs. But the forested setting and nearby coast are a magnet for outdoors adventure seekers. A 4km walk to the peak of Tully Mountain (356m) takes 40 minutes and offers uplifting ocean views.

Kylemore Abbey

◎ SIGHTS

Connemara
National Park
National Park

(☑076-100 2528; www.connemaranationalpark.ie; off N59; ⊘24hr) **FREE** Immediately southeast of Letterfrack, Connemara National Park spans 2000 dramatic hectares of bog, mountains, heath and woodlands.

The park encloses a number of the Twelve Bens, including Bencullagh, Benbrack and Benbaun. The heart of the park is Gleann Mór (Big Glen), through which the River Polladirk flows. There's fine walking up the glen and over the surrounding mountains along with short self-guided walks.

Guided nature walks (☑076-100 2528; www.connemaranationalpark.ie) **FREE** led by park rangers depart from the **visitor centre** (☑076-100 2528; www.connemaranationalpark.ie; off N59, Letterfrack; ⊘9am-5.30pm Mar-Oct).

Kylemore Abbey
Historic Building

(☑095-52001; www.kylemoreabbey.com; off N59; adult/child €13/free; ⊘9am-7pm Jul & Aug, 9.30am-5.30pm Sep & Oct, 9am-6pm Apr-Jun, 10am-4.30pm Nov-Mar) Photogenically perched on the shores of Pollacapall Lough, 4km east of Letterfrack, Kylemore is a crenellated 19th-century neo-Gothic fantasy. It was built for a wealthy English businessman, Mitchell Henry, who spent his honeymoon in Connemara. Ground-floor rooms are open to visitors, and you can wander down to the lake and the Gothic church. Admission includes entry to the extravagant Victorian walled gardens, around a 20-minute walk away (linked by a free shuttle bus from April to October).

❶ GETTING THERE & AWAY

Citylink (www.citylink.ie) bus 923 serves Letterfrack from Galway (€15, two hours, three daily), via Clifden (€5.50, 20 minutes).

BELFAST

Belfast

Belfast is in many ways a brand-new city. Once shunned by travellers unnerved by tales of the Troubles and sectarian violence, it has pulled off a remarkable transformation from bombs-and-bullets pariah to a hip-hotels-and-hedonism party town.

The Titanic Quarter's centrepiece, the stunning, star-shaped Titanic Belfast centre, has become the city's number-one tourist draw, adding to a list of attractions that includes beautifully& restored Victorian architecture, a glittering waterfront lined with modern art, a fantastic and fast-expanding foodie scene and music-filled pubs.

One Day in Belfast

Start with a free guided tour of **City Hall** (p230). Take a **black taxi tour** (p229) of the West Belfast murals, and ask the taxi driver to drop you off for lunch at **Holohan's** (p236). Afterwards, cruise the river on a **Lagan Boat Company tour** (p234), then spend the rest of the afternoon exploring **Titanic Belfast** (p226), before dinner at the **Muddlers Club** (p236).

Two Days in Belfast

On your second day, explore the fascinating exhibits in the **Ulster Museum** (p230) and take a stroll through the **Botanic Gardens** (p231). In the afternoon take a guided tour around historic **Crumlin Road Gaol** (p231), and spend the evening crawling traditional pubs such as **Kelly's Cellars** (p238), the **Duke of York** (p238) and **Crown Liquor Saloon** (p230).

Previous page:Belfast City Hall
MLENNY/GETTY IMAGES ©

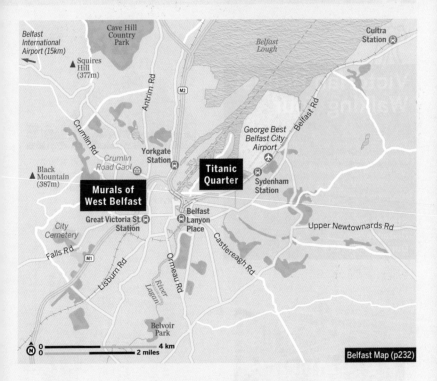

Belfast Map (p232)

Arriving in Belfast

Belfast International Airport Frequent buses to the city (return £11, 30 to 55 minutes) from 4.30am to 11.30pm.

George Best Belfast City Airport Frequent buses to the city (return £4, 15 minutes) from 5.15am to 9.30pm.

Europa Bus Station Buses from Dublin arrive here; located right in the city centre.

Belfast Central Station Trains from Dublin arrive here; rail ticket includes free bus ride into the city centre.

Where to Stay

From backpacker hostels to boutique havens, the range of places to stay widens every year. Most of Belfast's budget and midrange accommodation is south of the centre, in the leafy university district around Botanic Ave, University Rd and Malone Rd, around a 20-minute walk from City Hall. Business hotels and luxury boutiques proliferate in the city centre.

Book ahead on weekends, in summer and during busy festival periods.

Victorian Belfast Walking Tour

The Victorian era was a time of great prosperity in Belfast and the wealth generated by the city's industries is reflected in the elaborate architecture of the period.

Start St George's Market
Distance 2km
Duration One hour

4 Walk west to Donegall Sq, which has some fine Victorian architecture, including the **Robinson & Cleaver building** (1888).

6 Turn left onto Wellington Pl and then left onto Great Victoria St, to reach the 1895 **Grand Opera House**.

Take a Break...
Home (p236) makes an ideal lunch stop.

Classic Photo: Interior of the Crown Liquor Saloon.

7 Continue south on Great Victoria St to the **Crown Liquor Saloon** (p230), built in 1885.

Castle St

Queen St

Fountain St

Donegall Pl

College Sq N

College St

Wellington Pl

College Sq E

Upper Queen St

4

5

Grosvenor Rd

Howard St

Donegall Sq S

Bedford St

Linenhall St

6

FINISH
7

Great Victoria St

Brunswick St

Great Victoria St Station

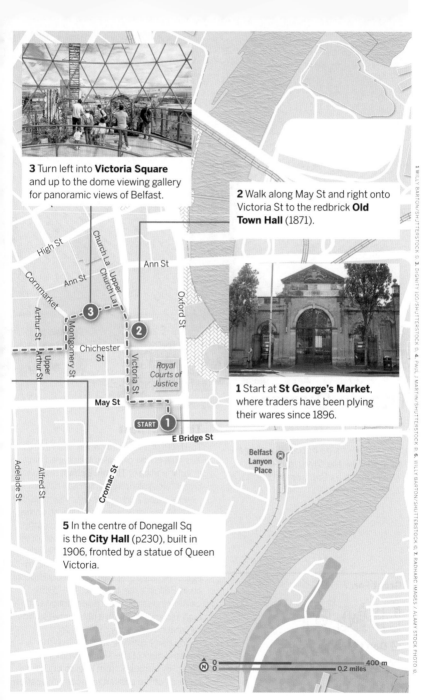

3 Turn left into **Victoria Square** and up to the dome viewing gallery for panoramic views of Belfast.

2 Walk along May St and right onto Victoria St to the redbrick **Old Town Hall** (1871).

1 Start at **St George's Market**, where traders have been plying their wares since 1896.

5 In the centre of Donegall Sq is the **City Hall** (p230), built in 1906, fronted by a statue of Queen Victoria.

START

E Bridge St

Belfast Lanyon Place

High St

Church La

Upper Church La

Ann St

Cornmarket

Ann St

Arthur St

Upper Arthur St

Montgomery St

Chichester St

Victoria St

Oxford St

Royal Courts of Justice

May St

Cromac St

Adelaide St

Alfred St

N

0   400 m
0   0.2 miles

Titanic Quarter

Belfast's former shipbuilding yards – the birthplace of RMS Titanic – stretch along the east side of the River Lagan, dominated by the towering yellow cranes known as Samson and Goliath.

Great For...

☑ Don't Miss...

Taking a peek at the first-class toilets aboard the SS *Nomadic*.

Titanic Belfast

The head of the slipway where the *Titanic* was built is now occupied by the gleaming, angular edifice of **Titanic Belfast** (www.titanic belfast.com; Queen's Rd; adult/child £18.50/8; ⏰9am-7pm Jun & Jul, to 8pm Aug, to 6pm Apr, May & Sep, 10am-5pm Oct-Mar; 🚋G2). It's an unmiss-able multimedia extravaganza that charts the history of Belfast and the creation of the world's most famous ocean liner. Cleverly designed exhibits enlivened by historic im-ages, animated projections and soundtracks chart Belfast's rise to turn-of-the-20th-century industrial superpower, followed by a high-tech ride through a noisy, smells-and-all re-creation of the city's shipyards.

You can explore every detail of the construction of the *Titanic*, from a com-puter 'fly-through' from keel to bridge, to replicas of the passenger accommodation.

CLAUDIO DIVIZIA/SHUTTERSTOCK ©

Titanic Quarter ◉

❶ Need to Know

A series of information boards along Queen's Rd describes items and areas of interest.

✕ Take a Break

There are cafes in both Titanic Belfast and the Thompson Pump House.

Perhaps most poignant are the few flickering images that constitute the only film footage of the ship in existence.

Behind the building you can see the massive slipways where the *Titanic* and her sister ship, *Olympic*, were built and launched.

SS Nomadic

Built in Belfast in 1911, the **SS Nomadic** (www.nomadicbelfast.com; Hamilton Dock, Queen's Rd; adult/child £7/5; ⊙10am-7pm Sun-Thu, to 8pm Fri & Sat Jul & Aug, 10am-7pm Jun, 10am-6pm Apr, May & Jun, 11am-5pm Oct-Mar; 🚌G2) is the last remaining vessel of the White Star Line. The little steamship ferried 1st- and 2nd-class passengers between Cherbourg Harbour and the ocean liners that were too big to dock at the French port. On 10 April 1912 it delivered

172 passengers to the ill-fated *Titanic*. Don't miss the luxurious 1st-class toilets. Entry to the SS *Nomadic* (valid for 24 hours) is included in the ticket for Titanic Belfast.

Titanic's Dock & Pump House

At the far end of Queen's Rd is the most impressive monument to the days of the great liners – the vast **Thompson Dry Dock** (www.titanicsdock.com; Queen's Rd; adult/child £5/3.50; ⊙10am-5pm Apr-Oct, 10.30am-4pm Nov & Dec, 10.30am-5pm Jan & Feb; 🚌G2) where the *Titanic* was fitted out.

Beside it is the Pump House, which has an exhibition on Belfast shipbuilding. Self-guided tours include a viewing of original film footage from the shipyards, a visit to the inner workings of the pump house and a walk along the floor of the dry dock.

The dry dock's huge size gives you some idea of the scale of the ship, which could only just fit into it.

EVERYONE
REPUBLICAN
OR OTHERWISE
HAS THEIR OWN
PARTICULAR
ROLE TO PLAY

...OUR
REVENGE
WILL BE THE
LAUGHTER
OF OUR
CHILDREN

Bobby Sands MP
POET, GAEILGEOIR, REVOLUTIONARY, IRA VOLUNTEER.

Murals of West Belfast

The political murals of West Belfast are one of the city's most compelling sights, a colourful and visceral reminder of the tensions that once tore the city apart.

Belfast's tradition of political murals is over a century old, dating from 1908 when images of King Billy (William III, Protestant victor over the Catholic James II at the Battle of the Boyne in 1690) were painted by Unionists protesting against home rule for Ireland. The tradition was revived in the late 1970s as the Troubles wore on, with murals used to mark out sectarian territory, make political points, commemorate historical events and glorify terrorist groups.

Republican Murals

The first Republican murals appeared in 1981, in support of Republican prisoners in Maze Prison during their hunger strike demanding recognition as political prisoners. In later years, Republican muralists broadened their scope to cover wider political issues, Irish legends and historical events.

Great For...

☑ Don't Miss

A visit to the Peace Line, the corrugated steel wall that divides West Belfast's Protestant and Catholic communities.

Mural representing political solidarity with Palestine

VANDERWOLF IMAGES/SHUTTERSTOCK © SOLIDARITY P.O.W.S MURAL BY DANNY DEVENNY AND CARLOS LATUFF

Peace Line

The most visible sign of the divisions that have scarred the area for so long is the so-called 'Peace Line' that controversially divides West Belfast's Protestant and Catholic communities. Begun in 1969 as a 'temporary measure', the 6m-high walls of corrugated steel, concrete and chain link have outlasted the Berlin Wall.

Loyalist Murals

Loyalist murals have traditionally been more militaristic and defiant in tone than the Republican murals. The Loyalist battle cry of 'No Surrender!' is everywhere, along with kerbstones painted red, white and blue, paramilitary insignia and images of King Billy, usually shown on a prancing white horse.

Murals Today

In recent years there has been a lot of debate about what to do with Belfast's murals. There's no doubt they have become an important tourist attraction, but there is now a move to replace the more aggressive and militaristic images with murals dedicated to local heroes and famous figures such as footballer George Best and *Narnia* author CS Lewis.

Taxi Tours

Black taxi tours of West Belfast's murals are offered by a large number of taxi companies and local cabbies. These can vary in quality and content, but in general they're an intimate and entertaining way to see the sights. Drivers will pick you up from anywhere in the city centre.

Paddy Campbell's Famous Black Cab Tours (☐07990-955227; www.belfastblack cabtours.co.uk; per person tour for 1-2 people £35, for 3-8 people £12) has popular 1½-hour tours; **Official Black Taxi Tours** (☐07702-449694, 028-9064 2264; www.belfasttours.com; 1-2 passengers £40, plus £17.50 per additional person) has 1½-hour customised political-murals tours.

◎ SIGHTS

◎ City Centre

City Hall   Historic Building

(📞028-9027 0456; www.belfastcity.gov.uk;
Donegall Sq; ⊙9.30am-5pm Mon-Fri, 10am-5pm
Sat & Sun, to 8pm Thu Jun-Sep; 🚌Donegall Sq)
FREE Belfast's classical Renaissance-style
City Hall was built in fine, white Portland stone in 1906. Highlights of the
free, 45-minute guided tour include the
sumptuous, wedding-cake Italian marble
of the rotunda; an opportunity to sit on the
mayor's throne in the council chamber;
and the idiosyncratic portraits of past
lord mayors. On the ground floor and
accessible outside tour times are a series
of commemorative stained-glass windows
and a visitor exhibition with displays on
Belfast's history spread across 16 rooms.

Crown Liquor Saloon Historic Building
(www.nationaltrust.org.uk/the-crown-bar; 46
Great Victoria St; ⊙11.30am-11pm Mon-Sat,
12.30-10pm Sun; 🚌8A to 8D, 9A to 9C) There
are not many historical monuments that
you can enjoy while savouring a pint of

Guinness, but the National Trust's Crown
Liquor Saloon is one of them. Belfast's
most famous bar was refurbished by Patrick Flanagan in the late 19th century and
displays Victorian decorative flamboyance
at its best (he was looking to pull in a posh
clientele from the train station and Grand
Opera House opposite). Despite being
a tourist attraction, the bar fills up with
locals come 6pm.

◎ South Belfast
(Queen's Quarter)

Ulster Museum   Museum
(www.nmni.com; Botanic Gardens, Stranmillis Rd;
⊙10am-5pm Tue-Sun; ♿; 🚌8A to 8D) **FREE** You
could spend hours browsing this state-of-
the-art museum, but if you're pressed for
time don't miss the Armada Room, with
artefacts retrieved from the 1588 wreck of
the Spanish galleon *Girona;* the Egyptian
Room, with Takabuti, a 2500-year-old
Egyptian mummy unwrapped in Belfast in
1835; and the Early Peoples Gallery, with
the bronze Bann Disc, a superb example of
Celtic design from the Iron Age.

Queen's University

CAPRI92X/GETTY IMAGES ©

Botanic Gardens — Gardens

(📞028-9031 4762; Stranmillis Rd; ⏱7.30am-sunset; 🚌8A to 8D) FREE The showpiece of Belfast's green oasis is Charles Lanyon's beautiful **Palm House** (⏱10am-5pm Apr-Sep, to 4pm Oct-Mar) FREE, built in 1839 and completed in 1852, with its birdcage dome, a masterpiece in cast-iron and curvilinear glass. Nearby is the 1889 **Tropical Ravine** (⏱10am-5pm Tue-Sun) FREE, a huge red-brick greenhouse designed by the garden's curator Charles McKimm. Inside, a raised walkway overlooks a jungle of tropical ferns, orchids, lilies and banana plants growing in a sunken glen. It reopened in 2018 following a £3.8 million renovation.

Queen's University — Historic Building

(www.qub.ac.uk; University Rd; 🚌8A to 8D) Northern Ireland's most prestigious university was founded by Queen Victoria in 1845. In 1908 the Queen's College became the Queen's University of Belfast and today its campus spreads across some 250 buildings.

Just inside the main entrance is the **Queen's Welcome Centre** (📞028-9097 5252; www.qub.ac.uk/welcomecentre; University Rd; ⏱8.30am-5.30pm Mon-Fri, 11am-4pm Sat & Sun; 🚌8A to 8D), with an information desk and souvenir shop. Pick up a free *Campus Walkbout* booklet that outlines a self-guided tour which highlights the beautiful architectural features of the buildings.

◎ Titanic Quarter

Harland & Wolff Drawing Offices — Historic Building

(www.titanichotelbelfast.com; Queen's Rd; 🚌G2) The designs for the *Titanic* were first drawn up here at the original Harland & Wolff drawing offices. Now part of the **Titanic Hotel** (📞028-9508 2000; d £110-270; ❄🛜), the drawing offices, Thomas Andrews' office, the old Harland & Wolff bathrooms and the room that received the news by telegram that the ship was in trouble, have all been preserved. Pop inside to take a look around and have a drink in **Drawing Office Two** (mains £12-18.50; ⏱kitchen noon-10pm), or see them on the **Titanic Discovery Tour** (📞028-9076 6386; adult/child £9/7.50; 🚌G2).

Crumlin Road Gaol

Guided tours of Belfast's notorious **Crumlin Road Gaol** (📞028-9074 1500; www.crumlinroadgaol.com; 53-55 Crumlin Rd; tour adult/child £12/7.50; ⏱10am-5.30pm, last tour 4.30pm; 🚌12B, 57) take you from the tunnel beneath Crumlin Rd, built in 1850 to convey prisoners from the courthouse across the street (and allegedly the origin of the judge's phrase 'take him down'), through the echoing halls and cramped cells of C-Wing, to the truly chilling execution chamber. Advance tour bookings are recommended. The gaol's pedestrian entrance is on Crumlin Rd; the car-park entrance is reached via Cliftonpark Ave to the north.

Entrance to Crumlin Road Gaol

If the hotel concierge is free he or she may be able to show you around; the best times are before noon or after 5pm. Don't miss John Kempster's photographs of the launch of the *Titanic;* the forgotten album was rediscovered in 2012.

HMS Caroline — Ship

(📞028-9045 4484; www.hmscaroline.co.uk; Alexandra Dock, Queen's Rd; adult/child £13.50/5; ⏱10am-5pm; 🚌G2) The UK's last surviving WWI Royal Navy cruiser has been converted into a floating museum, docked in Titanic Quarter. Audio tours take in the captain's quarters, officers' cabins, marines' mess, sick bay, engine room and galley kitchen, with interactive exhibits and a film dramatisation of HMS *Caroline's* role in the 1916 Battle of Jutland. Tickets are

Belfast

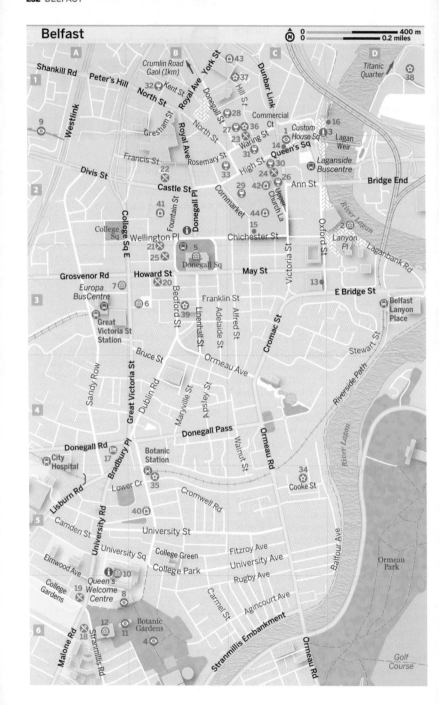

N

0 — 400 m
0 — 0.2 miles

Shankill Rd

Peter's Hill

Crumlin Road Gaol (1km)

Kent St

York St

Royal Ave

Dunbar Link

Titanic Quarter

38

9

Westlink

North St

Gresham St

Donegall St

North St

Royal Ave

Hill St

37

43

Commercial Ct

28

27 36

Waring St

23

31

High St

33

Rosemary St

Francis St

Divis St

22

Castle St

Donegall Pl

Cornmarket

Custom House Sq

14

Queen's Sq

1

16

13

Lagan Weir

Lagan Buscentre

Laganside Buscentre

Ann St

Bridge End

30

24

42

29

Upper Church La

26

River Lagan

41

Fountain St

44

15

Chichester St

Oxford St

2

Lanyon Pl

Langanbank Rd

College Sq

Wellington Pl

21

25

5

Donegall Sq

May St

Victoria St

13

E Bridge St

Grosvenor Rd

Howard St

20

Franklin St

Cromac St

Belfast Lanyon Place

Europa BusCentre

7

6

39

Adelaide St

Alfred St

Stewart St

Great Victoria St Station

Bedford St

Linenhall St

Ormeau Ave

Riverside Path

Bruce St

Great Victoria St

Dublin Rd

Maryville St

Apsley St

Donegall Pass

Walnut St

Ormeau Rd

Sandy Row

Donegall Rd

17

Bradbury Pl

Botanic Station

34

Cooke St

River Lagan

City Hospital

Lisburn Rd

Lower Cr

35

Cromwell Rd

Camden St

40

University St

Ormeau Park

University Rd

University Sq

College Green

Fitzroy Ave

University Ave

Elmwood Ave

College Gardens

Queen's Welcome Centre

10

19

8

College Park

Rugby Ave

Carmel St

Agincourt Ave

Balfour Ave

Malone Rd

12

18

11

Stranmillis Rd

Botanic Gardens

4

Stranmillis Embankment

Ormeau Rd

Golf Course

Belfast

valid for one year; buy them at the office in the pump house.

⊙ West Belfast (Gaeltacht Quarter)

Northwest of Donegall Sq, Divis St leads across the Westlink Motorway to Falls Rd and West Belfast. Though scarred by decades of civil unrest during the Troubles, this former battleground is one of the most compelling places to visit in Northern Ireland. Recent history hangs heavy in the air, but there is a noticeable spirit of optimism and hope for the future.

The main attractions are the powerful murals (p228) that chart the history of the conflict, as well as the political passions of the moment.

West Belfast grew up around the linen mills that propelled the city into late-19th-century prosperity. It was an area of low-cost, working-class housing, and even in the Victorian era was divided along religious lines. The advent of the Troubles in 1969 solidified the sectarian divide, and since 1970 the ironically named **Peace Line** (🚇G1) has separated the Loyalist and Protestant Shankill district (from the Irish *sean chill*, meaning 'old church') from the Republican and Catholic Falls district.

Despite its past reputation, the area is safe to visit. The best way to see West Belfast is on an informative and entertaining black taxi tour (p229), but there's nothing to stop you visiting under your own steam, either walking or using the shared black taxis that travel along the Falls and Shankill Rds. Alternatively, the G2 bus goes up the Falls Rd; buses 11A to 11D from Wellington Pl go along Shankill Rd.

Boat from Lagan Boat Company on the Lagan

🄖 TOURS

Belfast Food Tour   Food & Drink

(www.tasteandtour.co.uk; 4hr food tour per person £58; 🚇4C to 4E) Starting in St George's Market, these fun tours are a great way to tap into Northern Ireland's flourishing food scene, with plenty of samples of the region's most traditional dishes and innovative new produce along the way.

The company also runs other food and drink tours, including a gin jaunt (£63), Belfast whiskey walk (£60) and a beer crawl (£45). Book ahead.

Street Art Walking Tour   Walking

(www.seedheadarts.com; Commercial Ct; per person £10; ⊘noon-2pm Sun; 🚇3A, 4D, 5A, 6A) The Cathedral Quarter is covered with fascinating street art. This tour takes in some impressive works by a range of international artists, most of it commissioned as part of the **Hit the North festival** (www.capartscentre.com; ⊘May). Tours are guided by local street artists or the festival founder. The meeting point is outside the Duke of York on Commercial Ct (check availability online first).

Private tours available on request.

Lagan Boat Company   Boating

(📱028-9024 0124; www.laganboatcompany.com; Donegall Quay; adult/child £12/10; ⊘hours vary; 🚇G1, G2) The Lagan Boat Company's excellent Titanic Tour explores the docklands downstream of Lagan Weir, taking in the slipways where the liners *Titanic* and *Olympic* were launched and the huge dry dock where they could just fit, with just 23cm to spare. There's also a chance to spot seals. Tours depart from Donegall Quay near the **Bigfish sculpture** (Donegall Quay; 🚇3A, 4D, 5A, 6A). Book ahead.

Titanic Tours   Tours

(📱028-9065 9971; www.titanictours-belfast.co.uk; 3hr tour per adult/child £30/15) A three-hour luxury tour led by the great-granddaughter of one of the *Titanic's* crew, visiting various *Titanic*-related sites. For groups of two to five people; includes pickup and drop-off at your accommodation. Also offers custom full-day tours.

Belfast Pub Crawl — Tours

(📞07712-603764; www.belfastcrawl.co.uk; per person £10; ⊗8pm Fri & Sat; 🚌G2) A three-hour tour taking in four of the city's historic pubs (including a drink in each, plus live trad music), departing from the **Albert Memorial Clock Tower** (Queen's Sq; 🚌3A, 4D, 5A, 6A). Advance booking required.

🔒 SHOPPING

Space Craft — Arts & Crafts

(www.craftni.org; Fountain Centre, College St; ⊗10.30am-5.30pm; 🚌G1, G2) This shop and exhibition space displays the work of more than 40 local designers and artists. High-quality pieces include ceramics, artwork, cushions, greeting cards and jewellery. Information about each artist is displayed next to their work.

Studio Souk — Arts & Crafts

(www.studiosouk.com; 60-62 Ann St; ⊗9.30am-5.30pm Mon-Wed & Fri-Sat, to 8pm Thu, 1-5.30pm Sun; 🚌1, 2) With three floors filled with pieces by local artists and designers, Souk is the perfect place to pick up Belfast-themed items including pottery, printed canvas bags, tea towels and original artwork.

Unique Artshop — Arts & Crafts

(www.ulster.ac.uk/artshop; 25-51 York St, Ulster University; ⊗9am-5pm Mon-Fri, 11am-4pm Sat; 🚌2A to 2H) At Ulster University, this dynamic artshop sells pieces by students, alumni and other local designer makers, including graphics and prints, sculptures, pottery and ceramics, textiles, fine art, jewellery and furniture. It's also possible to commission work.

No Alibis Bookstore — Books

(www.noalibis.com; 83 Botanic Ave; ⊗9am-5.30pm Mon-Sat, 1-5pm Sun; 🚌7A to 7D) Specialising in crime fiction (and even appearing in print in Colin Bateman's *Mystery Man* series), this small, independent bookshop run by friendly and knowledgable staff hosts regular poetry readings and book signings.

Game of Thrones Tours

Game of Thrones Tours (📞028-9568 0023; www.gameofthronestours.com; adult/student £50/45; ⊗Wed-Sun Easter-Sep, reduced tours Oct-Easter; 🚌G1, G2) offers two full-day itineraries covering 11 iconic *Game of Thrones* filming locations: the Winterfell Locations Trek taking in Castle Ward and Tollymore Forest Park (where the Starks discover a dead direwolf and her pups), and the Iron Islands and Stormlands Adventure, covering sights in north Antrim including Ballintoy Harbour and the Dark Hedges.

Tours depart from **Victoria Square mall** (www.victoriasquare.com; btwn Ann & Chichester Sts; ⊗9.30am-6pm Mon-Tue, to 9pm Wed-Fri, 9am-6pm Sat, 1-6pm Sun; 🚌11A to 11D, 12A, 12B).

The drivers of the **McComb's Game of Thrones Tours** (📞028-9031 5333; www.mccombscoaches.com; 22-32 Donegall Rd; £35; ⊗office 8.30am-4.30pm; 🚌8A to 8D, 9A to 9C) have also driven the extras and equipment. Filming locations visited include the Dark Hedges (ie King's Road), Cushendun (the sea-cave where the shadow assassin was born), Ballintoy Harbour (Lordsport Harbour) and Larrybane (where the shadow assassin kills Renly). Pickup is from the **Belfast Youth Hostel** (📞028-9031 5435; www.hini.org.uk; 22-32 Donegall Rd; dm £13-16.50, tw with/without private bathroom £44/34; @🛜; 🚌8A to 8D, 9A to 9C) at 9am.

The Dark Hedges

Belfast's Titanic Connection

Perhaps the most famous vessel ever launched, RMS *Titanic* was built in Belfast's Harland & Wolff shipyard for the White Star Line. When the keel was laid in 1909, Belfast was at the height of its fame as a shipbuilding powerhouse, and the *Titanic* was promoted by White Star as the world's biggest and most luxurious ocean liner. Ironically, it was also claimed to be 'unsinkable'.

Titanic was launched from H&W's slipway No 3 on 31 May 1911, and spent almost a year being fitted out in the nearby Thompson Graving Dock before leaving Belfast for the maiden voyage on 2 April 1912. In one of the most notorious nautical disasters of all time, the ship hit an iceberg in the North Atlantic on 14 April 1912, and sank in the early hours of the following day. Of the 2228 passengers and crew on board, only 705 survived; there were only enough lifeboats for 1178 people.

Harland & Wolff shipyard
NAHLIK/SHUTTERSTOCK ©

✹ EATING
✪ City Centre
Holohan's at the Barge
Modern Irish **££**

(☏028-9023 5973; www.holohansatthebarge. co.uk; Belfast Barge, Lanyon Quay; mains lunch £9-14, dinner £16-25; ⏰1-4pm & 5-11pm Tue-Thu, 1-4pm & 5pm-midnight Fri & Sat, 1-7pm Sun; 🚌4, 6) Aboard the **Belfast Barge** (www.facebook. com/TheBelfastBarge; Lanyon Quay; adult/

child £4/3; ⏰10am-4pm Tue-Sat; 🚌3A, 5A, 5B), Holohan's is a sensational find for inspired twists on seafood and superb cooking of traditional Irish recipes such as *crabachain*, a mushroom, chestnut and tarragon fritter, and boxty, a kind of potato pancake. Desserts are excellent too, and wines from around the world are served by the glass.

Yūgo
Asian **££**

(☏028-9031 9715; www.yugobelfast.com; 3 Wellington St; mains £10-24; ⏰noon-3pm & 5-10pm; 🚌G1, G2) The contemporary styling at this compact restaurant – exposed brick walls, sleek industrial furniture and bamboo lanterns – sets the scene for fusion cooking that feels fresh and exciting; the dumplings, bao buns and rice dishes are particularly good. Service is excellent. Take a seat at the counter to watch the chefs at work.

Home
Modern Irish **££**

(☏028-9023 4946; www.homebelfast.co.uk; 22 Wellington Pl; mains £11-27; ⏰noon-4pm & 5-9.30pm Mon-Thu, noon-4pm & 5-10pm Fri, noon-3.30pm & 5-10pm Sat, 1-4pm & 5-9pm Sun; 🛜🍴; 🚌G1, G2) After beginning life as a pop-up restaurant that took the city's food scene by storm, Home moved into permanent premises where it continues to win fans for its creative use of seasonal ingredients. Its menus are tailored for vegetarians, vegans, gluten-free diners, slimmers and theatregoers.

Muddlers Club
Modern Irish **£££**

(☏028-9031 3199; www.themuddlersclubbelfast. com; Warehouse Lane, off Waring St; 6-course tasting menu £55, with wine pairings £90; ⏰noon-2.45pm & 5.30-10pm Tue-Sat; 🚌3A, 4D, 5A, 6A) Industrial-style decor, friendly service and rustic dishes that allow fresh local ingredients to shine are a winning combination at one of Belfast's best restaurants. The Muddlers Club is named after a society of Irish revolutionaries co-founded by Wolfe Tone who held meetings at the same spot in the 1790s; look for it in an alleyway between Waring St and Commercial Ct.

Holohan's at the Barge

Eipic
Modern Irish £££

(📞028-9033 1134; www.deaneseipic.com; 34-40 Howard St; lunch menu £30-45, dinner menu £45-70; ⏲noon-1.30pm Fri, 6-9.30pm Wed-Sat; 📶; 🚌G1, G2) The finest seasonal, local ingredients are given a creative twist at the flagship restaurant in Michael Deane's portfolio, the Michelin-starred Eipic. Head chef Alex Greene is originally from Dundrum in County Down; his tasting menus are full of theatrical surprises.

Mourne Seafood Bar
Seafood £££

(📞028-9024 8544; www.mourneseafood.com; 34-36 Bank St; mains £12-27.50; ⏲noon-4pm & 5-9.30pm Mon-Thu, noon-3.30pm & 5-9.45pm Fri & Sat, 1-4pm & 5-9pm Sun; 🚌10A, 10B) 🍴 Hugely popular, this informal, pub-like place is all red brick and dark wood with old oil lamps dangling from the ceiling. On the menu are oysters, meltingly sweet scallops, lobster and langoustines sourced from its own shellfish beds, along with luscious fish such as hake, seabream and sea bass. Book ahead for dinner.

🌐 South Belfast

Café Conor
Cafe £

(📞028-9066 3266; www.cafeconor.com; 11A Stranmillis Rd; breakfast £4.50-9, mains £6-13; ⏲9am-10pm Mon-Sat, to 9pm Sun; 🚌8A to 8C) Set in the glass-roofed former studio of Belfast artist William Conor, this light-filled, laid-back bistro offers a range of pastas, salads and burgers, along with favourites such as fish and chips with mushy peas and a daily pie special. The breakfast menu, which includes waffles with bacon and maple syrup, is served till 5pm.

★ Top Five Belfast Restaurants

Holohan's at the Barge (p236)

Muddlers Club (p236)

Mourne Seafood Bar (p237)

Saphyre (p238)

Eipic (p237)

Classic Victorian Pubs

Duke of York (📞028-9024 1062; www.dukeofyorkbelfast.com; 11 Commercial Ct; ⏱11.30am-11pm Mon, to 1am Tue & Wed, to 2am Thu & Fri, to midnight Sat, 3-9pm Sun; 🚌3A, 4D, 5A, 6A) In a cobbled alleyway off buzzing Hill St, the snug, traditional Duke feels like a living museum. There's regular live music; local band Snow Patrol played some of their earliest gigs here. Outside on Commercial Ct, a canopy of umbrellas leads to an outdoor area covered with murals depicting Belfast life; it takes on a street-party atmosphere in warm weather.

Kelly's Cellars (www.facebook.com/kellys. cellars; 30-32 Bank St; ⏱11.30am-1am Mon-Sat, 1pm-midnight Sun; 🚌10A, 10B) Kelly's is Belfast's oldest pub (1720) – as opposed to tavern – and was a meeting place for Henry Joy McCracken and the United Irishmen when they were planning the 1798 Rising. It pulls in a broad cross-section of Belfast society and is a great place to catch trad sessions on Saturday afternoons and during the week.

White's Tavern (www.whitesbelfast.com; 1-4 Wine Cellar Entry; ⏱noon-11pm Mon & Tue, to 1am Wed-Sat, to midnight Sun; 🚌1A to 1J, 2A to 2E) Established in 1630 but rebuilt in 1790, White's claims to be Belfast's oldest tavern (unlike a pub, a tavern provided food and lodging). It's a traditional Irish bar with an open peat fire and live music most nights.

The Duke of York
RICCAR/SHUTTERSTOCK ©

French Village Patisserie & Brasserie — Brasserie ££

(📞028-9066 4333; www.frenchvillagebakery. co.uk; 343-353 Lisburn Rd; mains lunch £8.50-11, dinner £14-22; ⏱kitchen 9am-3pm Mon-Wed, to 9pm Thu, to 10pm Fri & Sat, 11am-4pm Sun; 🚌9A to 9C) There's an air of sophistication at this excellent brasserie, serving plates like salmon nicoise and pea and shallot ravioli; the home-baked breads are worth the trip here alone. Lunch like an elegant Parisian before hitting Lisburn Rd's boutiques. Be sure to stop at the patisserie counter to pick up pastries and cakes to go.

Deanes at Queen's — Bistro ££

(📞028-9038 2111; www.michaeldeane.co.uk; 1 College Gardens; mains lunch £10-13.50, dinner £15-30; ⏱noon-3pm & 5.30-10pm Mon-Sat, 1-6pm Sun; 🚌8A to 8D) A chilled-out bar and grill from Belfast's top chef, Michael Deane, in what was once Queen's University's staff club. The menu focuses on what can be described as good-value, gourmet pub grub, taking full advantage of the Mibrasa charcoal grill. A three-course fixed price menu costs £22.

The outdoor terrace is perfect on a sunny day.

Saphyre — Modern Irish £££

(📞028-9068 8606; www.saphyrerestaurant. com; 135 Lisburn Rd; mains lunch £10, dinner £24-32; ⏱11am-3pm & 5-10pm Wed-Fri, 10am-3pm & 5-10pm Sat; 🚌9A to 9C) Spectacularly set inside the 1924 Ulsterville Presbyterian Church (behind an interior-design showroom), Saphyre serves some of the most sophisticated cooking in Belfast today. Menus change seasonally and include a five-course tasting menu (£50); each dish is a masterpiece. Brunch is available from 11am to 3pm and there's live music on Saturday from 1pm to 3pm.

🍸 DRINKING & NIGHTLIFE

Muriel's Cafe-Bar — Bar

(📞028-9033 2445; 12-14 Church Lane; ⏱11.30am-1am Mon-Fri, 10am-1am Sat, 11.30am-midnight Sun; 🚌G1, G2) Hats meet harlotry (ask who Muriel was) in this delightfully snug and welcoming bar with retro-chic decor, old sofas and armchairs, heavy fabrics in shades of olive and dark red, gilt-framed mirrors and a cast-iron fireplace. Gin is Muriel's favourite tipple and there's a range of more than 150 exotic brands to mix with your tonic.

Sunflower   Pub

(www.sunflowerbelfast.com; 65 Union St; 🕒noon-midnight Mon-Thu, to 1am Fri & Sat, 5pm-midnight Sun; 🚌2A to 2H) In a city full of buzzing bars, the Sunflower is an authentic corner pub, free from gimmicks and commercial glitz. There are local craft beers on tap, a beer garden with a pizza oven, and live music every night; check the website for the schedule. The Sunflower Folk Club meets on Thursday nights.

The security cage on the front door was once a common sight in 1980s Belfast; though it's no longer needed, the Sunflower has preserved it as a relic of Belfast's social history.

Babel Rooftop Bar   Rooftop Bar

(www.bullitthotel.com/eat-drink/babel; Ann St; 🕒3pm-1am Mon-Wed, noon-1am Thu-Sat, to midnight Sun; 🚌G1, G2) On a summer's night, a cocktail at the Bullitt Hotel's rooftop bar is hard to beat. Come on Sundays for boozy brunches (breakfast and bottomless cocktails) or tipsy tea (sandwiches, cakes, and cocktails served in a teapot).

Spaniard   Pub

(www.thespaniardbar.com; 3 Skipper St; 🕒noon-1pm Mon-Sat, to midnight Sun; 🚌3A, 4D, 5A, 6A) Specialising in rum (more than 30 kinds), this narrow, crowded bar has more atmosphere in one battered sofa than most 'style bars' have in their shiny entirety. Friendly staff, an eclectic crowd and cool tunes played at a volume that still allows you to talk: bliss. Nearby burger joint **Pablos** (www.pablosbelfast.com; 16 Church Lane; burgers £5.50-7.50; 🕒noon-10pm Tue-Thu, to 2am Fri & Sat, 2-10pm Sun; 🚌G1, G2) delivers to the bar.

Trad session at the Sunflower

 Van Morrison & CS Lewis

The little-explored neighbourhoods of East Belfast were once home to writer CS Lewis, footballer George Best and musician Van Morrison, whose former haunts have been mapped out in self-guided walking trails.

The star stop on the CS Lewis trail is a **square** (280 Newtownards Rd; 🚶; 🚌G1) dedicated to the author, with fabulous sculptures of characters from *The Chronicles of Narnia*.

Fans of 'Van the Man' Morrison can take a 3.5km neighbourhood walk past sights referenced in his lyrics, including the Hollow (immortalised in 'Brown Eyed Girl'), Cypress Ave and the modest house where he was born on Hyndford St (at number 125).

You can pick up maps at **EastSide Visitor Centre** (🕿028-9045 1900; www. eastsidepartnership.com; 278-280 Newtownards Rd; ☺8am-6pm Mon-Fri, 10am-5pm Sat & Sun; 🚌G1), or download them from www.connswatergreenway.co.uk/trails.

EastSide Visitor Centre
GERRY MCNALLY/ALAMY STOCK PHOTO ©

Love & Death Inc   Cocktail Bar
(www.loveanddeathbelfast.com; 10A Ann St; ☺4pm-1am; 🚌G1, G2) More like a cool inner-city house party than a bar, speakeasy-style Love & Death Inc is secreted up a flight of stairs above a pizza joint. Its living-room-style bar has outrageous decor, feisty cocktails and a wild nightclub in the attic on weekends.

John Hewitt   Pub
(www.thejohnhewitt.com; 51 Donegall St; ☺11.30am-1am Mon-Fri, noon-1am Sat, 7pm-1am Sun; 🚌3A, 4D, 5A, 6A) Named for the Belfast poet and socialist, the John Hewitt is one of those treasured bars that has no TV or gaming machines, just the murmur of conversation. There are trad sessions on Saturday afternoons and regular folk, jazz and bluegrass. It's owned by the Belfast Unemployed Research Centre.

✪ ENTERTAINMENT

Black Box   Arts Centre
(www.blackboxbelfast.com; 18-22 Hill St; 🚌3A, 4D, 5A, 6A) Black Box is an innovative arts venue, hosting a dynamic program of music, theatre, magic nights, spoken word events, comedy, film and more on Hill St in the heart of the Cathedral Quarter.

Belfast Empire   Live Music
(www.thebelfastempire.com; 42 Botanic Ave; entry live bands £3-22.50; ☺11.30am-1am Mon-Sat, 12.30pm-midnight Sun; 🚌7A to 7D) A converted late-Victorian church (reputed to be haunted) with three floors of entertainment, the Empire is a legendary live-music venue. Look out for stand-up comedy and quiz nights too.

MAC   Arts Centre
(Metropolitan Arts Centre; www.themaclive. com; 10 Exchange St West; 🚌3A, 4D, 5A, 6A) The MAC is a beautifully designed venue overlooking the neoclassical St Anne's Sq development, with its two theatres hosting regular performances of drama, stand-up comedy and talks, including shows for children. The centre's three galleries stage a rolling program of exhibitions, which are generally free. There's also a cafe here.

Ulster Hall   Concert Venue
(www.ulsterhall.co.uk; 34 Bedford St; 🚌7A to 7D) Dating from 1862, Ulster Hall is a popular venue for a range of events including rock concerts, lunchtime organ recitals and performances by the Ulster Orchestra (www.ulsterorchestra.org.uk).

MAC

An Droichead
Live Music

(www.androichead.com; 20 Cooke St, Lower Ormeau; ⊟7A to 7D) This Irish cultural centre is a great place to hear live Irish folk music performed by big names from around the country, as well as up-and-coming local talent. It also offers Irish-language courses, stages traditional dance and *céilidh* workshops.

ℹ INFORMATION

DANGERS & ANNOYANCES

Even at the height of the Troubles, Belfast wasn't a particularly dangerous city for tourists. It's still best, however, to avoid the so-called 'interface areas' – near the Peace Lines in West Belfast, Crumlin Rd and the Short Strand (just east of Queen's Bridge) – after dark.

If in doubt about any area, ask at your hotel or hostel.

You will notice a more obvious security presence than elsewhere in the UK and Ireland, such as armoured police Land Rovers and fortified police stations. There are door attendants at many city-centre pubs.

Dissident Republican groups continue a campaign of violent attacks aimed at police and military targets, but have very little public support. Security alerts usually have no effect on visiting tourists (other than roads being closed), but be aware of the potential danger. You can follow the Police Service of Northern Ireland (PSNI) on Twitter (@policeserviceni) and receive immediate notification of any alerts.

TOURIST INFORMATION

Visit Belfast Welcome Centre (☑028-9024 6609; www.visitbelfast.com; 9 Donegall Sq N; ⊙9am-7pm Mon-Sat, 11am-4pm Sun Jun-Sep, 9am-5.30pm Mon-Sat, 11am-4pm Sun Oct-May; 🛜; ⊟G1, G2) Stacks of information about Northern Ireland. Services include left luggage (not overnight), tour and accommodation bookings, bus-ticket sales and wi-fi.

GETTING THERE & AWAY

AIR

Belfast International Airport (Aldergrove; ☎028-9448 4848; www.belfastairport.com; Airport Rd) Located 30km northwest of the city. Flights serve the UK and Europe.

George Best Belfast City Airport (BHD; ☎028-9093 9093; www.belfastcityairport.com; Airport Rd) Located 6km northeast of Belfast city centre; flights serve the UK and Europe.

BUS

There is an **information point** (Great Victoria St, Great Northern Mall; ⊗8am-6pm Mon-Fri, 8.30am-5pm Sat) at Belfast's **Europa Bus Centre** (☎028-9066 6630; www.translink.co.uk; Great Victoria St, Great Northern Mall; ⊗5am-11pm Mon-Fri, 5.45am-11pm Sat, to 10.15pm Sun), where you can pick up regional bus timetables. Contact **Translink** (☎028-9066 6630; www.translink.co.uk; Great Victoria St, Europa Bus Centre) for timetable and fares information.

Laganside Buscentre (Oxford St) Near the River Lagan; mainly for buses to eastern County Down, including Bangor and Newtownards.

Aircoach (☎028-9033 0655; www.aircoach.ie; single/return adult £14/21, child £8/12) Offers an hourly bus service between Belfast and Dublin City Centre (2¼ hours) via Dublin Airport (1¾ hours). Discounted fares available when you book online. The bus stop is on Glengall St.

National Express (☎0871 781 8181; www.nationalexpress.com) Runs a daily coach service between Belfast and London (from £41 one-way, 15½ hours) via the Cairnryan ferry, Dumfries, Manchester and Birmingham. Buses depart from Glengall St.

Scottish Citylink (☎0871 266 3333; www.citylink.co.uk; Great Victoria St, Great Northern Mall) Operates three buses a day from Glasgow to Belfast (£28 to £32, six hours), via the Cairnryan ferry.

TRAIN

For information on train fares and timetables, contact **Translink** (☎028-9066 6630; www.translink.co.uk; Great Victoria St, Europa Bus Centre).

Belfast Lanyon Place (East Bridge St) East of the city centre. Trains run to Dublin and all destinations in Northern Ireland.

Donegall Sq, Belfast

Albert Memorial Clock Tower (p235)

Great Victoria Street Station (Great Victoria St, Great Northern Mall) Next to the Europa Bus Centre. Trains run to Portadown, Lisburn, Bangor, Larne Harbour and Derry.

Northern Ireland Railways (NIR; ☑028-9066 6630; www.translink.co.uk/Services/NI-Railways) Runs four routes from Belfast. One links with the system in the Republic via Newry to Dublin; the other three go east to Bangor, northeast to Larne and northwest to Derry via Coleraine.

❶ GETTING AROUND

Belfast's integrated public-transport system includes buses connecting both airports to the central bus and train stations.

Metro (☑028-9066 6630; www.translink.co.uk) bus services depart from various stops on and around Donegall Sq, at City Hall and along Queen St. You can pick up a free bus map (and buy tickets) from the **Metro kiosk** (Donegall Sq) at the northwest corner of the square.

The **Belfast Visitor Pass** (per one/two/three days £6.50/11/14.50) allows unlimited travel on bus and train services in Belfast and around, and discounts on admission to Titanic Belfast and other attractions.

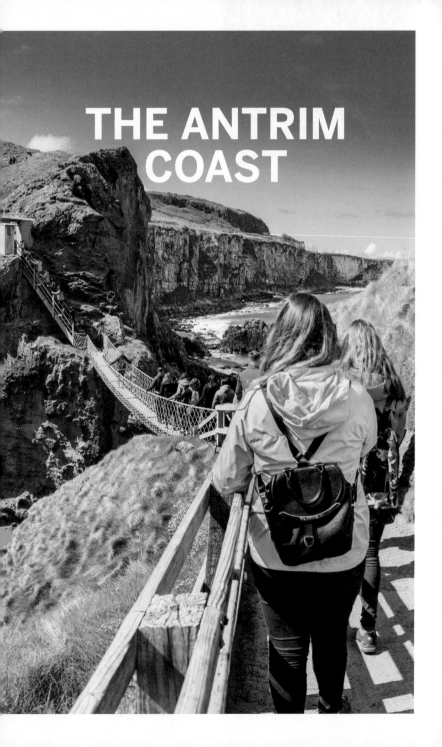

THE ANTRIM COAST

The Antrim Coast

Northern Ireland's north coast is a giant geology classroom. The ocean has laid bare the black basalt and white chalk that underlie much of County Antrim, and dissected the rocks into a scenic extravaganza of sea stacks, pinnacles, cliffs and caves. Extraordinary rock formations and ruined castles made the region an atmospheric backdrop for hit TV series Game of Thrones, filmed in numerous locations.

To the west lies the spirited city of Derry. Ireland's only walled city sits alongside a broad sweep of the River Foyle and echoes with centuries of often turbulent history.

One Day on the Antrim Coast

With one day to spare between Belfast and Derry, drive the Antrim coast road (including the Torr Head Scenic Road) to Ballycastle. After a lunch of fish and chips at **Morton's** (p259) continue to the Giant's Causeway and spend the afternoon exploring the fantastic coastal scenery before continuing the scenic drive to Derry.

Two Days on the Antrim Coast

With two days you can afford to relax with an overnight at the Giant's Causeway or Bushmills. On day one do the coastal drive to Ballycastle; in the afternoon visit **Carrick-a-Rede Rope Bridge** (p257) and the pretty harbour at Ballintoy. Explore the Causeway in the relative peace of evening and/or the following morning; next day take in **Dunluce Castle** (p255) and Portrush.

Previous page: Carrick-a-Rede Rope Bridge (p257)
VIOLETA MELETI/SHUTTERSTOCK ©

Derry (Londonderry) Map (p263)

Arriving at the Antrim Coast

Bus Ulsterbus services connect the region's towns and villages. Contact Translink for timetable and fare information. Additional connections are provided by the **Causeway Rambler** (p251) seasonal bus service.

Train The Londonderry Line links Derry to Belfast, stopping in Coleraine (with connections to Portrush), Ballymena and Antrim Town. For information on train fares and timetables, contact Translink.

Where to Stay

The greatest breadth of accommodation options can be found in Derry (Londonderry); as well as hotels, there are B&Bs aplenty, often located in beautiful Georgian or Victorian buildings. If you want to be closer to sights such as the Giant's Causeway and the Carrick-a-Rede Rope Bridge (particularly if you're relying on public transport), the coastal towns of Portrush and Ballycastle offer plenty of good lodgings.

S-F/SHUTTERSTOCK ©

Giant's Causeway

This spectacular rock formation – a national nature reserve and Northern Ireland's only Unesco World Heritage Site – is one of Ireland's most impressive and atmospheric landscape features.

When you first see it you'll understand why the ancients believed the Causeway was not a natural feature. The vast expanse of regular, closely packed, hexagonal stone columns gently beneath the waves looks for all the world like the handiwork of giants.

Visiting the Giant's Causeway itself is free of charge but you pay to use the car park on a combined ticket with the **Giant's Causeway Visitor Experience** (☎028-2073 1855; www.nationaltrust.org.uk; 60 Causeway Rd; adult/child £12.50/6.25; ⊘9am-7pm Jun-Sep, to 6pm Mar-May & Oct, to 5pm Nov-Feb) ☛; parking-only tickets aren't available.

The Making of the Causeway

The story goes that the Irish giant Finn McCool built the Causeway so he could cross the sea to fight the Scottish giant

Great For...

☑ **Don't Miss**

The clifftop views from the Chimney Tops headland.

ℹ Need to Know

www.nationaltrust.org.uk; ⊘dawn-dusk `FREE`

✕ Take A Break

There's a cafe in the visitor centre, but the nearby **Nook** (☑028-2073 2993; 48 Causeway Rd; mains £10.50-14; ⊘kitchen 11am-9pm Mar-Oct, to 6pm Nov-Feb) offers a more convivial atmosphere.

★ Top Tip

Try to visit midweek or out of season to experience the Causeway at its most evocative.

Benandonner. Benandonner pursued Finn back across the Causeway, but in turn took fright and fled back to Scotland, ripping up the Causeway as he went. All that remains are its ends – the Giant's Causeway in Ireland, and the island of Staffa in Scotland (which has similar rock formations).

The more prosaic scientific explanation is that the Causeway rocks were formed 60 million years ago, when a thick layer of molten basaltic lava flowed along a valley in the existing chalk beds. As the lava flow cooled and hardened – from the top and bottom surfaces inwards – it contracted, creating a pattern of hexagonal cracks at right angles to the cooling surfaces (think of mud contracting and cracking in a hexagonal pattern as a lake bed dries out). As solidification progressed towards the centre of the flow, the cracks spread down from the top and up from the bottom, until the lava was completely solid. Erosion has cut into the lava flow, and the basalt has split along the contraction cracks, creating the hexagonal columns.

Exploring the Causeway

From the car park, it's an easy 10- to 15-minute walk downhill on a tarmac road (wheelchair accessible) to the Giant's Causeway itself (a shuttle bus also plies the route). However, a much more interesting approach on foot is to follow the cliff-top path northeast for 2km to the **Chimney Tops** headland, which has an excellent view of the Causeway and the coastline to the west, including Inishowen and Malin Head.

This pinnacled promontory was bombarded by ships of the Spanish Armada in 1588, who thought it was Dunluce Castle, and the wreck of the Spanish galleon *Girona* lies just off the tip of the headland. Return towards the car park and about halfway back descend the **Shepherd's**

Steps (signposted) to a lower-level footpath that leads down to the Causeway. Allow 1½ hours for the round trip.

Alternatively, you can visit the Causeway first, then follow the lower coastal path as far as the **Amphitheatre** viewpoint at Port Reostan, passing impressive rock formations such as the **Organ** (a stack of vertical basalt columns resembling organ pipes), and return by climbing the Shepherd's Steps.

You can also follow the clifftop path east as far as Dunseverick or beyond.

The superb, ecofriendly Giant's Causeway Visitor Experience (p248), built into the hillside and walled in by tall black basalt slabs that mimic the basalt columns of the Causeway, houses an exhibition explaining the geology of the region, as well as a tourist information desk, restaurant and shop. It's cheaper if you arrive on foot, bicycle or by public transport; admission includes an audio guide.

Wreck of the Girona

The little bay 1km to the northeast of the Giant's Causeway is called Port na Spaniagh (Bay of the Spaniards). It was here, in October 1588, that the *Girona,* a ship of the Spanish Armada, was driven onto the rocks by a storm.

The *Girona* had escaped the famous confrontation with Sir Walter Raleigh's fleet in the English Channel but, along with many other fleeing Spanish ships, had been driven north around Scotland and Ireland by bad weather. Though designed for a crew of 500, when she struck the rocks she was loaded with 1300 people – mostly survivors gathered from other shipwrecks – including

the cream of the Spanish aristocracy. Barely a dozen survived.

Somhairle Buidhe (Sorley Boy) MacDonnell (1505–90), the constable of nearby Dunluce Castle, salvaged gold and cannons from the wreck, and used the money to extend and modernise his fortress – cannons from the ship can still be seen on the castle's landward wall. But it wasn't until 1968 that the wreck site was excavated by a team of archaeological divers. They recovered magnificent treasure of gold, silver and precious stones, as well as sailors' everyday possessions, which are now on display in Belfast's Ulster Museum (p230).

Getting There & Away

As well as the seasonal **Causeway Rambler** (Bus 402; ☎028-9066 6630; www. translink.co.uk; day ticket adult/child £9.50/4.75; ⊙Mar-Sep) and the Giant's Causeway & Bushmills Railway (p255), bus 172 from Ballycastle (£4.60, 30 minutes, eight daily Monday to Friday, three Saturday and Sunday) to Coleraine (£3.60, 25 minutes) and Bushmills (£2.10, five minutes) stops here year-round. From Coleraine, trains run to Belfast or Derry.

> ★ **Local Knowledge**
>
> A pleasant way to reach the Giant's Causeway is the 45-minute walk from Bushmills on the footpath running alongside the Giant's Causeway & Bushmills Railway.

SERG ZASTAVKIN/SHUTTERSTOCK ©

> ★ **Did You Know?**
>
> More than one million people visited the Giant's Causeway in 2018, making it Northern Ireland's most popular tourist attraction.

Causeway Coast Way

This spectacular stretch of the Causeway Coast Way is one of the finest coastal walks in Ireland. Be prepared: check tide times in advance.

Start Carrick-a-Rede Rope Bridge
Distance 16.5km
Duration Four to six hours

Take A Break...
Bring a picnic lunch with you and stop at one of the viewpoints along the way; if the weather isn't too wild, Dunseverick Castle is the perfect spot for a scenic meal.

4 The path at Dunseverick crosses a footbridge above a waterfall before reaching ruined **Dunseverick Castle**.

5 Named after an 18th-century clergyman and amateur geologist, **Hamilton's Seat** viewpoint enjoys a spectacular panorama of 100m-high sea cliffs, stacks and pinnacles.

6 The winding **Shepherd's Steps** (p248) cut a staircase into steep cliffs, descending to the shore where a path leads to the Giant's Causeway.

Classic Photo Carrick-a-Rede Rope Bridge

1 Test your nerve on the swaying **Carrick-a-Rede Rope Bridge** (p257) slung between sea cliffs and an island.

2 Next up is **White Park Bay** (p257), a dramatic 2km-long sweep of white sand. The going here is easiest at low tide, when you can walk on the firm sand.

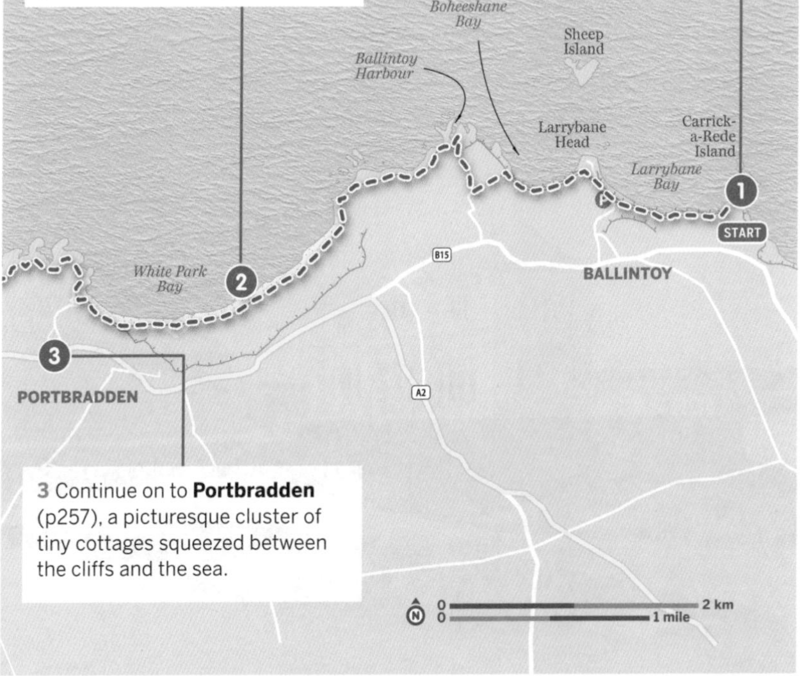

Boheeshane Bay

Sheep Island

Ballintoy Harbour

Larrybane Head

Carrick-a-Rede Island

Larrybane Bay

1

START

B15

White Park Bay **2**

BALLINTOY

3

PORTBRADDEN

A2

3 Continue on to **Portbradden** (p257), a picturesque cluster of tiny cottages squeezed between the cliffs and the sea.

N 0 —————— 2 km
0 —————— 1 mile

Portrush

The seaside resort of Portrush (Port Rois) bursts at the seams with holidaymakers in high season and, not surprisingly, many of its attractions are focused unashamedly on good old-fashioned family fun. However, it's also one of Ireland's top surfing centres and home to the North's most prestigious golf club, host of the 2019 Open Championship. In preparation for the tournament, money has been spent on beautifying the town centre with new granite paving, benches and lighting, and renovating the train station.

SIGHTS & ACTIVITIES

East Strand   Beach

(Curran Strand) Portrush's main attraction is the beautiful sandy East Strand beach that stretches for 3km to the east of town, ending at the scenic chalk cliffs of Whiterocks.

Royal Portrush Golf Club   Golf

(☎028-7082 2311; www.royalportrushgolfclub. com; Dunluce Rd; green fees Dunluce £90-220, Valley £25-50) Spectacularly situated alongside the Atlantic at the town's eastern edge, 1888-founded Royal Portrush first hosted the Open Championship in 1951. It's home to two courses: the Dunluce, with its water's-edge White Rock (5th) and ravine-set Calamity (14th) holes, and the Valley. Substantial improvements were made to the Dunluce Course ahead of hosting the Open Championship again in 2019, including the building of five new greens and two new holes. See the website for visitor times.

EATING

Arcadia   Cafe £

(www.arcadiaportrush.co.uk; East Strand; mains £3-6; ⊙9am-5pm Apr-Sep) A Portrush landmark, this 1920s art deco pavilion houses a breezy beach cafe on the ground floor, serving big breakfasts, bagels, salads and ice cream for a post-surf refuel, and a free art gallery on the upper floor, which also hosts workshops and classes (yoga, painting et al).

Arcadia

JOAQUIN OSSORIO CASTILLO/SHUTTERSTOCK ©

Ocho Tapas   Spanish ££

(📞028-7082 4110; www.ochotapas.com;
92-94 Main St; tapas £4-12; ☺5-9pm Mon-
Thu, 5-9.30pm Fri, 12.30-2.30pm & 5-9.30pm
Sat, 12.30-2.30pm & 5-9pm Sun) After living
in Spain for 20 years, chef Trudy Brolly
opened this authentic tapas restaurant in
her hometown of Portrush. Locally sourced
and Spanish ingredients are combined in
dishes such as Fivemiletown goat's cheese
croquettas with beetroot panna cotta and
cherry sour cream. Order three to four
tapas per person, or six of the smaller,
exquisite *pintxos*, with sherry pairings.

GETTING THERE & AWAY

The bus terminal is near the Dunluce Centre.
Buses 140A to 140D link Portrush with Portstewart
(£2.50, 10 minutes, every 20 minutes) and Coleraine (£2.80, 20 minutes). It's also served by the
seasonal Causeway Rambler (p251) bus service.

The train station is just south of the harbour.
Portrush is served by trains from Coleraine
(£2.40, 12 minutes, hourly), where there are
connections to Belfast and Derry.

Bushmills

The nearest town to the Giant's Causeway
(5km), Bushmills has long been a place
of pilgrimage for connoisseurs of Irish
whiskey, and is an attractive stop for hikers
exploring the Causeway Coast.

SIGHTS & ACTIVITIES

Old Bushmills Distillery   Distillery

(📞028-2073 3218; www.bushmills.com; 2
Distillery Rd; tour adult/child £9/5; ☺9.15am-
4.45pm Mon-Sat, noon-4.45pm Sun) Bushmills
is the world's oldest licensed distillery,
having been given permission to produce
whiskey by King James I in 1608. The
whiskey is made with Irish barley and water
from St Columb's Rill, a tributary of the River Bush, and matured in oak barrels. During
ageing, the alcohol content drops from
around 60% to 40%; the spirit lost through
evaporation is known as 'the angels' share'.

Dunluce Castle

The ruins of **Dunluce Castle** (87 Dunluce
Rd; adult/child £5.50/3.50; ☺10am-5pm
Feb-Nov, to 4pm Dec & Jan, last entry 30min
before closing) perch atop a dramatic
basalt crag 5km east of Portrush, a
one-hour walk away along the coastal
path. A narrow bridge leads from the
former guest lodgings and stables on
the mainland across a dizzying gap to
the main part of the fortress. Below, a
path leads down from the gatehouse to
the Mermaid's Cave beneath the castle
crag (the path was closed for repairs at
research time).

In the 16th and 17th centuries, the
castle was the seat of the MacDonnell
family (the earls of Antrim from 1620),
who built a Renaissance-style manor
house within the walls.

RAINBOW79/GETTY IMAGES ©

After the tour, you can try a free sample of
your choice from Bushmills' range.

Giant's Causeway
& Bushmills Railway   Train

(📞028-2073 2844; infogcbr@btconnect.com;
return adult/child £5/3) Trains run at noon,
2pm and 4pm from the Causeway, returning at 12.30pm, 2.30pm and 4.30pm from
Bushmills, daily in July and August, and on
weekends only from Easter to June and
September and October.

Brought from a private line on the shores
of Lough Neagh, the narrow-gauge line and
locomotives (two steam and one diesel)
follow the route of a 19th-century tourist

 **Portstewart
Strand**

Portstewart Strand (www.nationaltrust.
org.uk/portstewart-strand) The broad,
2.5km beach of Portstewart Strand is
a 20-minute walk south of the centre
along a coastal path, or a short bus ride
along Strand Rd. Parking is allowed on
the firm sand, which can accommodate
over 1000 cars (open year-round, £6.50
per car from Easter to October).

Harry's Shack (📞028-7083 1783; www.
facebook.com/HarrysShack; Portstewart
Strand; mains £12-19; ⏱11am-8.30pm
Mon-Thu, 11am-9pm Fri, 10am-9pm Sat,
10am-7pm Sun) Bang on Portstewart
Strand beach, this wooden shack has
one of the north coast's best restaurants (book ahead for lunch and
dinner). Harry's uses fruit, vegetables
and herbs from its own organic farm
plus local meat and seafood in simple
but sensational dishes like megrim sole
with cockles and seaweed butter, and
Mulroy Bay mussels in Irish cider.

WWW.DEIRDREGREGG.COM/GETTY IMAGES ©

tramway for 3km from Bushmills to below
the Giant's Causeway Visitor Experience.

A path alongside the full length of the
Giants Causeway & Bushmills Railway track
makes for a pleasant 5km walk or cycle.

❌ EATING

Bushmills Inn   Irish ££

(📞028-2073 3000; www.bushmillsinn.com; 9
Dunluce Rd; mains lunch £7-13, dinner £14-28;
⏱noon-9.30pm Mon-Sat, 12.30-3pm & 5-9.30pm

Sun; 📶) Set in the old 17th-century stables
of the Bushmills Inn, this haven has
intimate wooden booths and blazing fires,
and uses fresh local produce in dishes like
Greencastle cod, Laney Valley lamb and
traditional Dalriada Cullen skink (wood-
smoked haddock poached in cream, with
poached eggs and new potatoes). Book
ahead. There's trad music in the bar on
Saturday nights.

Tartine   Irish ££

(📞028-2073 1044; www.distillersarms.com;
140 Main St; mains £12-24; ⏱5-8pm Wed &
Thu, to 9pm Fri, to 9.30pm Sat, 12.30-2.15pm
& 5-7.30pm Sun) Inside a former pub, with
bare boards, exposed stone and glowing
fire, Tartine's three interconnecting dining
rooms are adorned with Irish art. Local
produce is given a French twist: Guinness
and molasses cured salmon on a baked
seafood thermidor and Irish oysters in a
Pernod-infused cream.

A two-course menu for £19, including a
drink, is available until 6.30pm.

Giant's Causeway
to Ballycastle

The pretty village of Ballintoy (Baile an
Tuaighe) tumbles down the hillside to a
picture-postcard harbour, better known to
Game of Thrones fans as the Iron Islands'
Lordsports Harbour (among other scenes
filmed here). The restored limekiln on
the quayside once made quicklime using
stone from the chalk cliffs and coal from
Ballymoney.

Ballintoy lies roughly halfway between
Ballycastle and the Giant's Causeway on
the most scenic stretch of the Causeway
Coast, with sea cliffs of contrasting black
basalt and white chalk, rocky islands and
broad sweeps of sandy beach.

The main attractions can be reached by
car or bus, but the 16.5km stretch between
the Carrick-a-Rede car park and the Giant's
Causeway is best enjoyed on a walk (p252)
following the waymarked **Causeway Coast
Way** (www.walkni.com).

STEFANO_VALERI/SHUTTERSTOCK ©

Portbradden

About 9.5km east of the Giant's Causeway is the tiny seaside hamlet of **Portbradden**, with half a dozen harbourside houses. Visible from Portbradden and accessible via the next junction off the A2 is the spectacular **White Park Bay**, with its wide, sweeping sandy beach. Some 3km further east is **Ballintoy**.

◎ SIGHTS

Carrick-a-Rede Rope Bridge   Bridge
(📞028-2073 3335; www.nationaltrust.org. uk/carrick-a-rede; 119 Whitepark Rd, Ballintoy; adult/child £9/4.50; ⊙9.30am-6pm Apr-Oct, to 3.30pm Nov-Mar) This 20m-long, 1m-wide bridge of wire rope spans the chasm between the sea cliffs and the little island of Carrick-a-Rede, swaying 30m above the rock-strewn water. Crossing the bridge is perfectly safe, but frightening if you don't have a head for heights, especially if it's breezy (in high winds the bridge is closed). From the island, views take in Rathlin Island and Fair Head to the east.

There's a small National Trust information centre and **cafe** (Whitepark Rd, Carrick-a-Rede; mains £3.50-6; ⊙9.30am-5.15pm) at the car park.

The impetus for the crossing first came from fishermen, who would stretch their nets out from the tip of the island to intercept the passage of salmon migrating along the coast to their home rivers.

Now firmly on the tour-bus route, Carrick-a-Rede has become so popular that the National Trust has introduced ticketed one-hour time slots to visit the bridge. Book your ticket online in advance, especially during high season. Mornings

Top Five Antrim Coast Photo Ops
Giant's Causeway (p248)

Dunluce Castle (p255)

White Park Bay

Carrick-a-Rede Rope Bridge (p257)

Torr Head Scenic Road (p260)

 Rathlin Island

Rathlin is famous for its spectacular coastal scenery and the seabirds, especially puffins, who nest on the sea cliffs at the island's western tip.

From the harbour in Church Bay, there are three main walking routes: 7km to the **Rathlin West Light Seabird Centre** (☎028-2076 3948; www.rspb.org.uk/rathlin island; adult/child £5/2.50; ☺10am-5pm May-Aug, 11am-4pm Apr & Sep), to the East Lighthouse (3km) and to the Rue Point Lighthouse in the south (4.5km). The roads are all suitable for cycling; **bikes** (☎028-2076 3954; john_jennifer@btinternet.com; per day £10; ☺10am-5pm May-Sep) can be hired at Soerneog View Hostel, south of the harbour (book ahead; cash only).

There are also some fabulous off-road walking trails including the Ballyconagan Trail to the Old Coastguard Station on the north coast.

Rathlin Island Ferry (☎028-2076 9299; www.rathlinballycastleferry.com; return trip adult/child/bicycle £12/6/3.30) operates daily from Ballycastle; advance bookings are essential. From April to mid-September there are up to 10 crossings a day, half of which are express services (25 minutes), the rest via a slower car ferry (40 minutes). In winter, the service is reduced.

McGinn's **Puffin Bus** (☎07752 861788, 07759 935192; adult/child £5/3) shuttles visitors between the ferry and Rathlin West Light Seabird Centre from April to September; contact the company for other transport requests.

Lighthouse on Rathlin Island
MIKEDRAGO.CZ/SHUTTERSTOCK ©

tend to be quieter; the coaches arrive in the afternoon.

🍴 EATING

Red Door Cottage
Irish £
(☎028-2076 9048; www.facebook.com/thered doortearoom; 14A Harbour Rd; mains £7-11; ☺11am-4pm Tue-Sun May-Oct, 10am-4pm Sat & Sun Mar & Apr) Fronted by a fire-engine-red door, this little cottage sits 200m off the main coast road along the side road to Ballintoy Harbour. Everything is homemade: soups, chowders, Irish stew, burgers and cakes. The garden's picnic tables are idyllic in the sunshine; when it's chilly there's a turf fire indoors. It's worth booking ahead in peak holiday season.

Roark's Kitchen
Cafe £
(Harbour Rd, Ballintoy Harbour; mains £4.25-9; ☺11am-5.30pm Apr-Sep, noon-4pm Oct-Mar; 🅿) On the quayside at Ballintoy Harbour, this cute little chalk-built tearoom serves teas, coffees, ice cream, home-baked apple, cherry and rhubarb tart, and lunch dishes such as Irish stew or chicken and ham pie. Cash only.

ⓘ GETTING THERE & AWAY

Bus 172 (eight daily Monday to Friday, three daily Saturday and Sunday) connects Ballintoy with Coleraine (£6.20, 40 minutes), Ballycastle (£3.10, 20 minutes), Giant's Causeway (£3.10, 20 minutes) and Bushmills (£3.60, 25 minutes). Causeway Rambler (p251) buses cover the route in season.

Ballycastle

The harbour town and holiday resort of Ballycastle (Baile an Chaisil) marks the eastern end of the Causeway Coast. It's a pretty town with a family-friendly promenade, a good bucket-and-spade beach and a thriving food scene. Ferries to Rathlin Island depart from here. Castle St and the Diamond are where most of the action is.

◉ SIGHTS

Kinbane Castle   Castle

(Whitepark Rd) FREE On a limestone headland jutting out from the basalt cliffs, with
stupendous views of Rathlin Island and
Scotland, sits this castle, now ruined. It
was built in 1547 by Colla MacDonnell (son
of Alexander MacDonnell, lord of Islay and
Kintyre, and Catherine, daughter of the
lord of Ardnamurchan), then rebuilt in 1555
following an English siege. It was inhabited
until the 17th century, when it was abandoned. From the car park, 140 steep steps
lead down to the castle.

Marconi Memorial   Monument

In the harbour car park, a plaque at the
foot of a rock pinnacle commemorates
the day in 1898 when Guglielmo Marconi's
assistants contacted Rathlin Island by
radio from Ballycastle to prove to Lloyds of
London that wireless communication was a
viable proposition. The idea was to send notice to London or Liverpool of ships arriving
safely after a transatlantic crossing – most

vessels on this route would have to pass
through the channel north of Rathlin.

✘ EATING

Morton's Fish & Chips   Fish & Chips £

(☎028-2076 1100; The Harbour, Bayview Rd;
dishes £2.30-7; ☺noon-8pm Sun-Thu, to 9pm Fri
& Sat) Fish and chips don't come fresher:
local boats unload their daily catch right
alongside this little harbourside hut. The
cod, haddock, scallops, scampi and crab
cakes, along with chips made from locally
farmed potatoes, draw long queues in
summer (expect to wait).

Thyme & Co   Cafe £

(☎028-2076 9851; www.thymeandco.co.uk;
5 Quay Rd; mains £6-9; ☺9am-4pm Mon-Tue,
Thu & Fri, 9am-3.30pm & 5-9pm Sat, 10am-3pm
Sun; 🛜📶) 🍃 Lush salads, shepherd's pie,
salmon and egg crumble and plenty of
vegetarian and vegan options are among
the homemade dishes prepared using local
produce at this welcoming cafe. Many of
its cakes and bakes are gluten free; there's

Ballycastle Harbour

Torr Head
Scenic Road

A few kilometres east of Ballycastle, a minor road signposted 'Scenic Route' branches north off the A2. This alternative route to Cushendun is not for the faint-hearted driver (nor for caravans), as it clings, precarious and narrow, to steep slopes high above the sea. Side roads lead off to the main points of interest. On a clear day there are superb views across the sea to Scotland, from the Mull of Kintyre to the peaks of Arran.

The first turn-off ends at the National Trust car park at Coolanlough, the starting point for a waymarked 5km return hike to **Fair Head**. The second turn-off leads steeply down to **Murlough Bay**. From the parking area at the end of this road, you can walk north along the shoreline to some ruined miners cottages (10 minutes); coal and chalk were once mined in the cliffs above, and burned in a limekiln (south of the car park) to make quicklime.

The third turn-off leads you past some ruined coastguard houses to the rocky headland of **Torr Head**, crowned with a 19th-century coastguard station (abandoned in the 1920s). This is Ireland's closest point to Scotland – the Mull of Kintyre is a mere 19km away across the North Channel. In late spring and summer, a fixed-net salmon fishery operates here. The ancient ice house beside the approach road was once used to store the catch.

SUSANNE POMMER/SHUTTERSTOCK ©

excellent coffee too. Saturday nights offer various specials, such as BYO pizza nights.

❶ GETTING THERE & AWAY

The bus station is on Station Rd, just east of the Diamond. Bus 217 links Ballycastle with Ballymena (£7.20, 50 minutes, hourly Monday to Friday, five Saturday), where you can connect to Belfast.

Bus 172 goes along the coast to Coleraine (£7.20, one hour, eight daily Monday to Friday, three Saturday and Sunday) via Ballintoy, the Giant's Causeway and Bushmills. The seasonal Causeway Rambler (p251) covers the same route.

Glens of Antrim

The northeastern corner of Antrim is a high plateau of black basalt lava overlying beds of white chalk. Along the coast, between Cushendun and Glenarm, the plateau has been dissected by a series of scenic, glacier-gouged valleys known as the Glens of Antrim.

Cushendun & Cushendall

The pretty seaside village of Cushendun is famous for its distinctive Cornish-style cottages, now owned by the National Trust. Built between 1912 and 1925 at the behest of the local landowner, Lord Cushendun, they were designed by Clough Williams-Ellis, the architect of Portmeirion in north Wales.

Cushendall is a holiday centre with a small and shingly beach. The village, which can be a traffic bottleneck, sits at the foot of Glenballyeamon, overlooked by the prominent flat-topped hill of Lurigethan.

◎ SIGHTS & ACTIVITIES

Cushendun has a wide sandy **beach**, various short **coastal walks** and some impressive **caves** – a *Game of Thrones* filming location – cut into the overhanging conglomerate sea cliffs south of the village (follow the trail around the far end of the holiday apartments south of the river mouth).

Some 6km north of the village on the A2 road to Ballycastle is **Loughareema**, also known as the Vanishing Lake. Three streams flow in but none flow out. The lough fills up to a respectable size (400m long and 6m deep) after heavy rain, but the water gradually drains away through fissures in the underlying limestone, leaving a dry lake bed.

From the car park beside the beach in Cushendall (follow the golf-club signs), a coastal path leads 1km north to the picturesque ruins of **Layd Old Church**, with views across to Ailsa Craig (a prominent conical island also known as 'Paddy's Milestone') and the Scottish coast. Founded by the Franciscans, it was used as a parish church from the early 14th century until 1790.

EATING

McCollam's

Pub

(Johnny Joe's; ☎028-2177 2849; www.johnny joes.co.uk; 23 Mill St; ⊙noon-11.30pm daily, kitchen noon-9pm Wed-Sun) Locally known as Johnny Joe's, this rhubarb-coloured pub is the town's liveliest. The original ground-floor bar was built in the 1800s; behind it is a tiny lounge dominated by an old range cooker. There are regular trad music sessions and great craic. The excellent restaurant **Upstairs at Joes** (mains £13 to £22) serves modern Irish dishes and daily seafood specials.

GETTING THERE & AWAY

Bus 150 links Cushendall with Cushendun (£2.80, 15 minutes, six daily Monday to Friday, three Saturday), Glenariff Forest Park (£3.10, 15 minutes) and Ballymena (£6.20, one hour).

Glenarm

Delightful little Glenarm (Gleann Arma) is the oldest village in the Glens of Antrim. It's well worth a visit for the fabulous gardens at Glenarm Castle, rows of pretty Georgian houses and forest park.

Cushendun Caves

◉ SIGHTS & ACTIVITIES

Glenarm Castle & Walled Garden   Castle

(www.glenarmcastle.com; 2 Castle Lane; walled garden adult/child £6/3; ⊗garden 10am-4pm Mar & Oct, to 5pm Apr-Sep) Since 1750 Glenarm has been the family seat of the McDonnell family, earls of Antrim; it's currently the home of Lord and Lady Dunluce. The castle itself is closed to the public – except during the Tulip Festival on the May bank-holiday weekend, and during the Dalriada Festival in July – but you can visit the lovely walled garden and take a walk around the estate along the castle trail. Admission is free for children under 12.

The estate's organic farm is renowned for its Glenarm shorthorn beef; the smokehouse produces organic smoked salmon. Both are sold at the Glenarm Castle Tea Room & Shop.

Derry (Londonderry)

Northern Ireland's second-largest city continues to flourish as an artistic and cultural hub. Derry's city centre was given a striking makeover for its year as the UK City of Culture 2013, with the construction of the Peace Bridge, Ebrington Sq, and the redevelopment of the waterfront and Guildhall area making the most of the city's splendid riverside setting.

There's lots of history to absorb here, along with taking in the burgeoning live-music scene in the city's lively pubs.

◉ SIGHTS

Derry's walled city is Ireland's earliest example of town planning. It's thought to have been modelled on the French Renaissance town of Vitry-le-François, designed in 1545 by Italian engineer Hieronimo Marino – both are based on the grid plan of a Roman military camp, with two main streets at right angles to each other, and four city gates, one at either end of each street.

Derry's City Walls   Walls

(⊗dawn-dusk) **FREE** The best way to get a feel for Derry's layout and history is to walk the 1.5km circumference of the city's

Derry

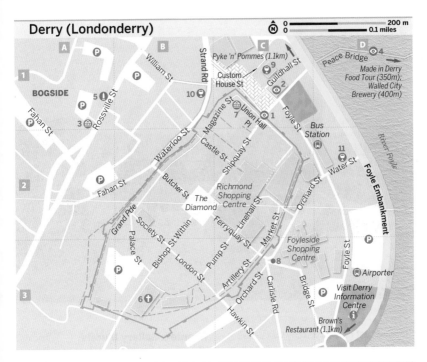

Derry (Londonderry)

walls. Completed in 1619, Derry's city walls are 8m high and 9m thick, and are the only city walls in Ireland to survive almost intact. The four original gates (Shipquay, Ferryquay, Bishop's and Butcher's) were rebuilt in the 18th and 19th centuries, when three new gates (New, Magazine and Castle) were added.

Tower Museum
Museum

(www.derrystrabane.com/towermuseum; Union Hall Pl; adult/child £3/1.50; ⊙10am-5.30pm, last entry 4pm) Head straight to the 5th floor of this award-winning museum inside a replica 16th-century tower house for a view from the top. Then work your way down through the excellent **Armada Shipwreck** exhibition, and the **Story of Derry**, where well-thought-out exhibits and audiovisuals lead you through the city's history, from the founding of the monastery of St Colmcille (Columba) in the 6th century to the Battle of the Bogside in the late 1960s. Allow at least two hours.

Guildhall
Notable Building

(☎028-7137 6510; www.derrystrabane.com/Guildhall; Guildhall St; ⊙10am-5.30pm) FREE

MICK HARPER/SHUTTERSTOCK ©

Peace Bridge

Standing just outside the city walls, the neo-Gothic Guildhall was originally built in 1890, then rebuilt after a fire in 1908. Its fine stained-glass windows were presented by the London livery companies, and its clock tower was modelled on London's Big Ben. Inside, there's a historical exhibition on the Plantation of Ulster, and a tourist information point.

St Columb's Cathedral   Cathedral
(www.stcolumbscathedral.org; 17 London St; suggested donation £2; ⊙9am-5pm Mon-Sat Mar-Oct, 10am-2pm Nov-Feb) Built between 1628 and 1633 from the same grey-green schist as the city walls, this was the first post-Reformation church to be erected in Britain and Ireland, and is Derry's oldest surviving building.

In the **porch** (under the spire, by the St Columb's Court entrance) you can see the original foundation stone of 1633 that records the cathedral's completion. The smaller stone inset comes from the original church built here in 1164.

People's Gallery Murals   Public Art
(Rossville St) The 12 murals that decorate the gable ends of houses along Rossville St, near Free Derry Corner, are popularly referred to as the People's Gallery. They are the work of 'the Bogside Artists' (Kevin Hasson, Tom Kelly, and William Kelly, who passed away in 2017). The three men lived through the worst of the Troubles in Bogside. The murals can be clearly seen from the northern part of the City Walls.

Museum of Free Derry   Museum
(www.museumoffreederry.org; 55 Glenfada Park; adult/child £6/5; ⊙9.30am-4.30pm Mon-Fri, 1-4pm Sat year-round, plus 1-4pm Sun Jul-Sep) Just off Rossville St, this excellent museum chronicles the history of the Bogside, the Civil Rights Movement and the events of Bloody Sunday through photographs, newspaper reports, film clips, interactive displays and the accounts of firsthand witnesses, including some of the original photographs that inspired the murals of the nearby People's Gallery.

Peace Bridge   Bridge

Sinuous and elegant, this 2011-completed, S-shaped pedestrian and cyclist bridge spans the River Foyle, linking the walled city on the west bank to Ebrington Sq on the east in a symbolic handshake.

 TOURS

City Walking Tours   Walking

(☑028-7127 1996; www.derrycitytours.com; Carlisle Rd; adult/under 12yr £4/free; ⊙Historic Derry tours 10am, noon, 2pm and 4pm year-round) One-hour Historic Derry walking tours start from outside the Carlisle Rd entrance to the Foyleside Shopping Centre. There are also tours of the Bogside and of Derry's murals. Recommended.

Free Derry Tours   Cultural

(☑07793 285972; www.freederry.tours) The Museum of Free Derry offers walking tours of the Bogside, taking in the People's Gallery murals, Free Derry Corner, the Hunger Strikers' Memorial and the Bloody Sunday Memorial.

Made in Derry
Food Tour   Food & Drink

(www.madeinderryfoodtour.com; per person £50; ⊙noon Sat) Four-hour tours of Derry's emerging artisan food and drink scene, meeting chefs and producers and sampling 20 local specialities – such as cheeses and craft beer – along the way. The tour starts outside the Eighty81 building on Ebrington Sq. Book ahead.

 EATING

Pyke 'n' Pommes   Street Food £

(No. 57; www.pykenpommes.ie; 57 Strand Rd; 1/2/3 tacos £5/8/10, burgers £8.50-13; ⊙noon-9pm Sun-Thu, to 10pm Fri & Sat; 🖋) For years **Pyke 'n' Pommes POD** (behind Foyle Marina, off Baronet St; mains £4-16; ⊙noon-8.30pm Fri & Sat, to 6pm Sun-Thu; 🖋) – a quayside shipping container – has been serving up the best food in Derry; in 2019 chef Kevin Pyke opened this licensed restaurant, serving a

 Walled City Brewery

Housed in the former army barracks on Ebrington Sq, **Walled City Brewery** (☑028-7134 3336; www.walledcitybrewery.com; 70 Ebrington Sq; mains £14-25; ⊙kitchen 5-11pm Tue-Thu, 12.30-3pm & 5-11pm Fri & Sat, 2-8pm Sun; 🖶) is a craft brewery and restaurant run by master brewer and Derry local James Huey. As well as having 10 craft beers on tap, Walled City serves top-notch grub, such as house-smoked pork neck and tandoori chargrilled rump of lamb. It also runs home-brewing courses.

ANDREW MONTGOMERY/LONELY PLANET ©

mouthwatering menu of tacos (fillings include fried cauliflower and Tequila battered haddock), and burgers like the Legenderry (made with wagyu beef) and the Veganderry (chickpeas, lemon and coriander).

The dining room has a street vibe, with industrial touches and roughly finished concrete walls.

Brown's Restaurant   Irish £££

(☑028-7134 5180; www.brownsrestaurant.com; 1 Bond's Hill, Waterside; 3 courses £35; ⊙noon-3pm Tue-Sat, 5.30-9pm Tue-Thu, 5-10pm Fri & Sat, noon-3pm Sun; 🖶) 🖋 From the outside, Brown's may not have the most promising appearance, but step inside and you're in an elegant little enclave of brandy-coloured banquettes and ornate metal light fittings, with vintage monochrome prints adorning the walls. The ever-changing menu is a gastronome's delight, making creative use of fresh local produce.

🍷 DRINKING & NIGHTLIFE

Peadar O'Donnell's   Pub

(www.facebook.com/Peadarsderry; 59-63 Waterloo St; ⊙11.30am-1.30am Mon-Sat, 12.30pm-12.30am Sun) Done up as a typical Irish pub and grocery (with shelves of household items, shopkeepers scales on the counter and a museum's worth of old bric-a-brac), Peadar's has rowdy traditional music sessions every night and often on weekend afternoons as well. The adjacent Gweedore Bar hosts live rock bands every night, and a Saturday-night disco upstairs.

Guildhall Taphouse   Bar

(www.facebook.com/Guildhalltaphouse; 4 Custom House St; ⊙noon-1am Mon-Sat, to midnight Sun) Housed in a wooden-beamed, 19th-century building brightened with fairy lights, the Taphouse is a cosy place to sample an excellent selection of local and international craft beers or a sophisticated cocktail. There's regular live music including trad sessions every Wednesday.

Sandino's Cafe-Bar   Bar

(www.sandinoscafebar.com; 1 Water St; ⊙11.30am-1am Mon-Sat, noon-midnight Sun) From the posters of Che to the Free Palestine flag to the fairtrade coffee and gluten-free beer, this relaxed cafe-bar exudes a liberal, left-wing vibe. DJs spin from Thursday to Saturday in Club Havana; there's regular live music, too.

ℹ️ INFORMATION

Visit Derry Information Centre (☎028-7126 7284; www.visitderry.com; 44 Foyle St; ⊙9am-7pm Mon-Fri, 9am-6pm Sat, 10am-5pm Sun Jun-Aug, shorter hours Sep-May; 🛜) A large tourist information centre with helpful staff and stacks of brochures for attractions in Derry and beyond. Also sells books and maps and can book accommodation.

Fish tacos from Pyke 'n' Pommes

ANDREW MONTGOMERY/LONELY PLANET ©

Peadar O'Donnell's

ℹ️ GETTING THERE & AWAY

AIR

City of Derry Airport (☎028-7181 0784; www.
cityofderryairport.com; Airport Rd, Eglinton) is
about 13km east of Derry along the A2 towards
Limavady. There are direct flights to London
Stansted (daily), Manchester (daily), Liverpool
(three days a week), Glasgow International (five
days a week) and Edinburgh (five days a week).

BUS

The **bus station** (☎028-7126 2261; Foyle St) is
just northeast of the walled city.

Services to Northern Ireland destinations are
operated by Translink (www.translink.co.uk);
destinations in the Republic are served by Bus
Éireann (www.buseireann.ie).

Belfast Europa Bus Centre £13, 1¾ hours,
half-hourly Monday to Friday, hourly Saturday
and Sunday

Galway £16.50, 5½ hours, four daily

Airporter (☎028-7126 9996; www.airporter.
co.uk; Foyleside Shopping Centre Coach Park,

Foyle St; single/return £20/30; 🛜) buses run
directly from Derry to Belfast International
Airport (£20, 1½ hours) and George Best
Belfast City Airport (£20, two hours) at least
once an hour Monday to Friday and slightly less
frequently Saturday and Sunday. Buses depart
from Foyleside Shopping Centre Coach Park,
near the Visit Derry Information Centre.

TRAIN

Derry's train station is on the eastern side of the
River Foyle. At research time, major works were
underway to create a new transport hub at the
site of the former Waterside Railway Station,
100m north of the current train station. The
new North-West Transport Hub, scheduled for
completion in 2020, will house the new train
terminus, bus stands, park-and-ride facilities and
a green way link to the city via the Peace Bridge.

Belfast £13, two hours, hourly Monday to
Saturday, six on Sunday

Coleraine £10, 40 minutes, hourly Monday to
Saturday, six on Sunday

Samuel Beckett Bridge, Dublin (p35)

In Focus

DERICK HUDSON/SHUTTERSTOCK ©

Ireland Today

On the threshold of the third decade of this millennium, Ireland has rediscovered the mojo that made it such a dynamic economic force in the final decade of the last. The tourist trade is booming and, in the Republic at least, the forces of liberalism continue to win battles against conservative traditionalism. Meanwhile, the spectre of Brexit casts a shadow over everything.

Tourism Boom

The year 2018 was a bumper one for Irish tourism, with a record 11.2 million visitors to the island. To meet the growing demand, dozens of new hotels are being added to the country's stock – at the end of 2018, 21 hotels were under construction across the country (70% more than at the same time in 2017), with at least another 20 to be built by 2020.

More hotels won't necessarily mean lower prices, however, as the government has raised value added tax (VAT) on the hospitality industry back to 13.5% – up from the 9.5% lifeboat thrown in 2011 to help the sector weather the effects of the global financial crisis. Many hoteliers and restaurateurs have responded negatively, arguing that the rise puts pressure on operators' margins already stretched by rising wage and rent costs.

if Ireland were 100 people

87 would be Irish
6 would be from the EU
2 would be British
3 would be Asian
1 would be American
1 would be other

If Northern Ireland were 100 people

40 would identify as British
25 would identify as Irish
21 would identify as Northern Irish
14 would identify as other

population per sq km

= 70 people

Republic of Ireland
Northern Ireland
England

What is almost certain is that the VAT hike will be passed on to the consumer. Many cafes and restaurants have already raised their prices, while hotel and B&B owners will be forced to mitigate what is effectively a 50% increase in their VAT bill by bumping up their room rates even more than the standard rate of year-on-year inflation.

Northern Ireland Politics

Without a working government since January 2017, Northern Ireland remains at a political impasse. The power-sharing agreement between the two largest blocs on either side of the sectarian divide – republican Sinn Féin and the Democratic Unionist Party (DUP) – was an improbable success for over a decade, but the years since 2017 have seen both sides retreat behind familiar positions of deep mistrust and antipathy. The main fault lines are the Irish language, which Sinn Féin wants recognised as having equal status with English, a concession firmly rejected by the DUP; and the latter's refusal on religious grounds to support the introduction of a marriage equality act that would bring it in line with the rest of the United Kingdom.

Paradoxically the pathway to restoration may have been carved by the tragic death of journalist and LGBT activist Lyra McKee in April 2019, killed during riots in Derry by members of the dissident republican group, the New IRA.

At her funeral, which was attended by party leaders from both sides of the political divide as well as the British and Irish prime ministers, the priest giving the homily received a standing ovation when he demanded to know why it took her death to unite politicians, tapping into the deep frustration felt by most in the province at their leaders' intransigence.

Brexit & the Border

What will Brexit bring? At the time of writing, this was the pressing political and economic question. Ireland has close socioeconomic ties with the UK, so most economists believe that 'the harder the Brexit, the worse the outcome', with bilateral trade taking a big hit.

But the biggest impact will be felt by Northern Ireland, which in a post-Brexit landscape will be divided from the Republic by the only land border between the UK and the EU. The majority of its citizens (56% to 44%) voted Remain, but the governing Democratic Unionist Party (DUP) favoured Leave, if only, they argued, to strenghten the province's ties to a UK that was out of the EU.

Hore Abbey (p130)

MNSTUDIO/SHUTTERSTOCK ©

History

Ireland's history is a search for identity, a search complicated by a long list of invaders, especially the English. Indeed, Ireland's fractious relationship with its nearest neighbour has occupied much of the last 1000 years, and it is through the prism of that relationship that a huge part of the Irish identity is reflected.

10,000–8000 BC
After the last ice age ends, the first humans arrive in Ireland.

700–300 BC
The Celtic culture and language arrive, ushering in a thousand years of cultural and political dominance.

AD 432–800
Arrival of St Patrick is followed by the flowering of early Christian monasticism in Ireland.

GPO, Dublin

ROY HARRIS/SHUTTERSTOCK ©

Who Are the Irish?

Hunters and gatherers may first have traversed the narrowing land bridge that once linked Ireland with Britain, but many more crossed the Irish Sea in small hide-covered boats.

In the 8th century BC, Ireland came to the attention of the fearsome Celts, who, having fought their way across Central Europe, established permanent settlements on the island in the 3rd century BC.

Getting into the Habit

Arguably the most significant import into Ireland came between the 3rd and 5th centuries AD, when Christian missionaries first brought the new religion of Rome. Everyone has heard of St Patrick, but he was merely the most famous of many who converted the local pagan tribes by cleverly fusing traditional pagan rituals with the new Christian teaching, creating an exciting hybrid known as Celtic (Insular) Christianity. The artistic and intellectual

795–841	1171	1350–1530
Vikings plunder Irish monasteries then establish settlements throughout the country.	King Henry II invades Ireland, forcing the Cambro-Norman warlords to accept him as their overlord.	Anglo-Norman barons establish power bases, English control recedes to an area around Dublin known as 'the Pale'.

Skellig Michael (p160)

★ **Monastic Sites**

Rock of Cashel (p126)

Clonmacnoise (p210)

Glendalough (p86)

Skellig Michael (p160)

credentials of Ireland's Christians were the envy of Europe and led to the moniker 'the land of saints and scholars'.

More Invaders

The Celts' lack of political unity made the island easy pickings for the next wave of invaders, Danish Vikings. Over the course of the 9th and 10th centuries, they established settlements along the east coast, intermarried with the Celtic tribes and introduced red hair and freckles to the Irish gene pool.

The '800 years' of English rule in Ireland began in 1171, when the English king Henry II sent a huge invasion force, at the urging of the pope, to bring the increasingly independent Christian missionaries to heel. It was also intended to curb the growing power of the Anglo-Norman lords, who had arrived in Ireland two years before Henry's army, and who had settled quite nicely into Irish life, becoming – as the old saying went – Hiberniores Hibernis ipsis (more Irish than the Irish themselves). By the 16th century they had divided the country into their own fiefdoms and the English Crown's direct control didn't extend any further than a cordon surrounding Dublin, known as 'the Pale'.

Divorce, Dissolution & Destruction

Henry VIII's failure to get the pope's blessing for his divorce augured badly for the Irish, who sided with the Vatican. Henry retaliated by ordering the dissolution of all monasteries in Britain and Ireland, and had himself declared King of Ireland. His daughter Elizabeth I went even further, establishing jurisdiction in Connaught and Munster before crushing the last of the rebels, the lords of Ulster, led by the crafty and courageous Hugh O'Neill, Earl of Tyrone.

With the native chiefs gone, Elizabeth and her successor, James I, could pursue their policy of Plantation with impunity. Though confiscations took place all over the country, Ulster was most affected both because of its wealthy farmlands and as punishment for being home to the primary fomenters of rebellion.

1536–41	1601	1649–53
Henry VIII declares war on the Irish Church and declares himself King of Ireland.	Following the Battle of Kinsale, Irish rebellion against the English Crown is broken.	Cromwell lays waste to Ireland after the Irish support Charles I in the English Civil War.

Bloody Religion

At the outset of the English Civil War in 1642, the Irish threw their support behind Charles I against the very Protestant parliamentarians in the hope that victory for the king would lead to the restoration of Catholic power in Ireland. When Oliver Cromwell and his Roundheads defeated the Royalists and took Charles' head off in 1649, Cromwell turned his attention to the disloyal Irish. His nine-month campaign was effective and brutal (Drogheda was particularly mistreated); yet more lands were confiscated – Cromwell's famous utterance that the Irish could 'go to hell or to Connaught' seems odd given the province's beauty, but there wasn't much arable land out there – and Catholic rights restricted even more.

St Patrick

Ireland's patron saint, St Patrick (AD 389–461), remembered all around the world on 17 March, wasn't even Irish. This symbol of Irish pride hailed from what is now Wales, which at the time of his birth was under Roman occupation. Kidnapped by Irish raiders when he was 16 and made a slave, he found religion, escaped from captivity and returned to Britain. He returned to Ireland vowing to make Christians out of the Irish, and within 30 years of his return his dream had come true.

So next St Paddy's Day, as you're swilling Guinness, think of who the man really was.

The Boyne & Penal Laws

Catholic Ireland's next major setback came in 1690. Yet again the Irish had backed the wrong horse, this time supporting James II after his deposition in the Glorious Revolution by the Dutch Protestant King William of Orange (who was married to James' daughter Mary!). After James had unsuccessfully laid siege to Derry for 105 days (the Loyalist cry of 'No surrender!', in use to this day, dates from the siege), in July he fought William's armies by the banks of the Boyne in County Louth and was roundly defeated.

The final ignominy for Catholics came in 1695 with the passing of the Penal Laws, which prohibited them from owning land or entering any higher profession. Irish culture, music and education were banned in the hope that Catholicism would be eradicated. Most Catholics continued to worship at secret locations, but some prosperous Irish converted to Protestantism to preserve their careers and wealth. Land was steadily transferred to Protestant owners, and a significant majority of the Catholic population became tenants living in wretched conditions. By the late 18th century, Catholics owned barely 5% of the land.

If at First You Don't Succeed...

With Roman Catholics rendered utterly powerless, the seeds of rebellion against autocracy were planted by a handful of liberal Protestants, inspired by the ideologies of the Enlightenment and the unrest provoked by the American War of Independence and then the French Revolution.

1690	1798	1801
Catholic King James II defeated by William of Orange in the Battle of the Boyne on 12 July.	The flogging and killing of potential rebels sparks a uprising of the United Irishmen led by Wolfe Tone.	The Act of Union unites Ireland politically with Britain, ending Irish 'independence'.

The first of these came in 1798, when the United Irishmen, led by a young Dublin Protestant, Theobald Wolfe Tone (1763–98), took on the British at the Battle of Vinegar Hill in County Wexford – their defeat was hastened by the failure of the French to land an army of succour in 1796 in Bantry Bay.

The Liberator

The Act of Union, passed in 1801, was the British government's vain attempt to put an end to any aspirations towards Irish independence, but the nationalist genie was out of the bottle, not least in the body of a Kerry-born Catholic named Daniel O'Connell (1775–1847).

In 1823 O'Connell founded the Catholic Association with the aim of achieving political equality for Catholics, which he did (in part) by forcing the passing of the 1829 Act of Catholic Emancipation, allowing some well-off Catholics voting rights and the right to be elected as MPs.

O'Connell's campaign now switched to the repeal of the Act of Union, but the 'Liberator' came to a sorry end in 1841 when he meekly stood down in face of a government order banning one of his rallies. His capitulation was deemed unforgivable given that Ireland was in the midst of the Potato Famine.

The Uncrowned King of Ireland

Charles Stewart Parnell (1846–91) was the other great 19th-century statesman. Like O'Connell, he too was a powerful orator, but the primary focus of his artful attentions was land reform, particularly the reduction of rents and the improvement of working conditions (conveniently referred to as the 'Three Fs': fair rent, free sale and fixity of tenure). Parnell championed the activities of the Land League, which instigated the strategy of 'boycotting' (named after one particularly unpleasant agent called Charles Boycott) tenants, agents and landlords who didn't adhere to the Land League's aims. In 1881 they won an important victory with the passing of the Land Act.

Parnell's other great struggle was for a limited form of autonomy for Ireland. Despite the nominal support of the Liberal leader William Gladstone, Home Rule bills introduced in 1886 and 1892 were uniformly rejected. Like O'Connell before him, Parnell's star plummeted dramatically: in 1890 he was embroiled in a divorce proceeding, and the 'uncrowned king of Ireland' was forced to resign; he died less than a year later.

Rebellion Once Again

Ireland's struggle for some kind of autonomy picked up pace in the second decade of the 20th century. The radicalism that had always been at the fringes of Irish nationalist aspirations was once again beginning to assert itself, partly in response to a hardening of attitudes in Ulster. Mass opposition to any kind of Irish independence had resulted in the formation of the Ulster Volunteer Force (UVF), a Loyalist vigilante group whose

1828–29
Daniel O'Connell's election to Parliament leads to the Catholic Relief Act; non-Protestants can now be MPs.

1845–51
Between 500,000 and one million die during the Potato Famine; two million more emigrate.

1884
The Gaelic Athletic Association (GAA) is founded to promote Gaelic games and culture.

100,000-plus members swore to resist any attempt to impose Home Rule on Ireland. Nationalists responded by creating the Irish Volunteer Force (IVF) and a showdown seemed inevitable.

Home Rule was finally passed in 1914, but the outbreak of WWI meant that its enactment was shelved for the duration. For most Irish, the suspension was disappointing but hardly unreasonable, and the majority of the volunteers enlisted to help fight the Germans.

Beyond the Pale

The expression 'beyond the pale' came into use when the Pale – defined as a jurisdiction marked by a clear boundary – was the English-controlled part of Ireland, which stretched roughly from Dalkey, a southern suburb of Dublin, to Dundalk, north of Drogheda. Inland, the boundary extended west to Trim and Kells. To the British elite, the rest of Ireland was considered uncivilised.

The Easter Rising

A few, however, did not heed the call.

Two small groups – a section of the Irish Volunteers under Pádraig Pearse and the Irish Citizens' Army led by James Connolly – conspired in a rebellion that took the country by surprise. A depleted Volunteer group marched into Dublin on Easter Monday 1916 and took over a number of key positions in the city, claiming the General Post Office on O'Connell St as its headquarters. From its steps, Pearse read out to passers-by a declaration that Ireland was now a republic and that his band was the provisional government. Less than a week of fighting ensued before the rebels surrendered to the superior British forces. The rebels weren't popular and had to be protected from angry Dubliners as they were marched to jail.

The Easter Rising would probably have had little impact on the Irish situation had the British not made martyrs of the rebel leaders. Of the 77 given death sentences, 15 were executed, including the injured Connolly. This brought about a change in public attitudes; support for the Republicans rose dramatically.

War with Britain

By the end of WWI, Home Rule was far too little, far too late. In the 1918 general election, the Republicans stood under the banner of Sinn Féin and won a large majority of the Irish seats. Ignoring London's Parliament, where technically they were supposed to sit, the newly elected Sinn Féin deputies – many of them veterans of the 1916 Easter Rising – declared Ireland independent and formed the first Dáil Éireann (Irish assembly or lower house), which sat in Dublin's Mansion House under the leadership of Éamon de Valera (1882–1975). The Irish Volunteers became the Irish Republican Army (IRA) and the Dáil authorised it to wage war on British troops in Ireland.

As wars go, the War of Independence was pretty small fry. It lasted two and a half years and cost around 1200 casualties. But it was a pretty nasty affair, as the IRA fought

1916	1919–21	1921–22
The Easter Rising rebels surrender to superior British forces in less than a week.	The Irish War of Independence, which ends in a truce; Anglo-Irish Treaty is signed.	Treaty grants independence to 26 counties, allowing six Ulster counties to remain part of Great Britain.

The Great Famine

As a result of the Great Famine of 1845–51, a staggering three million people died or were forced to emigrate from Ireland. This great tragedy is all the more inconceivable given that the scale of suffering was attributable to greed as much as to natural causes. Potatoes were the staple food of a rapidly growing, desperately poor population and, when a blight hit the crops, prices soared. The repressive Penal Laws ensured that farmers, already crippled with high rents, could ill afford to sell the limited harvest of potatoes not affected by blight or imported from abroad to the Irish. Mass emigration continued to reduce the population during the next 100 years and huge numbers of Irish emigrants found their way abroad.

a guerrilla-style, hit-and-run campaign against the British, whose numbers were swelled by returning veterans of WWI known as Black and Tans (on account of their uniforms, a mix of army khaki and police black).

A Kind of Freedom

A truce in July 1921 led to intense negotiations between the two sides. The resulting Anglo-Irish Treaty, signed on 6 December 1921, created the Irish Free State, made up of 26 of 32 Irish counties. The remaining six – all in Ulster – remained part of the UK. The Treaty was an imperfect document: not only did it cement the geographic divisions on the island that 50 years later would explode into the Troubles, it also caused a split among nationalists – between those who believed the Treaty to be a necessary stepping stone towards full independence, and those who saw it as capitulation to the British and a betrayal of Republican ideals. This division was to determine the course of Irish political affairs for virtually the remainder of the century.

Civil War

The Treaty was ratified after a bitter debate and the June 1922 elections resulted in a victory for the pro-Treaty side. But the anti-Treaty forces rallied behind de Valera, who, though president of the Dáil, had not been a member of the Treaty negotiating team (affording him, in the eyes of his critics and opponents, maximum deniability should the negotiations go pear-shaped) and objected to some of the Treaty's provisions, most notably the oath of allegiance to the British monarch.

Within two weeks of the elections, civil war broke out between comrades who, a year previously, had fought alongside each other. The most prominent casualty of this particularly bitter conflict was Michael Collins (1890–1922), mastermind of the IRA's campaign during the War of Independence and a chief negotiator of the Anglo-Irish Treaty – shot in an ambush in his native Cork.

1922–23
Brief and bloody civil war between pro-Treaty and anti-Treaty forces results in victory for the former.

1932
De Valera leads his Fianna Fáil party into government for the first time.

1948
The new Fine Gael declares the Free State to be a republic.

The Making of a Republic

The Civil War ground to an exhausted halt in 1923 with the victory of the pro-Treaty side, who governed the new state until 1932. Defeated but unbowed, de Valera founded a new party in 1926 called Fianna Fáil (Soldiers of Ireland) and won a majority in the 1932 elections; they would remain in charge until 1948. In the meantime, de Valera created a new constitution in 1937 that did away with the hated oath of allegiance, reaffirmed the special position of the Catholic Church and once again laid claim to the six counties of Northern Ireland. In 1948 Ireland officially left the Commonwealth and became a republic but, as historical irony would have it, it was Fine Gael, as the old pro-Treaty party was now known, that declared it – Fianna Fáil had surprisingly lost the election that year. After 800 years, Ireland – or at least a substantial chunk of it – was independent.

Growing Pains & Roaring Tigers

Unquestionably the most significant figure since independence, Éamon de Valera made an immense contribution to an independent Ireland. But, as the 1950s stretched into the 1960s, his vision for the country was mired in a conservative and traditional orthodoxy that was at odds with the reality of a country in desperate economic straits, where chronic unemployment and emigration were but the more visible effects of inadequate policy.

Partners in Europe

In 1972 the Republic (along with Northern Ireland) became a member of the European Economic Community (EEC). This brought an increased measure of prosperity thanks to the benefits of the Common Agricultural Policy, which set fixed prices and guaranteed quotas for Irish farming produce. Nevertheless, the broader global depression, provoked by the oil crisis of 1973, forced the country into yet another slump and emigration figures rose again, reaching a peak in the mid-1980s.

From Celtic Tiger...

In the early 1990s European funds helped kick-start economic growth. Huge sums of money were invested in education and physical infrastructure, while the policy of low corporate tax rates coupled with attractive incentives made Ireland very appealing to high-tech businesses looking for a door into EU markets. In less than a decade, Ireland went from being one of the poorest countries in Europe to one of the wealthiest: unemployment fell from 18% to 3.5%, the average industrial wage somersaulted to the top of the European league, and the dramatic rise in GDP meant that the country laid claim to an economic model of success that was the envy of the entire world. Ireland became synonymous with the term 'Celtic Tiger'.

1993	**1994**	**mid-1990s**
Downing Street Declaration signed by British prime minister John Major and Irish Taoiseach Albert Reynolds.	Sinn Féin leader Gerry Adams announces a cessation of IRA violence on 31 August.	The 'Celtic Tiger' economy transforms Ireland into one of Europe's wealthiest countries.

...to Rescue Cat

From 2002 the Irish economy was kept buoyant by a gigantic construction boom that was completely out of step with any measure of responsible growth forecasting. The out-of-control international derivatives market flooded Irish banks with cheap money, and they lent it freely.

Then American global financial services firm Lehman Bros and the credit crunch happened. The Irish banks nearly went to the wall, but were bailed out at the last minute, and before Ireland could draw breath, the International Monetary Fund (IMF) and the EU held the chits of the country's midterm economic future. Ireland found itself yet again confronting the familiar demons of high unemployment and emigration, but a deep-cutting program of austerity saw the corner turned by the end of 2014.

It's (Not So) Grim Up North

Making sense of Northern Ireland isn't that easy. It's not because the politics are so entrenched (they are), or that the two sides are at such odds with each other (they are): it's because the fight is so old.

It began in the 16th century, with the first Plantations of Ireland ordered by the English Crown, whereby the confiscated lands of the Gaelic and Hiberno-Norman gentry were awarded to English and Scottish settlers of good Protestant stock. The policy was most effective in Ulster, where the newly arrived Protestants were given an extra leg-up by the Penal Laws, which successfully reduced the now landless Catholic population to second-class citizens with little or no rights.

Irish Apartheid

But fast-forward to 1921, when the notion of independent Ireland moved from aspiration to actuality. The new rump state of Northern Ireland was governed until 1972 by the Protestant-majority Ulster Unionist Party, backed up by the overwhelmingly Protestant Royal Ulster Constabulary (RUC) and the sectarian B-Specials militia. As a result of tilted economic subsidies, bias in housing allocation and wholesale gerrymandering, Northern Ireland was, in effect, an apartheid state, leaving the roughly 40% Catholic and Nationalist population grossly underrepresented.

Defiance of Unionist hegemony came with the Civil Rights Movement, founded in 1967 and heavily influenced by its US counterpart. In October 1968 a mainly Catholic march in Derry was violently broken up by the RUC amid rumours that the IRA had provided 'security' for the marchers. Nobody knew it at the time, but the Troubles had begun.

The Troubles

Conflict escalated quickly: clashes between the two communities increased and the police openly sided with the Loyalists against a Nationalist population made increasingly militant

1998	2005	2008
After the Good Friday Agreement, the 'Real IRA' detonates a bomb in Omagh, killing 29 people and injuring 200.	The IRA orders all of its units to commit to exclusively democratic means.	The Irish banking system is declared virtually bankrupt following the collapse of Lehman Brothers.

by the resurgence of the long-dormant IRA. In August 1969 British troops went to Derry and then Belfast to maintain law and order; they were initially welcomed in Catholic neighbourhoods but within a short time they too were seen as an army of occupation: the killing of 13 innocent civilians in Derry on Bloody Sunday (30 January 1972) set the grim tone for the next two decades, as violence, murder and reprisal became the order of the day in the province and, occasionally, on the British mainland.

Overtures of Peace

By the early 1990s it was clear to Republicans that armed struggle was a bankrupted policy. Northern Ireland was a transformed society – most of the injustices that had sparked the conflict in the late 1960s had long since been rectified and most ordinary citizens were desperate for an end to hostilities.

A series of negotiated statements between the unionists, nationalists and the British and Irish governments – brokered in part by George Mitchell, Bill Clinton's special envoy to Northern Ireland – eventually resulted in the historic Good Friday Agreement of 1998.

The agreement called for the devolution of legislative power from Westminster (where it had been since 1972) to a new Northern Ireland Assembly, but posturing, disagreement, sectarianism and downright obstinance on both sides made slow work of progress, and the Assembly was suspended four times – the last from October 2002 until May 2007.

During this period, the politics of Northern Ireland polarised dramatically, resulting in the falling away of the more moderate UUP and the emergence of the hardline DUP, led by Ian Paisley; and, on the nationalist side, the emergence of the IRA's political wing, Sinn Féin, as the main torch-bearer of nationalist aspirations, under the leadership of Gerry Adams and Martin McGuinness.

2010
Ireland surrenders financial sovereignty to IMF and EU in exchange for bailout package of €85 billion.

2015
Ireland becomes the first country in the world to introduce marriage equality for same-sex couples by plebiscite.

2019
Brexit set to create an EU border between Northern Ireland (UK) and the Republic of Ireland (EU).

Soda bread

RRRAINBOW/SHUTTERSTOCK ©

Food & Drink

The 'local food' movement was pioneered in Ireland in the 1970s, notably at the world-famous Ballymaloe House. Since then it has gone from strength to strength, with dozens of farmers markets showcasing the best of local produce, and restaurants all over the country highlighting locally sourced ingredients. And with the growing sophistication of the Irish palate, it's now relatively easy to eat well in all budgets.

To Eat

Potatoes Still a staple of most traditional meals and presented in a variety of forms. The mashed-potato dishes colcannon and champ (with cabbage and spring onion, respectively) are two of the tastiest recipes in the country.

Meat and seafood Beef, lamb and pork are common options. Seafood is widely available in restaurants and is often excellent, especially in the west. Oysters, trout and salmon are delicious, particularly if they're direct from the sea or river rather than a fish farm.

Soda bread The most famous Irish bread is made with bicarbonate of soda, to make up for soft Irish flour that traditionally didn't take well to yeast. Combined with buttermilk, it makes a superbly tasty bread, and is often on breakfast menus at B&Bs.

Seafood chowder

HAOLIANG/GETTY IMAGES ©

The fry Who can say no to a plate of fried bacon, sausages, black pudding, white pudding, eggs and tomatoes? For the famous Ulster fry, common throughout the North, simply add fadge (potato bread).

Dare to Try

Ironically, while the Irish palate has become more adventurous, it is the old-fashioned Irish menu that features some fairly challenging dishes. Dare to try the following:

Black pudding Made from cooked pork blood, suet and other fillings; a ubiquitous part of an Irish cooked breakfast.

Boxty A Northern Irish starchy potato cake made with a half-and-half mix of cooked mashed potatoes and grated, strained raw potato.

Carrageen The typical Irish seaweed that can be found in dishes as diverse as salad and ice cream.

Corned beef tongue Usually accompanied by cabbage, this dish is still found on a traditional Irish menu.

Lough Neagh eel A speciality of Northern Ireland, typically eaten around Halloween; it's usually served in chunks with a white onion sauce.

Poitín It's rare to be offered a drop of the 'cratur', as illegally distilled whiskey (made from malted grain or potatoes) is called here. Still, there are pockets of the country – Donegal, Connemara and West Cork – with secret stills.

MARJA JANUS/SHUTTERSTOCK ©

To Drink

Stout While Guinness has become synonymous with stout the world over, few outside Ireland realise that there are two other major brands competing for the favour of the Irish drinker: Murphy's and Beamish, both brewed in Cork city.

Tea The Irish drink more tea, per capita, than any other nation in the world and you'll be offered a cup as soon as you cross the threshold of any Irish home. Taken with milk (and sugar, if you want) rather than lemon, preferred blends are very strong and nothing like the namby-pamby versions that pass for Irish breakfast tea elsewhere.

Whiskey As recently as the 1990s there were only three working distilleries in Ireland – Jameson's, Bushmills and Cooley's. An explosion in artisan distilling has seen the number grow to more than 30, exhibiting a range and quality that will make the connoisseur's palate spin while winning over many new friends to what the Irish call *uisce beatha* (water of life).

Craft Beer Revolution

Although mainstream lagers are most pubs' best-selling pints, the craft-beer revolution has seen around 100 microbreweries come into operation all over the island, making artisan beers that are served in more than 600 of Ireland's pubs and bars. Here's a small selection to whet the taste buds:

Devil's Backbone (4.9% alcohol by volume) Rich amber ale from County Donegal brewer Kinnegar

The Full Irish (6%) Single malt IPA by Eight Degrees Brewery outside Mitchelstown, County Cork

O'Hara's Leann Folláin (6%) Dry stout with vaguely chocolate notes produced by Carlow Brewing Company in Moneybeg, County Carlow

Metalman Pale Ale (4.3%) American-style pale ale by the much-respected Metalman Brewing Company in County Waterford – now available in cans

Saturate (8.0%) A double IPA with a hefty kick, from County Wicklow–based Whiplash Beer, voted Irish beer of the year in 2018

Twisted Hop (4.7%) Blond ale produced by Hilden, Ireland's oldest independent brewery, just outside Lisburn

When to Eat

Irish eating habits have changed over the last couple of decades, and there are differences between urban and rural practices.

Breakfast Usually eaten before 9am, as most people rush off to work (though hotels and B&Bs will serve until 10am or 11am Monday to Friday, and till noon at weekends in urban areas). Weekend brunch is popular in bigger towns and cities.

Lunch Urban workers eat on the run between 12.30pm and 2pm (most restaurants don't begin to serve lunch until at least midday). At weekends, especially Sunday, the midday lunch is skipped in favour of a substantial mid-afternoon meal (called dinner), usually between 2pm and 4pm.

Tea Not the drink, but the evening meal – also confusingly called dinner. This is the main meal of the day for urbanites, usually eaten around 6.30pm. Rural communities eat at the same time but with a more traditional tea of bread, cold cuts and, yes, tea. Restaurants follow international habits, with most diners not eating until at least 7.30pm.

Price Ranges

The following price ranges refer to the cost of a main course at dinner.

Budget	Republic	Dublin	Northern Ireland
€	less than €12	less than €15	less than £12
€€	€12–25	€15–28	£12–20
€€€	more than €25	more than €28	more than £20

Supper A before-bed snack of tea and toast or sandwiches, still enjoyed by many Irish folk, though urbanites increasingly eschew it for health reasons. Not a practice in restaurants.

Vegetarians & Vegans

Ireland has come a long, long way since the days when vegetarians were looked upon as odd creatures; nowadays, even the most militant vegan will barely cause a ruffle in all but the most basic of kitchens. Which isn't to say that travellers with plant-based diets are going to find the most imaginative range of options on menus outside the bigger towns and cities – or in the plethora of modern restaurants that have opened in the last few years. But you can rest assured that the overall quality of the homegrown vegetable is top-notch, and most places will have at least one dish that you can tuck into comfortably.

Dining Etiquette

The Irish aren't big on restrictive etiquette, preferring friendly informality to any kind of stuffy to-dos. Still, the following are a few tips to dining with the Irish:

Children All restaurants welcome kids up to 7pm, but pubs and some smarter restaurants don't allow them in the evening. Family restaurants have children's menus; others have reduced portions of regular menu items.

Returning a dish If the food is not to your satisfaction, it's best to politely explain what's wrong with it as soon as you can. Any respectable restaurant will offer to replace the dish immediately.

Paying the bill If you insist on paying the bill for everyone, be prepared for a first, second and even third refusal to countenance such an exorbitant act of generosity. But don't be fooled: the Irish will refuse something several times even if they're delighted with it. Insist gently but firmly and you'll get your way!

OLIVIER CIRENDINI/LONELY PLANET ©

The Pub

The pub is the heart of Ireland's social existence, and we're guessing that experiencing it ranks high on your list of things to do while you're here. But let's be clear: we're not just talking about a place to get a drink. Oh no. You can get a drink in a restaurant or a hotel, or wherever there's someone with a bottle of something strong. The pub is far more than just that.

The Role of the Pub

The pub is the broadest window through which you can examine and experience the very essence of the nation's culture, in all its myriad forms. It's the great leveller, where status and rank hold no sway, where generation gaps are bridged, inhibitions lowered, tongues loosened, schemes hatched, songs sung, stories told and gossip embroidered. It's a unique institution: a theatre and a cosy room, a centre stage and a hideaway, a debating chamber and a place for silent contemplation. It's whatever you want it to be, and that's the secret of the great Irish pub.

Spirit Groceries

The 'spirit grocery' is a combined pub and grocer's shop. Found all over Ireland, they usually have a bar counter on one side and a general store counter on the other, a combination that has engendered the international image of the Irish pub as littered with old signs and bric-a-brac. There are pubs today where you can buy a bag of nails, a tin of peas or a pair of wellies as well as a pint.

Talk

Talk – whether it is frivolous, earnest or incoherent – is the essential ingredient. Once tongues are loosened and the cogs of thought oiled, the conversation can go anywhere and you should let it flow to its natural conclusion. An old Irish adage suggests you should never talk about sport, religion or politics in unfamiliar company. But as long as you're mindful, you needn't restrict yourself too much. While it's a myth to say you can walk into any pub and make a friend, you probably won't be drinking on your own for long – unless that's what you want, of course. There are few more spiritual experiences than a solitary pint in an old country pub in the mid-afternoon.

Tradition

Aesthetically, there is nothing better than the traditional haunt, populated by flat-capped pensioners bursting with delightful anecdotes and always ready to dispense a kind of wisdom distilled through generations' worth of experience. The best of them have stone floors and a peat fire; the chat barely rises above a respectful murmur save for appreciative laughter; and most of all, there's no music save the kind played by someone sitting next to you. Pubs like these are a disappearing breed, but there are still plenty of them around to ensure that you will find one, no matter where you are.

Etiquette

The rounds system – the simple custom where someone buys you a drink and you buy one back – is the bedrock of Irish pub culture. It's summed up in the Irish saying: 'It's impossible for two men to go to a pub for one drink'. Nothing will hasten your fall from social grace here like the failure to uphold this pub law.

Another golden rule about the system is that the next round starts when the first person has finished (preferably just about to finish) their drink. It doesn't matter if you're only halfway through your pint – if it's your round, get your order in.

Craft Beer

In the last decade there has been a swing away from the big international brands – even Guinness is now part of the multinational Diageo drinks group – in favour of beers made by small, local breweries – so-called 'craft beers'. Many of these have their own pubs, or even combine pub and brewery in one place.

Claddagh ring

GRACEPHOTOS/SHUTTERSTOCK ©

Irish Mythological Symbols

Ireland's collection of icons serves to exemplify the country – or a simplistic version of it – to an astonishing degree. It's referred to by the Irish as 'Oirishness', which is what happens when you take a spud, shove it in a pint of Guinness and garnish it with a shamrock.

The Shamrock

Ireland's most enduring symbol is the shamrock, a three-leafed white clover known diminutively in Irish as *seamróg*, which was anglicised as 'shamrock'. According to legend, when St Patrick was trying to explain the mystery of the Holy Trinity to the recently converted Celtic chieftains, he plucked the modest little weed and used its three leaves to explain the metaphysically challenging concept of the Father, the Son and the Holy Spirit as being separate but part of the one being. This link is what makes the shamrock a ubiquitous part of the St Patrick's Day celebrations.

The Leprechaun

The country's most enduring cliché is the myth of the mischievous leprechaun and his pot of gold, which he jealously guards from the attentions of greedy humans. Despite the twee aspect of the legend, its origin predates the Celts and belongs to the mythological Tuatha dé Danann (peoples of the Goddess Danu), who lived in Ireland 4000 years ago. When they were eventually defeated, their king Lugh (the demigod father of Cúchulainn) was forced underground, where he became known as Lugh Chromain, or 'little stooping Lugh' – the origin of leprechaun.

The Irish can get visibly irritated if asked whether they believe in leprechauns (you might as well ask them if they're stupid), but many rural dwellers are a superstitious lot. They mightn't necessarily believe that malevolent sprites who dwell in faerie forts actually exist, but they're not especially keen to test the theory either, which is why there still exist trees, hills and other parts of the landscape that are deemed to have, well, supernatural qualities, and as such will never be touched.

The Luck of the Irish?

Nearly a millennium of occupation, a long history of oppression and exploitation, a devastating famine, mass emigration...how exactly are the Irish 'lucky'? Well, they're not, or at least not any more so than anybody else. The expression was born in the mid-19th century in the US during the gold and silver rush, when some of the most successful miners were Irish or of Irish extraction. It didn't really seem to matter that the Irish were recent escapees from famine and destitution in Ireland and were over-represented among the miners; the expression stuck. Still, the expression was always a little derisory, as though the Irish merely stumbled across good fortune.

The Harp

The Celtic harp (clársach) is meant to represent the immortality of the soul, which is handy given that it's been a symbol of Ireland since the days of Henry VIII and the first organised opposition to English rule. The harp was the most popular instrument at the Celtic court, with the harpist (usually blind) ranked only behind the chief and bard in order of importance. In times of war, the harpist played a special, jewel-encrusted harp and served as the cheerleading section for soldiers heading into battle.

During the first rebellions against the English, the harp was once again an instrument of revolutionary fervour, prompting the crown to ban it altogether. This eventually led to its decline as the instrument of choice for Irish musicians but ensured its status as a symbol of Ireland.

The Claddagh Ring

The most famous of all Irish jewellery is the Claddagh ring, made up of two hands (friendship) clasping a heart (love) and usually surmounted by a crown (loyalty). Made in the eponymous fishing village of County Galway since the 17th century, the symbolic origins are much older and belong to a broader family of rings popular since Roman times known as the fede rings (from mani in fede, or 'hands in trust'), which were used to symbolise marriage. Nevertheless, their popularity is relatively recent, and almost entirely down to their wearing by expat Americans who use them to demonstrate their ties to their Irish heritage.

Brendan Behan memorial, Royal Canal, Dublin

YULIA PLEKHANOVA/SHUTTERSTOCK © SCULPTOR: JOHN COLL

Literary Ireland

Of all their national traits, characteristics and cultural expressions, it's perhaps the way the Irish speak and write that best distinguishes them. Their love of language and their great oral tradition have contributed to Ireland's legacy of world-renowned writers and storytellers. All this in a language imposed on them by a foreign invader.

The Mythic Cycle

Before there was anything like modern literature there was the Ulaid (Ulster) Cycle – Ireland's version of the Homeric epic – written down from oral tradition between the 8th and 12th centuries. The chief story is the Táin Bó Cúailnge (Cattle Raid of Cooley), about a battle between Queen Maeve of Connaught and Cúchulainn, the principal hero of Irish mythology. He appears in the work of Irish writers to the present day, from Samuel Beckett to Frank McCourt.

Modern Literature

From the mythic cycle, zip forward 1000 years, past the genius of Jonathan Swift (1667–1745) and his *Gulliver's Travels,* stopping to acknowledge acclaimed dramatist Oscar

Wilde (1854–1900), *Dracula* creator Bram
Stoker (1847–1912) – some have claimed
that the name of the count may have come
from the Irish *droch fhola* (bad blood) –
and the literary giant that was James Joyce
(1882–1941), whose name and books elicit
enormous pride in Ireland.

The majority of Joyce's literary output
came when he had left Ireland for the
artistic hotbed that was Paris, which was
also true for another great experimenter of

Contemporary Fiction

Brooklyn (Colm Tóibín)
The Thrill of it All (Joseph O'Connor)
Spill Simmer Falter Wither
(Sara Baume)
The Glorious Heresies (Lisa McInerney)
The Gamal (Ciarán Collins)

language and style, Samuel Beckett (1906–89). Beckett's work centres on fundamental existential questions about the human condition and the nature of self. He is probably best known for his play *Waiting for Godot,* but his unassailable reputation is based on a series of stark novels and plays.

Of the dozens of 20th-century Irish authors to have achieved published renown, some names to look out for include playwright and novelist Brendan Behan (1923–64), who wove tragedy, wit and a turbulent life into his best works including *Borstal Boy, The Quare Fellow* and *The Hostage* before dying young of alcoholism.

Belfast-born CS Lewis (1898–1963) died a year earlier, but he left us *The Chronicles of Narnia,* a series of allegorical children's stories, three of which have been made into films. Other Northern writers have, not surprisingly, featured the Troubles in their work: Bernard MacLaverty's *Cal* (also made into a film) and his more recent *The Anatomy School* are both wonderful.

Contemporary Scene

'I love James Joyce. Never read him, but he's a true genius'. Yes, the stalwarts are still great, but ask your average Irish person who their favourite home-grown writer is and they'll most likely mention someone who's still alive.

They might say Roddy Doyle (1958–), whose mega-successful Barrytown trilogy *The Commitments, The Snapper* and *The Van* – have all been made into films; his latest book, *The Guts* (2013), saw the return of *The Commitments* protagonist Jimmy Rabbitte older, wiser and battling illness. Doyle's novel *Paddy Clarke, Ha Ha Ha* won the Booker Prize in 1993.

Sebastian Barry (1955–) has been shortlisted twice for the Man Booker Prize, for his WWI drama *A Long Long Way* (2005) and the absolutely compelling *The Secret Scripture* (2008), about a 100-year-old inmate of a mental hospital called Roseanne who decides to write an autobiography.

Anne Enright (1962–) did nab the Booker for *The Gathering* (2007), a zeitgeist tale of alcoholism and abuse – she described it as 'the intellectual equivalent of a Hollywood weepie'. Her latest novel, *The Green Road* (2015), continues to mine the murky waters of the Irish family. Another Booker Prize winner is heavyweight John Banville (1945–), who won it for *The Sea* (2005); we also recommend either *The Book of Evidence* (1989) or the masterful roman-à-clef *The Untouchable* (1997), based loosely on the secret-agent life of art historian Anthony Blunt. Banville's literary alter-ego is Benjamin Black, author of a series of seven hard-boiled detective thrillers set in the 1950s starring a troubled pathologist called Quirke – the latest book is *Even the Dead* (2015).

Another big hitter is Wexford-born Colm Tóibín (1955–), author of nine novels including *Brooklyn* (2009; made into a film in 2015 starring Saoirse Ronan) and, most recently, *Nora Webster* (2014), a powerful study of widowhood.

The Gaelic Revival

While Home Rule was being debated and shunted, something of a revolution was taking place in Irish arts, literature and identity. The poet William Butler Yeats (1865–1939) and his coterie of literary friends (including Lady Gregory, Douglas Hyde, John Millington Synge and George Russell) championed the Anglo-Irish literary revival, unearthing old Celtic tales and writing with fresh enthusiasm about a romantic Ireland of epic battles and warrior queens. For a country that had suffered centuries of invasion and deprivation, these images presented a much more attractive version of history.

The Troubles have been a rich and powerful subject for Northern Irish writers. The novels of Derry native Sean O'Reilly (1969–) are populated by characters freed from sectarianism but irreparably damaged by it: his last novel was *Watermark* (2005), about a young woman on the edge of desire and reason in an unnamed Irish town. Eoin McNamee (1961–) has written a series that explores the conflict directly, teasing out the effects of religion and history on the lives of individuals. His latest novel, *Blue is the Night* (2014), is the final book of a trilogy that also includes *The Blue Tango* (2001) and *Orchid Blue* (2010).

The second novel from Paul Murray (1975–), *Skippy Dies* (2010), is about a group of privileged students at an all-boys secondary school. It won him lots of critical praise (and an upcoming movie version directed by Neil Jordan) but his follow-up, *The Mark and the Void* (2015), which is set against the backdrop of the financial crisis, met with far more lukewarm praise. Not so Shane Hegarty (1976–), who in 2015 published the first volume of *Darkmouth*, a YA novel set in a fictional Irish town where young Finn is learning about girls and fighting monsters.

Belfast-born Anna Burns is the first Northern Irish author to win the Booker Prize, picking up the award in 2018 for her third novel, *Milkman*, about an 18-year-old girl being stalked by a much older paramilitary figure. Emilie Pine burst onto the scene in 2018 with a superb collection of nonfiction essays, *Notes to Self*, an unflinching look at addiction, sexual assault and mental health.

Melatu Oche Okorie was born in Nigeria, but moved to Ireland in 2006, where she spent 8½ years in direct provision (the processing system for asylum seekers); she recounts her experiences in the three stories of *This Hostel Life* (2018), which cast an important light on the migrant experience in Ireland.

Sinéad Gleeson is another important voice on the literary scene. Her 2019 memoir, *Constellations: Reflections from a Life*, is a stunning collection of linked essays exploring the fraught relationship between the physical body and identity. Dubliner Karl Geary left home for New York in the late '80s, but tells the story of a love affair between a teenager and an older woman in his debut novel, *Montpelier Parade* (2017).

Chick Lit

Authors hate the label and publishers profess to disregard it, but chick lit is big business, and few have mastered it as well as the Irish. Doyenne of them all is Maeve Binchy (1940–2012), whose mastery of the style saw her outsell most of the literary greats – her last novel before she died was *A Week in Winter* (2012). Marian Keyes (1963–) is another author with a long line of bestsellers, including *The Woman Who Stole My Life* (2014). She's a terrific storyteller with a rare ability to tackle sensitive issues such as alcoholism and depression, issues that she herself has suffered from and is admirably honest about. Former agony aunt Cathy Kelly has turned out novels at the rate of one a year since 1997: her most recent book is *The Year That Changed Everything* (2018), a heartwarming tale of three women passing their 30th, 40th and 50th birthdays.

Traditional music in O'Donoghue's pub (p76)

ANDREW MONTGOMERY/LONELY PLANET ©

Traditional Music

Irish music (known in Ireland as traditional music, or just trad) has retained a vibrancy not found in other traditional European forms, which have lost out to the overbearing influence of pop music. Although it has kept many of its traditional aspects, Irish music has itself influenced many forms of music, most notably American country music.

Instruments

Despite popular perception, the harp isn't widely used in traditional music (it *is* the national emblem, but that probably has more to do with the country traditionally being run by people pulling strings). The Bodhrán (*bow*-rawn) goat-skin drum is much more prevalent, although it makes for a lousy symbol. The uillean pipes, played by squeezing bellows under the elbow, provide another distinctive sound, although you're not likely to see them in a pub. The fiddle isn't unique to Ireland but it is one of the main instruments in the country's indigenous music, along with the flute, tin whistle, accordion and bouzouki (a version of the mandolin). Music fits into five main categories (jigs, reels, hornpipes, polkas and slow airs), while the old style of singing unaccompanied versions of traditional ballads and airs is called *sean-nós*.

★ **Traditional Albums**

The Quiet Glen (Tommy Peoples)

Paddy Keenan (Paddy Keenan)

The Chieftains 6: Bonaparte's Retreat (The Chieftains)

Old Hag You Have Killed Me (The Bothy Band)

ANATOLII BRONOVSKYI/SHUTTERSTOCK ©

Tunes

The music was never written down, it was passed on from one player to another and so endured and evolved – regional 'styles' only developed because local musicians sought to play just like the one who seemed to play better than everybody else. The blind itinerant harpist Turlough O'Carolan (1670–1738) 'wrote' more than 200 tunes – it's difficult to know how many versions their repeated learning has spawned. This characteristic of fluidity is key to an appreciation of traditional music, and explains why it is such a resilient form today.

Popular Bands

In the 1960s composer Seán Ó Riada (1931–71) tried to impose a kind of structure on traditional music. His ensemble group, Ceoltóirí Chualann, was the first to reach a wider audience, and from it The Chieftains were born, arguably the most important traditional group of them all. They started recording in 1963 – any one of their nearly 40 albums are worth a listen, but you won't go wrong with their 10-album eponymous series.

The other big success of the 1960s were The Dubliners. More folksy than traditional, they made a career out of bawdy drinking songs that got everybody singing along. Other popular bands include The Fureys, comprising four brothers originally from the travelling community (no, not like the Wilburys) along with guitarist Davey Arthur. And if it's rousing renditions of Irish rebel songs you're after, you can't go past The Wolfe Tones.

Since the 1970s various bands have tried to blend traditional with more progressive genres, with mixed success. The Bothy Band formed in 1975 and were a kind of trad supergroup: bouzouki player Dónal Lunny, uillean piper Paddy Keenan, flute and whistle player Matt Molloy (later a member of The Chieftains), fiddler Paddy Glackin and accordion player Tony MacMahon were all superb instrumentalists and their recordings are still as electrifying today as they were four decades ago.

Musicians tend to come together in collaborative projects. A contemporary group worth checking out are The Gloaming, who've taken traditional reels and given them a contemporary sound – their eponymous debut album (2011) is sensational. A key member of the group, fiddler Caoimhín Ó Raghallaigh, is also worth checking out in his own right; his latest album, *The Gloaming 3*, displays both his beautiful fiddle playing and his superb understanding of loops and electronic texturing.

And if you want to check out a group that melds rock, folk and traditional music, you won't go far wrong with The Spook of the Thirteenth Lock, who've released a couple of albums since 2008; in 2017 they released an EP called *The Bullet in the Brick*.

Gap of Dunloe (p167)

BENJAMIN B/SHUTTERSTOCK ©

Survival Guide

Directory A–Z

Accessible Travel

All new buildings have wheelchair access, and many hotels (especially urban ones that are part of chains) have installed lifts, ramps and other facilities such as hearing loops. Others, particularly B&Bs, have not invested in making their properties accessible.

In big cities most buses have low-floor access and priority spaces on board, but only 63% of the Bus Éireann coach fleet that operates on Commuter and Expressway services is wheelchair-accessible. Note,

too, that many of its rural stops are not accessible.

Trains are accessible with help. Call 1850 366 222 (outside Republic of Ireland +353 1 836 6222) or email access@irishrail. ie 24 hours in advance to arrange assistance with boarding, alighting and transferring at intermediate stations. Note that there is a limited number of wheelchair-accessible spaces on each train. Newer trains have audio and visual information systems for visually impaired and hearing-impaired passengers. Assistance dogs may travel without restriction. A full list of station facilities as at 2019 can be downloaded from www.irishrail. ie/travel-information/ disabled-access.

○ For an informative article with links to accessibility information for transport and tourist attractions, visit www.ireland.com/en-us/ accommodation/articles/ accessibility.

○ Two review sites covering accommodation, eating and drinking and places of interest that are worth checking out are https:// mobilitymojo.com, which has a searchable database that's expanding outside its base of Dublin and Galway; and www.accessibleireland. com, which also hosts short introductions to public transport.

○ Download Lonely Planet's free Accessible Travel guides

from http://lptravel.to/ AccessibleTravel.

○ The **Citizens' Information Board** (☑0761 079 000; www.citizensinformationboard. ie) in the Republic and **Disability Action** (☑028-9029 7880; www.disabilityaction. org; 189 Airport Rd W, Portside Business Pk; ☐28) in Northern Ireland can give some advice to travellers with disabilities.

Accommodation

Accommodation options range from bare and basic to pricey and palatial. The spine of the Irish hospitality business is the ubiquitous B&B, in recent years challenged by a plethora of midrange hotels and guesthouses. Ireland-specific online resources for accommodation include the following:

Daft.ie (www.daft.ie) Online property portal includes holiday homes and short-term rentals.

Elegant Ireland (www.elegant. ie) Specialises in self-catering castles, period houses and unique properties.

Imagine Ireland (www. imagineireland.com) Holiday cottage rentals throughout the whole island, including Northern Ireland.

Irish Landmark Trust (www. irishlandmark.com) Not-for-profit conservation group that rents self-catering properties of historical and cultural significance, such as castles, tower houses, gate lodges, schoolhouses and lighthouses.

Dream Ireland (www.dream ireland.com) Lists self-catering holiday cottages and apartments.

B&Bs & Guesthouses

Bed and breakfasts are small, family-run houses, farmhouses and period country houses, generally with fewer than five bedrooms. Standards vary enormously, but most have some bedrooms with private bathroom at a cost of roughly €40 to €60 (£35 to £50) per person per night (at least €100 in Dublin). In luxurious B&Bs, expect to pay €70 (£60) or more per person. Off-season rates – usually October through to March – are usually lower, as are midweek prices.

Guesthouses are like upmarket B&Bs, but a bit bigger. Facilities are usually better and sometimes include a restaurant.

Other tips:

◦ Facilities in B&Bs range from basic (bed, bathroom, kettle, TV) to beatific (whirlpool baths, rainforest showers) as you go up in price. Wi-fi is standard and most have parking (but do check).

◦ Most B&Bs take credit cards, but the occasional rural one might not; check when you book.

◦ Advance reservations are strongly recommended, especially in peak season (June to September).

◦ Some B&Bs and guesthouses in more remote regions may only be open from Easter to September or similar.

◦ If full, B&B owners may recommend another house in the area (possibly a private house taking occasional guests, not in tourist listings).

◦ To make prices more competitive at some B&Bs, breakfast may be optional.

Hotels

Hotels range from the local pub to a medieval castle. Booking online or negotiating directly will almost always net you a better rate than the published one, especially out of season or midweek (except for business hotels, which offer cheaper weekend rates).

The bulk of the country's hotels are of the midrange variety, with clean rooms and a range of facilities, from restaurants to gyms. The trend towards offering free wi-fi is stubbornly resisted by many – usually more expensive hotels – that still charge for the privilege.

House Swapping

House swapping can be a popular and affordable way to enjoy a real home away from home. There are several agencies in Ireland that, for an annual fee, facilitate international swaps. The fee pays for access to a website and a book giving house descriptions, photographs and the owners' details. After that it's up to you to make arrangements. Use of the family car is sometimes included.

Homelink International House Exchange (www.homelink.ie)

Accommodation Prices

Accommodation prices vary according to demand – or have different rates for online, phone or walk-in bookings. B&B rates are more consistent, but virtually every other accommodation will charge wildly different rates depending on the time of year, day, festival schedule and even your ability to do a little negotiating. The following price ranges are based on a double room with private bathroom in high season.

Budget	Republic	Dublin	Northern Ireland
€/£	less than €80	under €150	less than £50
€€/££	€80–180	€150–250	£50–120
€€€/£££	more than €180	over €250	more than £120

Home exchange service running for more than 60 years.
Intervac International Holiday Service (www.intervac-homeexchange.com) Long-established, with agents all over the world.

Rental Accommodation

Self-catering accommodation is often rented on a weekly basis and usually means an apartment, a house or a cottage where you look after yourself. The rates vary from one region and season to another.
Fáilte Ireland (Republic 1850 230 330, UK 0800 039 7000; www.discoverireland.ie) publishes a guide for registered self-catering accommodation; you can check listings on its website.

Climate

Belfast

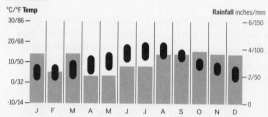

Dublin

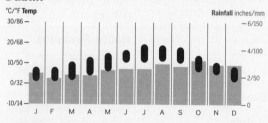

Galway

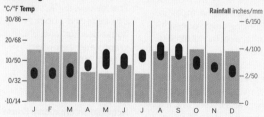

Customs Regulations

Both the Republic of Ireland and Northern Ireland have a two-tier customs system: one for goods bought duty-free outside the EU, the other for goods bought in another EU country where tax and duty is paid. There is technically no limit to the amount of goods transportable within the EU, but customs will use certain guidelines to distinguish personal use from commercial purpose. Allowances are as follows:

Duty-free For duty-free goods from outside the EU, limits include 200 cigarettes, 1L of spirits or 2L of wine, 60mL of perfume and 250mL of eau de toilette.

Tax and duty paid Amounts that officially constitute personal use include 3200 cigarettes (or 400 cigarillos, 200 cigars or 3kg of tobacco) and either 10L of spirits, 20L of fortified wine, 60L of sparkling wine, 90L of still wine or 110L of beer.

Food

Our cafe and restaurant listings appear in budget order, with the cheapest budget range first. Within the ranges, listings are given in preference order.

For more information, see the Food & Drink chapter.

Electricity

Type G
230V/50Hz

Health

No jabs are required to travel to Ireland.

Excellent health care is readily available. For minor, self-limiting illnesses, pharmacists can give valuable advice and sell over-the-counter medication. They can also advise when more specialised help is required and point you in the right direction.

EU citizens equipped with a European Health Insurance Card (EHIC), available from health centres or, in the UK, post offices, will be covered for most medical care – but not nonemergencies or emergency repatriation. While other countries, such as Australia, also have reciprocal agreements with Ireland and Britain, many do not.

In Northern Ireland everyone receives free emergency treatment at accident and emergency (A&E) departments of state-run NHS hospitals, irrespective of nationality.

Insurance

Comprehensive travel insurance to cover theft, loss and medical problems is highly recommended. Worldwide travel insurance is available at www.lonelyplanet.com/travel-insurance. You can buy, extend and claim online anytime – even if you're already on the road.

Internet Access

Wi-fi and 3G/4G networks are making internet cafes largely redundant (except to gamers). The few that are left will charge around €6 per hour. Most accommodation places have wi-fi, either free or for a daily charge (up to €10 per day).

Legal Matters

Illegal drugs are widely available, especially in clubs. The possession of small quantities of marijuana attracts a fine or warning, but harder drugs are treated more seriously. Public drunkenness is illegal but commonplace – the police will usually ignore it unless you're causing trouble. Should you find yourself under arrest, you have the right to remain silent and to contact either an attorney or your embassy.

Once you are charged and cautioned you will either be released on bail (known as 'station bail') or, in the event of a more serious offence, transferred from the police station to the District Court as early as possible (usually within 12 hours), where you will either be bailed or remanded in custody by the judge.

Contact the following for assistance:

Legal Aid Board (☏066-947 1000, in Republic 1890 615 200; www.legalaidboard.ie; ☉9am-5pm Mon-Fri) Has a network of local law centres.

Legal Services Agency Northern Ireland (☏028-9076 3000; www.justice-ni.gov.uk/topics/legal-aid) Administers the statutory legal-aid scheme for Northern Ireland, but cannot offer legal advice.

LGBT+ Travellers

Ireland is a pretty tolerant place for gays and lesbians. Bigger cities such as Dublin, Galway and Cork have well-established gay scenes, as do Belfast and Derry in Northern Ireland. In 2015 Ireland overwhelmingly backed same-sex marriage in a historic referendum, whereas Northern Ireland is the only part of the United Kingdom where it's not legal.

While the cities and main towns tend to be progressive and tolerant, you'll still find pockets of homophobia throughout the island, particularly in smaller towns and rural areas. Resources include the following:

Gaire (www.gaire.com) Message board and info for a host of gay-related issues.

Gay & Lesbian Youth Northern Ireland (www.cara-friend.org.uk/projects/glyni) Voluntary counselling, information, health and social-space organisation for the gay community.

Gay Men's Health Project (☎01-660 2189; www.hse.ie/go/GMHS) Practical advice on men's health issues.

National Lesbian & Gay Federation (NLGF; ☎01-671 9076; http://nxf.ie) Publishes the monthly *Gay Community News* (www.gcn.ie).

Northern Ireland Gay Rights Association (☎028-9066 4111; www.nigra.org.uk; Belfast LGBT Centre, 23-31 Waring St) Represents the rights and interests of the LGBTQ community in Northern Ireland. It offers phone and online support, but is not a call-in centre.

Outhouse (☎01-873 4932; www.outhouse.ie; 105 Capel St; ◷10am-6pm Mon-Fri, noon-5pm Sat; ◻all city centre) Top gay, lesbian and bisexual resource centre. Great stop-off point to see what's on, check noticeboards and meet people. It publishes Ireland's free *Pink Pages*, a directory of gay-centric services, which is also accessible on the website.

Maps

Michelin's 1:400,000-scale Ireland map (No 923) is a decent single sheet map, with clear cartography and most of the island's scenic roads marked. The four maps – North, South, East and West – that make up the Ordnance Survey Holiday map series at 1:250,000 scale are useful for more detail.

The Ordnance Survey Discovery series covers the whole island in 89 maps at a scale of 1:50,000, also available as digital versions. These are all available through Ordnance Survey Ireland (www.osi.ie) and many bookshops around Ireland.

Collins also publishes a range of maps covering Ireland, also available at bookshops.

Money

The Republic of Ireland uses the euro (€), while Northern Ireland uses the pound sterling (£), although the euro is also accepted in many places.

ATMs

All banks have ATMs that are linked to international money systems such as Cirrus, Maestro or Plus. Each transaction incurs a currency-conversion fee, and credit cards can incur immediate and exorbitant cash-advance interest-rate charges. Watch out for ATMs that have been tampered with, as card-reader scams ('skimming') have become a real problem.

Credit & Debit Cards

Visa and MasterCard credit and debit cards are widely accepted. American Express is only accepted by the major chains, and virtually no one will accept Diners or JCB. Chip-and-PIN is the norm for card transactions – only a few places will accept a signature.

Smaller businesses, such as pubs and some B&Bs, prefer debit cards (and will charge a fee for credit cards) and a small number of rural B&Bs only take cash.

Taxes & Refunds

Most goods come with value-added tax (VAT) of 21% (20% in Northern Ireland), which non-EU residents can claim back so long as the store in which the goods are purchased operates either the Cashback or Taxback refund programme (the Tax-Free Shopping refund scheme in Northern Ireland), usually indicated by a display sticker on the window.

Tipping

Hotels A tip of €1/£1 per bag is standard; tip cleaning staff at your discretion.

Pubs Not expected unless table service is provided, then €1/£1 for a round of drinks.

Restaurants For decent service 10%; up to 15% in more expensive places.

Taxis Tip 10% or round up fare to nearest euro/pound.

Toilet attendants Loose change; no more than 50c/50p.

Opening Hours

Banks 10am–4pm Monday to Friday (to 5pm Thursday)
Pubs 10.30am–11.30pm Monday to Thursday, 10.30am–12.30am Friday and Saturday, noon–11pm Sunday (30 minutes 'drinking up' time allowed); closed Christmas Day and Good Friday

Practicalities

Newspapers *Irish Independent* (www.independent.ie), *Irish Times* (www.irishtimes.com), *Irish Examiner* (www.examiner.ie), *Belfast Telegraph* (www.belfasttelegraph.co.uk).

Radio RTE Radio 1 (88MHz–90MHz), Today FM (100MHz–103MHz), Newstalk 106-108 (106MHz–108MHz), BBC Ulster (92MHz–95MHz; Northern Ireland only).

Smoking It is illegal to smoke indoors everywhere except private residences and prisons.

Weights & Measures The metric system is used; the exception is for liquid measures of alcohol, where pints are used.

Restaurants noon–10.30pm; many close one day of the week
Shops 9.30am–6pm Monday to Saturday (to 8pm Thursday in cities), noon–6pm Sunday

Photography

● Natural light can be very dull, so use higher ISO speeds than usual, such as 400 for daylight shots.

● In Northern Ireland get permission before taking photos of fortified police stations, army posts or other military or quasi-military paraphernalia.

● Don't take photos of people in Protestant or Catholic strongholds of West Belfast without permission; always ask and be prepared to accept a refusal.

● Lonely Planet's *Guide to Travel Photography* is full of helpful tips for photography while on the road.

Public Holidays

Public holidays can cause road chaos as everyone tries to get somewhere else for the break. It's wise to book accommodation in advance for these times.

The following are public holidays in both the Republic and Northern Ireland:

New Year's Day 1 January
St Patrick's Day 17 March
Easter (Good Friday to Easter Monday inclusive) March/April
May Holiday 1st Monday in May
Christmas Day 25 December
St Stephen's Day (Boxing Day) 26 December

St Patrick's Day and St Stephen's Day holidays are taken on the following Monday when they fall on a weekend. Nearly

Telephone

When calling Ireland from abroad, dial your international access code, followed by 353 and the area code (dropping the 0). Area codes in the Republic have three digits, eg 021 for Cork, 091 for Galway and 061 for Limerick. The only exception is Dublin, which has a two-digit code (01).

To make international calls from Ireland, first dial 00 then the country code, followed by the local area code and number. Always use the area code if calling from a mobile phone, but you don't need it if calling from a fixed-line number within the area code.

In Northern Ireland the area code for all fixed-line numbers is 028, but you only need to use it if calling from a mobile phone or from outside Northern Ireland. To call Northern Ireland from the Republic, use 048 instead of 028, without the international dialling code.

	Republic	Northern Ireland
Country Code	☎353	☎44
International Access Code	☎00	☎00
Directory Enquiries	☎11811/ ☎11850	☎118 118/ ☎118 192
International Directory Enquiries	☎11818	

Mobile Phones

○ Both the Republic and Northern Ireland use the GSM 900/1800 cellular phone system, which is compatible with European and Australian, but not North American or Japanese, phones.

○ Pay-as-you-go mobile-phone packages with any of the main providers start at around €40 and usually include a basic handset and credit of around €10.

○ SIM-only packages are also available, but make sure your phone is compatible with the local provider.

everywhere in the Republic closes on Good Friday even though it isn't an official public holiday. In the North most shops open on Good Friday, but close the following Tuesday.

Northern Ireland

Spring Bank Holiday Last Monday in May

The Twelfth 12 July

August Holiday Last Monday in August

Republic of Ireland

June Holiday 1st Monday in June

August Holiday 1st Monday in August

October Holiday Last Monday in October

Safe Travel

Ireland is safer than most countries in Europe, but normal precautions should be observed.

○ Don't leave anything visible in your car when you park.

○ Skimming at ATMs is an ongoing problem; be sure to cover the keypad with your hand when you input your PIN.

○ In Northern Ireland exercise extra care in 'interface' areas where sectarian neighbourhoods adjoin.

○ Best avoid Northern Ireland during the climax of the Orange marching season on 12 July. Sectarian passions are usually inflamed and even many Northerners leave the province at this time.

Time

In winter Ireland is on Greenwich Mean Time (GMT), also known as Universal Time Coordinated

(UTC), the same as Britain. In summer the clock shifts to GMT plus one hour, so when it's noon in Dublin and London, it's 4am in Los Angeles and Vancouver, 7am in New York and Toronto, 1pm in Paris, 7pm in Singapore and 9pm in Sydney.

Toilets

There are no on-street facilities in Ireland. All shopping centres have public toilets (either free or 20c/20p). If you're stranded, go into any bar or hotel.

Tourist Information

In both the Republic and the North there's a tourist office or information point in almost every big town. Most can offer a variety of services, including accommodation and attraction reservations, currency-changing services, map and guidebook sales and free publications.

In the Republic the tourism purview falls to **Fáilte Ireland** (Republic 1850 230 330, UK 0800 039 7000; www.discoverireland. ie); in Northern Ireland, it's **Discover Northern Ireland** (head office 028-9023 1221; www.discovernorthernireland. com). Outside Ireland both organisations unite under the banner Tourism Ireland (www.tourismireland.com).

Visas

If you're a European Economic Area (EEA) national, you don't need a visa to

Border Crossings

Border crossings between Northern Ireland and the Republic are unnoticeable; there are no formalities of any kind. However, this may change once Brexit occurs.

visit (or work in) either the Republic or Northern Ireland. Citizens of Australia, Canada, New Zealand, South Africa and the US can visit the Republic for up to three months, and Northern Ireland for up to six months. They are not allowed to work, unless sponsored by an employer.

Full visa requirements for visiting the Republic are available online at www.dfa.ie; for Northern Ireland's visa requirements see www.gov.uk/ government/organisations/ uk-visas-and-immigration.

To stay longer in the Republic, contact the local *garda* (police) station or the **Garda National Immigration Bureau** (01-666 9100; www.garda.ie; 13-14 Burgh Quay, Dublin; 8am-9pm Mon-Fri; all city centre). To stay longer in Northern Ireland, contact the Home Office (www.gov.uk/govern ment/organisations/ uk-visas-and-immigration).

Climate Change & Travel

Every form of transport that relies on carbon-based fuel generates CO_2, the main cause of human-induced climate change. Modern travel is dependent on aeroplanes, which might use less fuel per kilometre per person than most cars but travel much greater distances. The altitude at which aircraft emit gases (including CO_2) and particles also contributes to their climate change impact. Many websites offer 'carbon calculators' that allow people to estimate the carbon emissions generated by their journey and, for those who wish to do so, to offset the impact of the greenhouse gases emitted with contributions to portfolios of climate-friendly initiatives throughout the world. Lonely Planet offsets the carbon footprint of all staff and author travel.

Women Travellers

Ireland should pose no problems for women travellers. Finding contraception is not the problem it once was, though anyone on the pill should bring adequate supplies.

Rape Crisis Network Ireland (☏091-563 676; www.rcni.ie) In the Republic. App available.

Transport

Getting There & Away

Entering the Country

Dublin is the primary point of entry for most visitors to Ireland, although some do choose Shannon or Belfast.

○ The overwhelming majority of airlines fly into Dublin.

○ For travel to the US, Dublin and Shannon airports operate preclearance facilities, which means you pass through US immigration *before* boarding your aircraft.

○ Dublin is home to two seaports that serve as the main points of sea transport with Britain; ferries from France arrive in the southern ports of Rosslare and Cork.

○ Dublin is the nation's rail hub.

Air

Cork Airport (☏021-431 3131; www.corkairport.com) Airlines servicing the airport include Aer Lingus and Ryanair.

Dublin Airport (☏01-814 1111; www.dublinairport.com) Ireland's major international gateway airport, with direct flights from the UK, Europe, North America and the Middle East.

Shannon Airport (SNN; ☏061-712 000; www.shannonairport. ie; ☏) Has a few direct flights from the UK, Europe and North America.

Belfast International Airport (Aldergrove; ☏028-9448 4848; www.belfastairport.com; Airport Rd) Has direct flights from the UK, Europe and North America.

Land

Eurolines (www.eurolines.com) has a daily coach and ferry service from London's Victoria Station to Dublin Busáras.

Sea

The main ferry routes between Ireland and the UK and mainland Europe are as follows:

○ Belfast to Liverpool (England; eight hours)

○ Belfast to Cairnryan (Scotland; 2½ hours)

○ Cork to Roscoff (France; 14 hours; April to October only)

○ Dublin to Liverpool (England; fast ferry four hours, slow ferry 8½ hours)

○ Dublin to Holyhead (Wales; fast ferry two hours, slow ferry 3½ hours)

○ Dublin to Roscoff (France; 18 hours)

○ Larne to Cairnryan (Scotland; two hours)

○ Rosslare to Cherbourg (France; 18 hours)

○ Rosslare to Fishguard and Pembroke (Wales; 3½ hours)

Competition from budget airlines has forced ferry operators to discount heavily and offer flexible fares.

A useful website is www. aferry.co.uk, which covers all sea-ferry routes and operators to Ireland.

Main operators include the following:

Brittany Ferries (☏021-427 7801; www.brittanyferries.ie; 42 Grand Pde) Cork to Roscoff; April to October.

Irish Ferries (☏0818 300 400; www.irishferries.com; Ferryport, Terminal Rd South) Dublin to Holyhead (up to five per day year-round) and Dublin to France (four times per week).

P&O Ferries (☏01-686 9467; www.poferries.com; Terminal 3, Dublin Port) Daily sailings year-round from Dublin to Liverpool, and Larne to Cairnryan.

Stena Line Daily sailings from Holyhead to Dublin,

Road Distances (km)

	Athlone	Belfast	Cork	Derry	Donegal	Dublin	Galway	Kilkenny	Killarney	Limerick	Rosslare Harbour	Shannon Airport	Sligo	Waterford
Belfast	242													
Cork	219	424												
Derry	209	117	428											
Donegal	183	180	402	69										
Dublin	127	167	256	237	233									
Galway	93	306	209	272	204	212								
Kilkenny	116	284	148	335	309	129	172							
Killarney	232	436	87	441	407	304	193	198						
Limerick	363	323	105	328	287	202	98	113	111					
Rosslare Harbour	201	330	208	397	391	153	274	98	275	211				
Shannon Airport	133	346	128	351	282	218	93	135	135	25	234			
Sligo	117	206	336	135	66	214	138	245	343	227	325	218		
Waterford	164	333	126	383	357	163	220	48	193	129	82	152	293	
Wexford	184	309	187	378	372	135	253	80	254	190	19	213	307	61

Belfast to Liverpool and Cairnryan, and Rosslare to Fishguard and Cherbourg.

Getting Around

The big decision in getting around Ireland is whether to go by car or use public transport. Your own car will make the best use of your time and help you reach even the most remote of places. It's usually easy to get very cheap rentals – €30 per day, or even less, is common – and if two or more are travelling together, the fee for rental and petrol can be cheaper than bus fares.

The bus network, made up of a mix of public and private operators, is extensive and generally quite competitive, though journey times can be slow and lots of the points of interest outside towns are not served. The rail network is quicker but more limited, serving only some major towns and cities. Both buses and trains get busy during peak times; you'll need to book in advance to be guaranteed a seat.

Air

Ireland's size makes domestic flying unnecessary, but there are flights between Dublin and Belfast, Cork, Derry, Donegal, Galway, Kerry, Shannon and Sligo aimed at passengers connecting from international flights. Flights linking the mainland to the Aran Islands are popular.

Bicycle

Ireland's compact size and scenic landscapes make it a good cycling destination. However, unreliable weather, very narrow roads and some very fast drivers are

Bus & Train/Ferry Combos

It's possible to combine bus, ferry and train tickets from major UK centres to most Irish towns. This might not be as quick as flying on a budget airline but leaves less of a carbon footprint. The journey between London and Dublin takes about 12 hours by bus, eight hours by train; the London to Belfast trip takes 13 to 16 hours by bus. Both can be had for as little as £29 one way. Eurolines (www.eurolines.com) has bus-ferry combos while Virgin Trains (www.virgintrains.co.uk) has combos that include London to Dublin. For more options, look for SailRail fares.

major concerns. Special tracks such as the 42km Great Western Greenway in County Mayo are a delight. A good tip for cyclists in the west is that the prevailing winds make it easier to cycle from south to north.

Buses will carry bikes, but only if there's room. For trains, bear the following in mind:

◦ Intercity trains charge up to €10.50 per bike.

◦ Book in advance (www. irishrail.ie), as there's only room for two bikes per service.

Companies that arrange cycle tours in Ireland include the following:

Go Visit Ireland (066-976 2094; www.govisitireland.com) Guided and independent tours.

Irish Cycling Safaris (01-260 0749; www.cyclingsafaris. com; tours from €860) Organises numerous tours across Ireland.

Boat

Ireland's offshore islands are all served by boat.

Ferries also operate across rivers, inlets and loughs, providing useful shortcuts, particularly for cyclists.

Bus

Private buses compete – often very favourably – with Bus Éireann in the Republic and also run where the national buses are irregular or absent.

Distances are not especially long: few bus journeys will last longer than five hours. Bus Éireann bookings can be made online, but you can't reserve a seat for a particular service. Dynamic pricing is in effect on many routes, so book early to get the lowest fares.

Note the following:

◦ Bus routes and frequencies are slowly contracting in the Republic.

◦ The National Journey Planner app by Transport for Ireland is very useful for planning bus and train trips. The main bus services in Ireland are as follows:

Bus Éireann (1850 836 6111; www.buseireann.ie) The Republic's primary bus line.

Translink (028-9066 6630; www.translink.co.uk) Northern Ireland's main bus service; includes Ulsterbus and Goldline.

Car & Motorcycle

Travelling by car or motorbike means greater flexibility and independence. The road system is extensive and the network of motorways has cut driving times considerably. Also note, however, that many secondary roads are very narrow and at times rather perilous.

All cars on public roads must be insured. If you are bringing your own vehicle, check that your insurance will cover you in Ireland.

Hire

Advance hire rates start at around €20 a day for a small car (unlimited mileage). Shop around and use price-comparison sites as well as company sites (which often have deals not available on booking sites).

Other tips:

◦ Most cars are manual; automatic cars are available, but they're more expensive to hire.

◦ If you're travelling from the Republic into Northern Ireland, it's important to be sure that your insurance covers journeys to the North.

◦ The majority of hire companies won't rent you

a car if you're under 23 and haven't had a valid driving licence for at least a year.

Parking

All big towns and cities have covered and open short-stay car parks that are conveniently signposted.

○ On-street parking is usually by 'pay and display' tickets available from on-street machines or disc parking (discs, which rotate to display the time you park your car, are usually provided by rental agencies). Costs range from €1.50 to €6 per hour; all-day parking in a car park will cost around €25.

○ Yellow lines (single or double) along the edge of the road indicate restrictions. Double yellow lines mean no parking at any time. Always look for the nearby sign that spells out when you can and cannot park.

Roads & Rules

Ireland may be one of the few countries where the posted speed limits are often much faster than you'll find possible.

○ Motorways (marked by M+number on a blue background): modern, divided highways.

○ Primary roads (N+number on a green background in the Republic, A+number in Northern Ireland): usually well-engineered two-lane roads.

○ Secondary and tertiary roads (marked as R+number in the Republic, B+number in Northern Ireland): can be very winding and exceedingly narrow.

○ Tolls are charged on many motorways, usually by machine at a plaza. On the M50, pay the automated tolls between junctions 6 and 7 at www.eflow.ie.

○ Directional signs are often not in evidence.

○ GPS navigation via your smartphone or device is very helpful.

○ EU licences are treated like Irish licences.

○ Non-EU licences are valid in Ireland for up to 12 months.

○ If you plan to bring a car from Europe, it's illegal to drive without at least third-party insurance.

The basic rules of the road are as follows:

○ Drive on the left; overtake to the right.

○ Safety belts must be worn by the driver and all passengers.

○ Children aged under 12 aren't allowed to sit in the front passenger seat.

○ When entering a roundabout, give way to the right.

○ In the Republic, speed-limit and distance signs are in kilometres; in the North, speed-limit and distance signs are often in miles.

Speed limits:

Republic 120km/h on motorways, 100km/h on national roads, 80km/h on regional and local roads, and 50km/h or as signposted in towns.

Northern Ireland 70mph (112km/h) on motorways, 60mph (96km/h) on main roads, 30mph (48km/h) in built-up areas.

Drinking and driving is taken very seriously. You're allowed a maximum blood-alcohol level

Bus & Rail Passes

There are a few bus, rail and bus-and-rail passes worth considering:

Irish Explorer Offers customers five days of unlimited Irish Rail travel within 15 consecutive days (adult/child €160/80).

Open Road Pass Three days' travel out of six consecutive days (€60) on Bus Éireann; extra days cost €16.50.

Sunday Day Tracker One day's unlimited travel (adult/child £8/4) on Translink buses and trains in Northern Ireland, Sunday only.

Trekker Four Day Four consecutive days of unlimited travel (€110) on Irish Rail.

Note that Eurail's one-country pass for Ireland is a poor deal in any of its permutations.

Motoring Organisations

The following comprise Ireland's two main motoring organisations:

Automobile Association (AA; ☑Northern Ireland breakdown 00 800 8877 6655, Republic breakdown 1800 66 77 88; www.theaa.ie)

Royal Automobile Club (RAC; ☑Northern Ireland breakdown 0333 200 0999, Republic breakdown 0800 015 6000; www.rac.ie)

of 50mg/100mL (0.05%) in the Republic, and 35mg/100mL (0.035%) in Northern Ireland.

Local Transport

Dublin and Belfast have comprehensive local bus networks, as do some other large towns.

○ The Dublin Area Rapid Transport (DART) rail line runs roughly the length of Dublin's coastline, while the Luas tram system has two popular lines.

○ Taxis tend to be expensive: flagfall is daytime/ night-time €3.60/4 plus €1.10/1.40 per kilometre after the first 500m.

○ Uber is in Dublin but is not as popular as the taxi app MyTaxi (www.mytaxi.com).

Tours

Organised tours are a convenient way of exploring the country's main highlights if your time is limited. Tours can be booked through travel agencies, tourist offices, or through the tour companies.

Bus Éireann (☑01-836 6111; www.buseireann.ie) Offers day trips from Dublin and Cork to popular destinations.

CIE Tours International (www.cietours.com) Runs multiday bus tours of the Republic and the North.

Paddywagon Tours (☑01-823 0822; www.paddywagontours.com) Activity-filled tours all over Ireland.

Railtours Ireland (☑01-856 0045; www.railtoursireland.com) All-Ireland tours for train enthusiasts.

Touristy (☑087-631 2682; www.touristy.ie) One- to 14-day custom tours with your own vehicle and driver.

Train

Given Ireland's relatively small size, train travel can be quick and advance-purchase fares are competitive with buses.

○ Many of the Republic's most beautiful areas, such as whole swaths of the Wild Atlantic Way, are not served by rail.

○ Most lines radiate out from Dublin, with limited ways of interconnecting between lines, which can complicate touring.

○ There are four routes from Belfast in Northern Ireland, one links with the system in the Republic via Newry to Dublin.

○ True 1st class only exists on the Dublin–Cork and Dublin–Belfast lines. On all other trains, seats are the same size as in standard class, despite any marketing come-ons such as 'Premier' class.

Irish Rail (Iarnród Éireann; ☑01-836 6222; www.irishrail.ie) Operates trains in the Republic.

Translink NI Railways (☑028-9066 6630; www.translink.co.uk) Operates trains in Northern Ireland.

Language

Irish (Gaeilge) is Ireland's official language. In 2003 the government introduced the Official Languages Act, whereby all official documents, street signs and official titles must be either in Irish or in both Irish and English. Despite its official status, Irish is really only spoken in pockets of rural Ireland known as the Gaeltacht, the main ones being Cork (*Corcaigh*), Donegal (*Dún na nGall*), Galway (*Gaillimh*), Kerry (*Ciarraí*) and Mayo (*Maigh Eo*).

Ask people outside the Gaeltacht if they can speak Irish and nine out of 10 of them will probably reply '*ah, cupla focal*' (a couple of words) – and they generally mean it. Irish is a compulsory subject in schools for those aged six to 15, but Irish classes have traditionally been rather academic and unimaginative, leading many students to resent it as a waste of time. As a result, many adults regret not having a greater grasp of it. In recent times, at long last, a new Irish curriculum has been introduced cutting the hours devoted to the subject but making the lessons more fun, practical and celebratory.

For in-depth language information and a witty insight into the quirks of language in Ireland, check out Lonely Planet's *Irish Language & Culture*. To enhance your trip with this title or a phrasebook, visit **lonely planet.com**. Lonely Planet's Fast Talk app is available through the Apple App store.

Pronunciation

Irish divides vowels into long (those with an accent) and short (those without an accent), and distinguishes between broad (**a**, **á**, **o**, **ó**, **u**) and slender (**e**, **é**, **i** and **í**) vowels, which can affect the pronunciation of preceding consonants.

Other than a few odd-looking clusters, like **mh** and **bhf** (both pronounced as 'w'), consonants are generally pronounced as they are in English.

Irish has three main dialects: Connaught Irish (in Galway and northern Mayo), Munster Irish (in Cork, Kerry and Waterford) and Ulster Irish (in Donegal). The pronunciation guides given here are an anglicised version of modern standard Irish, which is essentially an amalgam of the three – if you read them as if they were English, you'll be able to get your point across in Gaeilge without even having to think about the specifics of Irish pronunciation or spelling.

Basics

Hello. (greeting)
Dia duit. — deea gwit

Hello. (reply)
Dia is Muire duit. — deeas moyra gwit

Good morning.
Maidin mhaith. — mawjin wah

Good night.
Oíche mhaith. — eekheh wah

Goodbye. (when leaving)
Slán leat. — slawn lyat

Goodbye. (when staying)
Slán agat. — slawn agut

Excuse me.
Gabh mo leithscéal. — gamoh lesh scale

I'm sorry.
Tá brón orm. — taw brohn oruhm

Thank you (very) much.
Go raibh (míle) — goh rev (meela)
maith agat. — mah agut

Do you speak Irish?
An bhfuil Gaeilge — on wil gaylge
agat? — oguht

I don't understand.
Ní thuigim. — nee higgim

What is this?
Cad é seo? — kod ay shoh

What is that?
Cad é sin? — kod ay shin

I'd like to go to ...
Ba mhaith liom — baw wah lohm
dul go dtí ... — dull go dee ...

I'd like to buy ...
Ba mhaith liom ... — bah wah lohm ...
a cheannach. — a kyanukh

..., (if you) please.

más é do thoil é.	... maws ay do hall ay	

Yes.

Tá. — taw

No.

Níl. — neel

It is.

Sea. — sheh

It isn't.

Ní hea. — nee heh

another/ one more

ceann eile — kyawn ella

nice

go deas — goh dyass

Making Conversation

Welcome.

Ceád míle fáilte. — kade meela fawlcha
(lit: 100,000 welcomes)

How are you?

Conas a tá tú? — kunas aw taw too

I'm fine.

Táim go maith. — thawm go mah

What's your name?

Cad is ainm duit? — kod is anim dwit

My name is (Sean Frayne).

(Sean Frayne) is ainm dom. — (shawn frain) is anim dohm

Impossible!

Ní féidir é! — nee faydir ay

Nonsense!

Ráiméis! — rawmaysh

That's terrible!

Go huafásach! — guh hoofawsokh

Take it easy.

Tóg é gobogé. — tohg ay gobogay

Cheers!

Slainte! — slawncha

I'm never ever drinking again!

Ní ólfaidh mé go brách arís! — knee ohlhee mey gu brawkh ureeshch

Bon voyage!

Go n-éirí an bóthar leat! — go nairee on bohhar lat

Happy Christmas!

Nollaig shona! — nuhlig hona

Happy Easter!

Cáisc shona! — kawshk hona

Days of the Week

Monday	*Dé Luaín*	day loon
Tuesday	*Dé Máirt*	day maart
Wednesday	*Dé Ceádaoin*	day kaydeen
Thursday	*Déardaoin*	daredeen
Friday	*Dé hAoine*	day heeneh
Saturday	*Dé Sathairn*	day sahern
Sunday	*Dé Domhnaigh*	day downick

Numbers

1	*haon*	hayin
2	*dó*	doe
3	*trí*	tree
4	*ceathaír*	kahirr
5	*cúig*	kooig
6	*sé*	shay
7	*seacht*	shocked
8	*hocht*	hukt
9	*naoi*	nay
10	*deich*	jeh
20	*fiche*	feekhe

Behind the Scenes

Acknowledgements

Climate map data adapted from Peel MC, Finlayson BL & McMahon TA (2007) 'Updated World Map of the Köppen-Geiger Climate Classification', *Hydrology and Earth System Sciences*, 11, 1633–44.

Cover photograph: Kylemore Abbey, Ester Lo Feudo/Shutterstock©

This Book

This 3rd edition of Lonely Planet's *Best of Ireland* guidebook was researched and written by Neil Wilson, Isabel Albiston, Fionn Davenport, Belinda Dixon and Catherine Le Nevez. The previous edition was researched and written by Neil Wilson, Isabel Albiston, Fionn Davenport, Damian Harper and Catherine Le Nevez. This guidebook was produced by the following:

Destination Editor Clifton Wilkinson

Senior Product Editor Jessica Ryan

Regional Senior Cartographer Mark Griffiths

Product Editor Amy Lynch

Book Designer Fergal Condon

Assisting Editors Andrew Bain, Imogen Bannister, Nigel Chin, Carly Hall, Kellie Langdon, Anne Mulvaney, Rosie Nicholson, Kristin Odijk, Maja Vatrić, Simon Williamson

Assisting Cartographer Anthony Phelan

Cover Researcher Naomi Parker

Thanks to Melanie Dankel, Shona Gray, Sandie Kestell, Sarah Stewart

Send Us Your Feedback

We love to hear from travellers – your comments keep us on our toes and help make our books better. Our well-travelled team reads every word on what you loved or loathed about this book. Although we cannot reply individually to postal submissions, we always guarantee that your feedback goes straight to the appropriate authors, in time for the next edition. Each person who sends us information is thanked in the next edition, the most useful submissions are rewarded with a selection of digital PDF chapters.

Visit lonelyplanet.com/contact to submit your updates and suggestions or to ask for help. Our award-winning website also features inspirational travel stories, news and discussions.

Note: We may edit, reproduce and incorporate your comments in Lonely Planet products such as guidebooks, websites and digital products, so let us know if you don't want your comments reproduced or your name acknowledged. For a copy of our privacy policy visit lonelyplanet.com/privacy.

Index

Symbols & Map Key

Look for these symbols to quickly identify listings:

- ◉ Sights
- ✪ Activities
- ✪ Courses
- ✪ Tours
- ✪ Festivals & Events
- ✪ Eating
- ✪ Drinking
- ✪ Entertainment
- ✪ Shopping
- ✪ Information & Transport

These symbols and abbreviations give vital information for each listing:

🌿 Sustainable or green recommendation

FREE No payment required

- ☎ Telephone number
- ⊙ Opening hours
- P Parking
- ⊗ Nonsmoking
- ❄ Air-conditioning
- @ Internet access
- 🛜 Wi-fi access
- 🏊 Swimming pool
- 🚌 Bus
- ⛴ Ferry
- 🚊 Tram
- 🚆 Train
- 📖 English-language menu
- 🥗 Vegetarian selection
- 👪 Family-friendly

Find your best experiences with these Great For... icons.

 Art & Culture
 Beaches
 Budget
Cafe/Coffee
Cycling
Detour
 Drinking
 Entertainment
 Events
Family Travel
 Food & Drink

History
Local Life
Nature & Wildlife
 Photo Op
 Scenery
 Shopping
Short Trip
 Sport
 Walking
 Winter Travel

Sights
- 🏖 Beach
- Bird Sanctuary
- Buddhist
- Castle/Palace
- Christian
- Confucian
- Hindu
- Islamic
- Jain
- Jewish
- Monument
- Museum/Gallery/Historic Building
- Ruin
- Shinto
- Sikh
- Taoist
- Winery/Vineyard
- Zoo/Wildlife Sanctuary
- Other Sight

Points of Interest
- Bodysurfing
- Camping
- Cafe
- Canoeing/Kayaking
- Course/Tour
- Diving
- Drinking & Nightlife
- Eating
- Entertainment
- Sento Hot Baths/Onsen
- Shopping
- Skiing
- Sleeping
- Snorkelling
- Surfing
- Swimming/Pool
- Walking
- Windsurfing
- Other Activity

Information
- Bank
- Embassy/Consulate
- Hospital/Medical
- Internet
- Police
- Post Office
- Telephone
- Toilet
- Tourist Information
- Other Information

Geographic
- Beach
- Gate
- Hut/Shelter
- Lighthouse
- Lookout
- Mountain/Volcano
- Oasis
- Park
- Pass
- Picnic Area
- Waterfall

Transport
- Airport
- BART station
- Border crossing
- Boston T station
- Bus
- Cable car/Funicular
- Cycling
- Ferry
- Metro/MRT station
- Monorail
- Parking
- Petrol station
- Subway/S-Bahn/Skytrain station
- Taxi
- Train station/Railway
- Tram
- Underground/U-Bahn station
- Other Transport

Belinda Dixon

Only happy when her feet are suitably sandy, Belinda has been (gleefully) travelling, researching and writing for Lonely Planet since 2006. It's seen her navigating mountain passes and soaking in hotpots in Iceland's Westfjords, marvelling at Stonehenge at sunrise; scrambling up Italian mountain paths; horse riding across Donegal's golden sands; gazing at Verona's frescoes; and fossil hunting on Dorset's Jurassic Coast. Then there's the food and drink: truffled mushroom pasta in Salo; whisky in Aberdeen, Balti in Birmingham, grilled fish in Dartmouth; wine in Bardolino. And all in the name of research. Belinda is also a podcaster and adventure writer and helps lead wilderness expeditions. See her blog posts at https://belindadixon.com.

Catherine Le Nevez

Catherine's wanderlust kicked in when she roadtripped across Europe from her Parisian base aged four, and she's been hitting the road at every opportunity since, travelling to some 60 countries and completing her Doctorate of Creative Arts in Writing, Masters in Professional Writing, and postgrad qualifications in Editing and Publishing along the way. Over the past decade-and-a-half she's written scores of Lonely Planet guides and articles covering Paris, France, Europe and far beyond. Her work has also appeared in numerous online and print publications. Topping Catherine's list of travel tips is to travel without any expectations.

Our Story

A beat-up old car, a few dollars in the pocket and a sense of adventure. In 1972 that's all Tony and Maureen Wheeler needed for the trip of a lifetime – across Europe and Asia overland to Australia. It took several months, and at the end – broke but inspired – they sat at their kitchen table writing and stapling together their first travel guide, *Across Asia on the Cheap*. Within a week they'd sold 1500 copies. Lonely Planet was born.

Today, Lonely Planet has offices in Franklin, London, Melbourne, Oakland, Dublin, Beijing, and Delhi, with more than 600 staff and writers. We share Tony's belief that 'a great guidebook should do three things: inform, educate and amuse'.

Our Writers

Neil Wilson

Neil was born in Scotland and has lived there most of his life. Based in Perthshire, he has been a full-time writer since 1988, working on more than 80 guidebooks for various publishers, including the Lonely Planet guides to Scotland, England, Ireland and Prague. He has climbed and tramped in four continents, including ascents of Jebel Toubkal in Morocco, Mount Kinabalu in Borneo, the Old Man of Hoy in Scotland's Orkney Islands and the Northwest Face of Half Dome in California's Yosemite Valley.

Isabel Albiston

After six years working for the *Daily Telegraph* in London, Isabel left to spend more time on the road. A job as writer for a magazine in Sydney, Australia was followed by a four-month overland trip across Asia and five years living and working in Buenos Aires, Argentina. Isabel started writing for Lonely Planet in 2014 and has contributed to 12 guidebooks. She's currently based in Ireland.

Fionn Davenport

Irish by birth and conviction, Fionn has spent the last two decades focusing on the country of his birth and its nearest neighbour, England, which he has written about extensively for Lonely Planet and others. In between writing gigs he's lived in Paris and New York, where he was an editor, actor, bartender and whatever else paid the rent. He moved to Manchester a few years ago where he lives with his wife, Laura, but he commutes back and forth to Dublin, only 40 minutes away. He posts his travel shots on instagram – @fionndavenport.

--- More Writers ---

STAY IN TOUCH LONELYPLANET.COM/CONTACT

AUSTRALIA The Malt Store, Level 3, 551 Swanston St, Carlton, Victoria 3053
📞 03 8379 8000,
fax 03 8379 8111

IRELAND Digital Depot, Roe Lane (off Thomas St), Digital Hub, Dublin 8, D08 TCV4, Ireland

USA 155 Filbert St, Suite 208, Oakland, CA 94607
📞 510 250 6400,
toll free 800 275 8555,
fax 510 893 8572

UK 240 Blackfriars Road, London SE1 8NW
📞 020 3771 5100,
fax 020 3771 5101

 twitter.com/lonelyplanet

 facebook.com/lonelyplanet

 instagram.com/lonelyplanet

 youtube.com/lonelyplanet

 lonelyplanet.com/newsletter